Anointed for Battle

The Warrior Chronicles

Anointed for Battle

The Warrior Chronicles

Bryan Porter

ARPress
ILLUMINATING IDEAS.
EMPOWERING VOICES

ARPress
45 Dan Road Suite 5
Canton MA 02021
Hotline: 1(888) 821-0229
Fax: 1(508) 545-7580

Ordering Information:

Quantity sales. Special discounts are available on quantity purchases by corporations, associations, and others. For details, contact the publisher at the address above.

Printed in the United States of America.

ISBN-13:	Paperback	979-8-89676-538-7
	eBook	979-8-89676-539-4

Library of Congress Control Number: 2024927100

ENDORSEMENTS

From a childhood friendship, to co-laborers in the ministry. We were ordained together engaging on this spiritual journey, as we walked in life the pages of this book. One putting 1,000 to flight; and two putting 10,000 through the anointing of God. *Anointed for Battle* shares some of our struggles, as we all shared in victory. For many are called but few are chosen. *Anointed for Battle* shows believers can persevere through insurmountable odds.

> Rev. Stephen E Bryant, Sr, M.A., M.Div. Pastor at Heard AME Church in Roselle NJ. Chairman, Rev. Dr. D Albert Turk Ministry of Evangelism New Jersey Annual Conference. *former* pastor of St James AME, St Mark AME, & St James AME.

∞∞∞∞

Anointed for Battle answers are revealed, and the reader is immersed on a powerful journey with the author as he rebuilds his life, after being beaten into a coma, and left for dead with amnesia. Bryan's story is a true testament to the human spirit and the power of faith. May this book, *Anointed for Battle* serve as a source of inspiration to all who face adversity. This author shows us, that with faith, all things are possible.

> Michele Sargent, Educator, Notary Public, Executive Director of the Brad Sargent Institute for Mental Health Charitable Institute, Kindness Ambassador for 'Life Vest Inside', *former* Jersey City 9-11 Committee Music Director

∞∞∞∞

Bryan Porter's latest book *Anointed for Battle* is the perfect sequel to his first book "Warrior for Christ." As you read you will be captivated by his life's constant spiritual warfare, as well as, his physical battles, and struggles against the medical & mental health communities. Seeing how he overcame the obstacles, persevered through the pain, showed exuberant strength in the struggle and in the midst of the predicament he never lost his praise. You will be truly blessed and moved by his story declaring that the only way he could have made it through, God has Anointed him for Battle!

> Errold Lanier, Sr., Pastor and Minister of Music of Good News Bible Mission in New Jersey, Dean of Good News Bible College

DEDICATION

In loving memory: to the late great Reverend Doctor Erwin Lanier, Sr. and wife Missionary Shirley Lanier, Elder David Alexander Porter (Boo-Jack/Grand Dad), Arlene Porter (Bebe/Nana), Demetrius Trè Porter, Sonya 'Nini' Williams, Ann 'Big Momma' McKinnon. To the Lee Family: Percy, Rudolph, Ben, Howard, Clara, Joe, and Willie. And to a host of bereaved family, saints, and friends. Many who are mentioned.

To the living: Missionary Marva Jean Lee-Porter, (my Sweet Sweet, my confidant, my friend, to my loving Daughter), my Bestie Michele Costello-Sargent, and the many mentioned throughout this book.

The *Warrior Chronicles* are an auto-biographical reflection of the author's recollections of experiences from over two decades. Many of the names, identifying characteristics, and relationship status have been changed. If anyone feels there are similarities to any character in these tales, are purely coincidental please disregard (wink). The occurrence of certain events may have been moved for poetic license. Thank you Holy Spirit.

Table of Contents

CHAPTER 1
Filling in the Blanks

Italian Inn, Route 450, Hyattsville Maryland - April 22, 2000,

S o now begins the next round of my warrior tales. How did I get to this point? I survived a coma, was beaten, left for dead, battling amnesia and depression. Thank God, what doesn't kill you only makes you stronger. So many questions still remained unanswered about the 9/11 attacks, the war on terror, and the mysterious anthrax attacks. What truly happened that night at the Italian Inn? Will reconciliation be possible with my wife? What will happen with my daughter? Once my medical settlement comes, everything will be different. Thank God.

I remember things well from my coma days. Whether in the body or without, I cannot tell. God took me to the beginning of time and space. And the earth was without form and void, and there was darkness. I was suspended up in the deepness of space. There was no sun or moon, yet I had vision, I still saw. There was no gravitational pull. I floated. I felt the cold for there was no warmth. Fore there was no sun. Then the warmth and fire started. One wouldn't appreciate warmth unless they first felt the cold. People used to ask me about what I saw while in a coma. It was hard to explain. I never told them about Creation. They would neither understand nor believe. When I told them about the flying hotdog cart, they laughed. They could not comprehend how God took me to a place of peace. He let me fly like a bird and reach for the sky. One day, we will mount up eagle's wings and eat all the hotdogs we want.

As David was prepared to defeat Goliath, God sent the lion first. Next, God sent the bear for him to fight in order to build his courage and confidence. As Job was tested, he lost everything he had. Including: his children, wealth, health, and social status. I went from working for the Department of Justice to hauling trash. Tests come in our lives to prepare us. We may not understand the test. The stress may feel overwhelming at times. Still God promised that He would not allow more on us than we are able to stand. I can't image the pain of losing a child, a spouse, or a parent. But if you feel the burden on your shoulders, remember, "You can handle it. Take the pain!" Believers can make it with God on their side. That is my testimony. Yet God allowed me to face all my fears, face my own mortality, not being loved, not being able to see my children, being in jail for crimes I did not commit, unemployment, and homelessness. We Christians proclaim that Jesus is the Lord of the resurrection. To be absent from the body is to be present with the Lord. When I was absent from my body in the coma, I was in a safe place. My mind, will, and emotions were still active. I felt at peace, comforted, and loved. The Bible promises Jesus will one day change 'mortal' to 'immortality.' This is my faith, I boast it to non-believers that 'I am immortal.' I said that even when I was threatened. 'You can't kill, what can't be killed.' That always throws them for a loop. 'Only God can kill me,' I'll say as a witness but normally it just gets weird. Jesus said, "No one takes it from me, but I lay it down of my own accord. I have *authority* to lay it down and *authority* to take it up again. This command I received from my Father" (John 10:18 *New Living Translation*). Since I have faced my greatest fears, I shall fear no evil. Through Christ, I am immortal, for I am anointed for battle; and I am a warrior for Christ!

Peter, my Lawyer, called excited about a tremendous break in our lawsuit against the Italian Inn. The Private Investigator had made two huge breaks. Sugar had supplied the name of Carl Jackson who witnessed everything from the inside of the Italian Inn. Another man had put his name and telephone number on Sugar's car windshield. His name was Andrew Thomas and he witnessed the entire assault that night outside of the Italian Inn. Thank God the pieces were coming together at last. God had supplied me a witness from the inside and outside. Peter informed me that copies of their testimonies were being sent to me. Every day, I earnestly checked the mail anticipating their arrival.

Then, my divorce attorney called and told me that something strange had developed. At first, Sugar filed for divorce. 'Good' were my thoughts about it. Curiously, he stated, she withdrew her filing for divorce. I requested for him to re-file on my behalf. When I told my Mother about our conversation, she was curious why Sugar withdrew. Maybe to her it meant hope for our marriage.

"Who cares," I said angrily, "I told him to just re-file," wishing to keep the ball rolling. Finally, the mail arrived. As I read the testimony of Andrew Thomas, the mysteries of my assault were finally being answered. Andrew said he was out jogging that Saturday night on April 22, 2000, when he heard some talking. He looked down and saw me talking with two bouncers at the doorway of the Italian Inn. He said they were telling me to leave and I kept telling them that my credit card was inside. They told me to come back tomorrow but I stood there insisting they return my credit card. The testimonies from inside the Italian Inn claim I wrestled the two bouncers and went crashing through the door into the manager's office. Dazed, confused, and with a nose bleeding; I sat Indian style. On the outside finally, one of the bouncers grew frustrated, reached back and punched me in the face. Immediately, I dropped and was knocked out cold. But while I lay on the ground lifeless and defenseless, Andrew said they both started stomping me repeatedly in the face and head. They kept stomping me all over my body. Andrew just stood there horrified because he couldn't look away. He couldn't believe how they kept brutally attacking me. He commented that you wouldn't beat an animal like that. Then the female owner came outside and saw me lying there on the ground bloody. She told them to get me off the property. So they dragged me into the left lane of the eastbound highway of Route 450 in an attempt to claim I was run over by a car. As a car approached, I laid there helpless on the highway in the dead of night. A Lady stopped and got out. She wondered how I got there in the middle of the road. She remained there blocking the oncoming traffic with her car protecting me as I laid there still lifeless and bleeding. God sent me a Guardian Angel. Next, she asked Andrew, the jogger, if he would help move me into the grass before someone ran me over. She said that I was too heavy for her to move and too bloody. One of the bouncers came over pretending to be innocent of what happened. He helped Andrew move me into the grassy medium.

Just then the police and ambulance arrived on the scene. They were dispatched earlier when Carl called 911 from the inside of the Italian Inn. The police told Andrew to get on the ground until the Lady came forward telling them that he helped move my body off the highway. From there, we know Detective Fenner took my wallet and identification, informing no one that I was in a coma laying in the hospital. He could have done some police work and asked Carl or Andrew what happened. Instead, he recognized these Ex-Bowie State Football players and covered up for them. It felt strange and cold as I read how they beat me so severely. On the other hand, it felt good to finally fill in the blank spots of what happened.

For a month, I laid in a coma. It took me another two months to learn how to walk again. Suffering from amnesia, unable to remember what happened or how I got there, and unable to recall the faces of who had done this to me, I did remember that I trusted in the Lord. He would reveal light in the darkness of this situation.

The Protective Order against me expired on Friday. It was merely a rouge for Sugar to hide behind from contacting her or Gabriel. Her 'no contact' rule was what she wanted and supervised visitation was just another tool for her to manipulate. As long as the child support checks kept rolling in, she didn't care if I had any role in Charity's life. Avoiding me for the rest of her life was preferred rather than co-parenting or any communication she wasn't in control of. I missed my daughter daily and the calling in music ministry had me constantly preparing for praise songs and solos. Daily I meditated anticipating musical practice with Joel. Meaning several independent practices, perfecting bass lines before our collaboration, despite it being a praise song, the melancholy of the notes and pain reflected the depression I struggled against. This particular psalm was a lament of David. Laments are meant to acknowledge the pain so that God's victory will be seen.

The FBI announced, "there was no prime suspect in this case at this time," addressing the 2001 Anthrax Attacks. Thank God a legal temp firm called Access Legal called me to work in New York. God had me working back as a paralegal again. Maybe this endeavor would finally have me return to stable employment in the legal field. Redemption after my legal career was destroyed back in Maryland. It took me five years to build up my resume in the field but a five-year plan is hard to manage while being married to Sugar.

The Bower Law Firm forward me a copy of the letter sent to the Circuit Court Clerk of PG County, Maryland, regarding the State's case against me being placed on the Stet Docket. This docket means an indefinite postponement of a non-guilty verdict. In the event of a future violation, the case may be re-opened within one year. I could have the pending child abuse charge technically still pending. At least I could handle a weapon again and go on temporary duty (TDY) on military assignments again. It cost me $1,000 in attorney fees, though.

Judgment came against Citi-Markets. The Black owned supermarket we championed for to employ the Blacks of the community was no more. They say employee theft and Mr. Banks were misappropriating funds. My belief, given the way they had me arrested and almost assaulting me, was 'Don't put my name in it.'

Mom let me use her car to make it to Drill this weekend out in Pennsylvania. Even though I just started working again, I didn't see how I was going to be able to acquire a car to continue with the Pennsylvania Air National Guard. With me I brought the testimony of Andrew Thomas for my Commander to read. He followed the case from the beginning and appreciated the updates. I knew someone must have stomped me the way my hips were disjointed. It took me months of therapy to learn how to walk again, while using wheelchairs and walkers, and undergoing physical therapy. When I told Sugar they must have stomped me, she told me that 'my brain was just telling me that.'

My Commander eagerly read Andrew Thomas's testimony. Everyone else being Eagles fans was smugly smiling because the Rams lost to the Patriots in the Superbowl. Three points never hurt so bad. Mike Martz should have stayed an Offensive Coordinator and not a Head Coach. Later my Commander called me back at the end of the weekend. He handed back Andrew's testimony, shaking his head now that more of the blanks were being filled. We knew the efforts of Detective Fenner to hide my wallet in his desk and the owners of the Italian Inn to tell people I was hit by a car. Major Palmer tried to encourage me to apply for an Officer's position opening up in our Unit. My dream was to obtain a commission. 'Captain Porter' had a nice ring to it but this was not the time. The shame of me being arrested, the dirtiness of divorce proceedings, the protective order, supervised visitation, and my financial woes had me totally embarrassed to apply. He reminded me of my qualifications and bachelor's degree but my focus remained on my troubles. Not to mention the financial hole I was sinking in and not having my own vehicle to use. I told him that I'd think about it but I had little hope for possibility at this time.

Skadden & Arps were a premiere New York law firm in Manhattan. I started working with the Temporary Legal firm. They had an office right off Times Square. Some lunches I would just walk around with some co-workers cruising down Broadway and 42nd Street. It was now time to take advantage of my legal training and restore my good name. My Godchild's Mother worked in the library and showed me a kit that was designed to expunge your legal records clean. It had all the proper forms with all the proper language. All I had to do was fill in all the blanks with the dates, the charges, and the proper courts to have the charges dismissed. It even provided the New Jersey Statue Code authorizing the Clerks and all relevant criminal justice and law enforcement services of the State to expunge from their records all evidence in these matters. The FBI or any other law enforcement agency outside of New Jersey were informed to retain control and not to release any records of this. My rights were finally restored, I should have never been arrested in the first place.

After work in the daytime, I would try and get a couple of hours of sleep before I reported to work down at Newport for Central Parking. I was only getting about four hours of sleep for the past three months, plus the drive to Guard Drill and the two weekends of supervised visitation a month. The fatigue and financial drain was starting to catch up to me. I decided to call the Family Crisis Center and reduce me down to one visit per month. The Director didn't want to budge and insisted that there be two visits per month. I explained my financial dilemma and unlike most parents involved in the PG County Family Crisis Center, I was not a resident of PG County or the state. It was a costly trip with gas and tolls. With much resistance, I was eventually granted a reduction to one visitation per month.

Monthly visits didn't stop me from missing my daughter, especially on the weekends. Normally, I would just stay in my room. Depression started kicking in. I didn't want to go out and face anyone. A letter came informing me that my bankruptcy attorney sent a letter to Peter's law firm down in Maryland. He informed Peter that I had filed for Chapter 7 bankruptcy. He also wanted to know the expected range of recovery. Though I was curious, I preferred to keep this information from him.

Peter was preparing us for a legal battle. He sent me a letter personally naming the owners of the Italian Inn and the bouncers. Members of this joint enterprise are jointly and severely liable for the tortuous acts, omissions, and conduct.

Glad for May's Air National Guard Drill because legal assignments were getting inconsistent. This month we had our annual weapons training. Firing the M-16 on the target showed me proficient up to 200 meters. I would have shot better if the smoke didn't discharge into my eyes while shooting left handed. My contact lenses would get cloudy so I couldn't see too far after awhile.

The House of Ruth sent me a letter informing me that thirty days passed since their Request for Production of Documents had been served. She wanted a response by next week. How was I going to get a lawyer this quickly? They asked if an attorney was retained to have them contact them immediately. Immediately, I contacted Peter who sensed the urgency. He called and secured a divorce attorney for me. McGrady was a former Air Force General, he was willing to wait, acknowledging my ability to make prompt payment. His rate was $200 an hour.

Following our conversation, I wrote him a letter requesting representation for divorce and child custody proceedings. I mentioned Gabriel's truancy in school and supporting documents of Sugar's emails attesting his rebellious behavior. I informed McGrady of Gabriel's school suspensions, assaulting teachers and a youth pastor, his Mother's decision to home drug testing, him failing it, and the possibility of him being on drugs when he assaulted me. Vehemently, I denied any physical or verbal abuse of Sugar or the children. I challenged Sugar's mental status for making these false allegations to satisfy her legal support and delusions that I've been attempting to kidnap my daughter when I've been sleeping in my car and hotels. I expressed not fighting for sole custody as long as visitation with Charity be unsupervised, my parental right to have knowledge of her address, school, and the right to freely call her.

Her lawyers sent me yet another letter pressuring me to respond. Why weren't they pursuing legitimate cases of abuse to women as they were funded to do? Why do they concentrate on me to keep me away from my daughter? McGrady sent a letter requesting the date the responses are actually due. Despite that, he suggested I provide him with written responses as quickly as possible.

Father's Day came and I didn't get a call from the children. It felt hurtful after all the years I took care of Gabriel and she didn't even teach him to be thankful or respectful for that. Everything was always about them. Then my nephews, Ice and Double K, called. It made me feel good again. Then AJ and Kyle called, too. Everybody but my children called and wished me a Happy Father's Day. My sisters gave me the best present ever. They gave me my first 'George Foreman Electric Grill. 'Now I can cook my meat in five minutes on the grill. This was showing some real love.

Regular assignments from Access Legal stopped. None of the paralegal, legal assistant, legal receptionist, business assistant, document coder or legal secretary jobs were calling me in for interviews. Stable employment with benefits is what I needed. Maybe

I could become a schoolteacher using my bachelor's degree. First, I would give substitute teaching a try and see whether I liked it or not.

Charity's birthday came up and I tried to celebrate it with her during our supervised visit. The Visitation Monitor told me that my daughter and I didn't 'belong in there 'and that I needed to get her out of there. How was I supposed to accomplish that? I couldn't talk directly to my daughter about it. When I asked why did we have to meet here at the Family Crisis Center and was she afraid of Daddy, she never replied back to me so I didn't push.

My brother had now entered the world of parenthood. He and his girlfriend Stacey had a little boy. Shakur had a baby of his own now. Stacey named him after his father but his middle name was Trè, which we used.

Peter, my medical lawsuit attorney, told me about the deposition coming up tomorrow for Sugar. Thank God she was cooperating. It embarrassed me that no one in the family could keep an open relationship with her or simply because I asked them. I kept one up with my brother-in-law and sisters' boyfriends whether I cared for them or not. When I asked Peter how was he able to get Sugar to testify and was he worried she would try and hurt our case, he said that he just asked and prayed with her reminding her to tell the truth.

The next day I had my Pennsylvania Air National Guard trip. The trip was difficult; I made the decision to start talking to my Commander about transferring to the New Jersey Air National Guard. It would be easier to travel to, even by mass transit. Major Palmer didn't like my request but he understood. He was a true leader among men and a mentor that I would miss. I told Mom that I was making the switch to New Jersey and I wouldn't be putting extra mileage on her car. She said that it was alright and that she didn't mind but it was my way of not taking advantage of her kindness. As usual, she didn't support my decision to transfer.

Peter sent me a copy of Sugar's deposition. God was protecting me documenting a lot of truths under oath that supported not only my character but also truths about my marriage. The opposing counsel, Mr. Stevens, asked what marital problems specifically led to us separating in September of 1999, prior to the coma?

"We just were two different people," Sugar answered. "We just...," she paused in deep reflection, "I just decided it was better not being together." That was a startling revelation. Sugar tried to elicit sympathy from whomever she could that I had left since I moved out. But I moved with her consent thinking we were still together but she knew in her mind that she didn't love me anymore and tricked me into still sending her money paying bills like we were still a couple. This was the first admission that 'I just decided.'

Stevens asked her directly if I ever been violent with her or hit her prior to our separation in September of 1999. She answered no. I was not surprised. He asked if I ever been violent with her or hit her in any way. Sugar answered no, again. Then he asked if I ever struck or hit any of the children. Sugar answered yes. I continued reading eagerly to get clarification on who was hit and what were the circumstances.

"Gabriel, just on your normal disciplinary type, you know, spanking, things along that line." I was shocked. Thank God she was finally telling the truth. "Nothing like a violent temper type thing. That would be outside of normal."

Great! I loved my son, step-son or not. I wouldn't have even needed to discipline him if he wasn't such a handful. Sugar, Gabriel, and I all talked about the behavior expected of him. I never disciplined him because I was having a bad day. It was always over something he understood beforehand wouldn't be tolerated.

Stevens continued to ask questions about me disciplining Gabriel. In retrospect, I couldn't see what bearing it had with me being beaten to death and dragged to the middle of the road. These questions could nullify Sugar as a helpful witness if she continued previous claims of my alleged violence in our domestic case. Now he was asking if I ever spanked Gabriel in her presence where she observed it to be violent in nature. Peter asked to specify 'ever or prior to?' Stevens answered that he could put some time scope but it was a general question.

"There were..., I mean, the..., I don't know what you're considering like excessive. I mean, it just seemed you know, it was just the...," Sugar pondered seeming to choose her words wisely on my behalf. "I guess court systems today might think it was excessive, but it was just a normal spanking. There's one or two instances where he seemed like it was a little more than what, you know, was normal, but not, you know, like bruises or, you know, no scarring or anything like that." I never knew Sugar to sound so nervous before. She was making a great conscious effort not to paint me as violent toward our son.

"Did he ever cause any type of injury to Gabriel?" asked Stevens.

"No, never," she answered. Well, the hospital records would verify that, I thought.

"Did he ever cause any type of injury to Charity?" I wondered what Stevens was fishing for. He must have hoped since we were separated that he could use something from the Italian Inn against me.

"No," she answered him. "I can't even remember a time where he spanked her." This was true but thank God she didn't do anything wrong or else I would have disciplined her as well.

After further questioning about her employment to include a part-time job, she had taken over for me when I left. I was working two jobs when I took a paralegal job in New Jersey, hoping to relocate the family back to that area. Sugar took over my second job at the video rental store at her request. Everyone was concerned that Sugar worked a day job and with this second job, no one would be home with two young children. Charity was only in the first grade. Ruth, Sugar's Mom, felt so concerned for the children that she came down from Pennsylvania to stay with them because she didn't want the children to be home alone at night. I didn't want Sugar to work the second job. either. But what could I do? She was a grown woman and we all know despite the Gary Smalley books that women today do what they want to do. Neither Ruth nor I wanted her to work this second job. When anyone asked, she never had a valid reason.

"Why did you leave that work?" Stevens asked.

"It was just evening hours for a little extra cash. When we first separated, I was trying to get a little extra cash," Sugar answered. Funny how the truth eventually comes out. As her husband, I was sending practically my entire paycheck home. I didn't know we were *separated*. But more of her true feelings were coming out in this deposition than the six months of space I gave her to search herself and move with me. I can't feel like a total fool for trusting her but I took her at her word, knowing and trusted in the Lord. She was building a war chest for divorce. When she finally made it clear that she left me, I was devastated. I knew she always struggled in her love for me but I loved my wife and hoped that would have been enough.

Sorry, HC Pastor and Gary Smalley. God didn't place all the weight on my shoulders. Sugar has to bear some responsibility for her own actions and choices. It's not always the father and the husband. So women have some boyfriends and other men in between but again it's from their choices made.

Stevens did as most lawyers do. He asked the same questions over and over. He asked Sugar about some college courses she had before we even got married. What does this have to do with bouncers beating me into a coma? Then he moved back to 'did we live continuously separate and apart from since September of 1999?' Sugar answered no, and that we moved back together after the incident at the Italian Inn. Stevens asked for how long. Sugar answered that I came back in June and I left in January. Stevens asked prior to April 2000, before the incident, if she in her dealing with me find that I had a temper. This question was asked and answered previously but as with most people in depositions, more eventually comes out in their answers.

"He was excitable. I mean, he could be loud and, you know, some people might call that temper.""Yes maybe," was her final answer. Prior to April 2000, we weren't even living together. I would pick Charity up from the babysitters three to four times a week because Sugar had her big promotion at work. The same daughter I now needed supervised visitation. Now she says that I was excitable and that I had a temper.

After he played up the anger, he asked how often we would argue back in September 1999. Sugar answered that we argued probably three days a week, mainly on Saturdays, when it came around to paying bills. This guy was good. He got her worked up over bills by jumping back in time. Then he asked if any of those arguments ever involved any type of physical threat. She answered no without hesitation. Stevens wasn't satisfied, he tried to fish for more. He asked if there was any type of threat or physical act taken against her that was threatening her safety.

"No," Sugar replied. "I never felt that my safety was threatened, no." She reaffirmed her position and remained unshaken about her answer. "I would just leave, or he would leave." Truthfully, I don't even remember us arguing very much. Either we had money for a bill or it waited until we did. There is no way to argue what people have in their hearts though. A lot of unresolved emotions were tangled in her answers.

"Did he ever strike you in any way?" Stevens asked, not satisfied with her previous answers.

"No," Sugar fired back.

"Objection, asked and answered. You can answer," interjected Peter.

"Only in January when he left…, the incident that he left." Finally Stevens was getting to the one incident of an eight year marriage. Again, what did it have to do with the Italian Inn was beyond me. "He got into an altercation with our son Gabriel, and I went to separate them. It was a physical altercation. I went to separate them, and at that moment he kind of turned and came after me, and he, with his forearm, kind of had me up against a closet door in my bedroom, and then kind of tossed me to the ground, and him and Gabriel continued to go at it," Sugar had finally given him the one incident he hoped to build his case on. Still, from her perspective, it was how I put my hands on her, not her putting her hands on me and Gabriel repeatedly punching me in the face and head while she held me. Still, she played the innocent victim.

She said that I 'came after her with my forearm,' that I 'kind of had her up against the closet door,' and that I 'then kind of tossed her to the ground?' Me! Me! Me! What about the truth? Sugar was holding my arms down while Gabriel kept swinging haymakers at my head. I was having real injuries and she heard me bring this up and documenting this in writing. Her refusal to acknowledge my injuries was mocking and unsympathetic.

"Were Gabriel and Bryan exchanging blows?" Stevens asked with blood lust.

"Yes," she answered.

"Punches?"

"Yes."

"What part of the body was involved?" Stevens kept fishing.

"I'd say upper body, mainly upper body," she said.

"Were you injured in any way as a result of this altercation in January of 1999?"

"My ego," she added with some humor. However, Stevens smelled blood in the water. He wasn't even getting the years right. The domestic incident happened in January of 2001.

"Did you ever go to the doctor?" He asked. No, she answered. Funny, I couldn't say the same but no one ever asked me the question and even more importantly, no one cared. He asked if she has any bruises or scratches or marks on her body.

"I may have had a small black and blue on my hip from falling on the closet door," she told him, which was different from her original answers of no.

"Was your son Gabriel injured in any way as a result of this altercation?" Stevens keep pursuing.

"Yes he was," Sugar was turned again.

"What was his injuries?" Like a blood thirty shark, he finally found his prey.

"He had two black eyes," she answered. Two black eyes? I only punched him once to get him off of me. "He had some scrapes, some bruises to his arms and shoulders and back and stomach." Wow! Were there any parts of the body I missed?

"Did he go to a hospital?" He asked to which she answered, yes. "For medical attention?" Again she answered, yes. "What was the name of the hospital?"

"Doctors Community Hospital."

"He was admitted?" He asked. "Did he receive medical care after being evaluated at the emergency room?"

"What do you mean?" Sugar asked. That's what I was thinking. What do you mean? The Children's Protective Services did not record any injuries or bruises. All they could write was his nose and lips were bloody when he came in. Now he had two black eyes, scrapes, and multiple bruises. "Like follow-up type thing?" Sugar continued to ask.

"Was he seen for follow-up with any physician or orthopedic doctors or any specialist, or anything of that type?" The blood thirsty lawyer was casting a very wide net. When were they going to get to the part of me at the Italian House when my eye sockets were crushed or my nose being broken? When were they going to ask if I was injured by Gabriel and Sugar?

Sugar told them that they went back for a follow-up because their papers indicated to do so. Why would you follow-up to a Doctor when you had no notable injuries in the first place? It was just a further attempt to muddy up me in the domestic case.

"Did Bryan receive any medical attention or checkups or evaluation after this altercation?" Stevens asked. Finally, it was asked, even if it was unsympathetic.

"I couldn't tell you, because he was no longer in the home at that point," was her answer. Very early I learned from the people at HC church who hides behind 'didn't know.' There is little difference in not knowing something and not caring to know.

"Prior to January of 1999, had your husband had any physical altercations or physical contact, fights with your son Gabriel?"

"No. That was the first and only time," replied Sugar. Stevens asked what led to this altercation. Sugar answered, "A misunderstanding about a progress report which Bryan interpreted to be a report card that was supposed to be brought home from school that evening, and it wasn't, and the argument kind of ensued from that point. That led to the physical." What a load of crap! The Mothers of today constantly make excuses for their children. This teenager was failing at that time and he failed yet again for that entire academic year.

No admittance to her yelling that 'he didn't have to listen to me.' Placing me on the same level as a sixteen year old like we were equals. Failing to mention that we already had his failing grades so there was no misunderstanding there.

They went into the Protective Order and asked how long it lasted. Stevens was getting into all the details of the Protective Order. Clearly, he was avoiding the only topic that mattered, the beat down at the Italian Inn. Sugar gave her interpretation of the protective order, which according to her included that I wasn't permitted to go to Charity's school with the intentions of trying to remove her from the school. I wasn't permitted to take Charity out of the D.C. Metropolitan area. Sugar also brought up supervised visitations in the protective order after she already made false claims about the school.

"If I may interject, just for my clarification," Peter finally spoke up. "When did this altercation between Bryan and Gabriel take place?"

"1999, is that right?" Stevens asked. He was so bloodthirsty he botched the year in question.

"Was it before or after the Italian Inn?" Finally someone mentioned the reason we are here today. Peter was earning his $200 an hour.

"After it was," Sugar replied. "It was…, I'm sorry. It was January of…, the protective order expired this year. So, it would have had to be 2001."

Then Stevens asked about divorce papers being filed. Sugar replied yes with excitement. They asked about the status and she responded it was pending. They asked if she had any anticipation as to when a final order would come. Sugar said she didn't know but wished that she did. She said that she had initiated an absolute divorce pushed by the incident with Gabriel. Stevens the shark asked if there were any other grounds for divorce. Was there adultery or anything like that? Sugar responded that there was no adultery.

"I object to the form of the question," Peter interjected. Stevens rephrased the question on the grounds for divorce. Why was Sugar so adamant about getting a divorce?

"I'm not sure. I'm not sure what to say to be honest with you. They just state the fact that, you know, I'm requesting a divorce and custody of the children, the same thing as far as no contact. They kind of put that same wording in there. As far as, you know, no harassment or, you know, other than the only contact would be in regards to the children. That he wouldn't harass me. He wasn't…, things like that are all written in there."

Stevens asked about my paralegal job and how often I consumed alcohol. Sugar had the nerve to say I drank on a weekly basis. We never had alcohol in the home. I went years without drinking. The only friends that we visited who drank alcohol were her friends, like Raven. But while a church remained silent these lies could continue. If 'no contact' persisted, she would never have to confront truth or reality.

Finally, they started asking about the Italian Inn. Sugar mentioned how we used to visit there as a family. Then she was asked if she had any knowledge of my activities of April 22, 2000.

"Yes. He worked in the morning and he went shopping. He was trying to contact me by cell phone. He was going to come over to spend time with the children and paint Easter eggs."

"When he spoke to you around 7-ish where did he inform you as to where he was?" Stevens asked.

"The Air Force base, he was coming from the Air Force base. He had been shopping and he was going to go get…, he had just got his dry cleaning, and he was wondering where I was, he had been trying to call me all day," Sugar answered. This was vaguely filling in memories of that day.

"How did you first hear about anything occurring to Bryan Porter after April 22nd, 2000?" Stevens was finally getting to the juicy parts but he was still careful not to claim any negligence on the part of the Italian Inn or how I ended up in the hospital.

"How did I hear about it? I didn't hear about it. I figured it out. I ultimately found him in a coma in the hospital through a lot of investigation and questions. I found him in the intensive care unit in P.G. Hospital Center. I learned about him through the grace of God. I was on the cell phone with my son coming home from work. He hadn't shown up, and hadn't shown up to paint the eggs, he didn't go to church the next day, which was…, his favorite group was at the church, and his daughter was going to be dancing, and he loved his Daughter, and he didn't show up for either of those dances. I just really felt like something was wrong, because it wasn't like him not to at least call, especially when he told the children he was going to come over. I was on the phone with my son and, just out of the corner of my eye. I see his van parked in the Italian Inn's parking lot." Sugar told how she skillfully found me and like she said, by the grace of God, since the Detective had my wallet sitting in his desk, informing no one.

Stevens kept asking when she saw the van, whether she noticed a toolbox, and whether any tools were missing. Sugar repeatedly answered him no. This must have been fishing about the alleged screwdriver I threatened the bouncers with. It was an excuse given to beat me inches from my life. Then he returned to what happened at the Italian Inn.

"I had a picture of him and asked the staff if anybody had seen him," Sugar said. "Nobody thought they recognized him. I asked them to check in the men's room to see if he was in there because his van was in the parking lot. So at that point my friend and I went over next door to check at the hotel to see if, you know, possibly he had checked into the hotel, and they had said, no. There was no listing with his name in the hotel there. So we went back to the Italian Inn restaurant and, you know, really explained that we - - he was - - it had been a couple of days since we talked to him and we were really worried. We weren't sure what was going on and we're not sure if the van had been parked there all those days. And as we continued, we were more intense in our conversations with the woman. She mentioned that there had been a fight in the bar area, and I said, well, can you remember what, took place, what happened? And she explained that there was an argument inside the bar and the people were asked to leave, and I, the woman who was with me, I guess, asked her what the people were drinking. Were they drunk, that type of thing, and she remembered that the drink was a Blue Hawaiian, he likes girly drinks. So, I said that had to be him. Then I asked and she said that they left, that they were told to leave the establishment at that point. And it wasn't until later, again when we were talking trying to get more out of this woman, that she said, well, and I also believe she said I think someone got hit by a car, she said, because later there was an ambulance, and I think someone got hit by a car.

I went outside, got on the telephone, and called home because I scheduled the police to come over to take a missing person's report. My friend tried calling the hospitals since they said someone might have been hit by a car. We were making assumptions it might have been him.

I was on the phone with Prince George's Hospital and asked did the 911 people have somebody brought in the other night. It was an assault case. At that point we went to the hospital and that's how I know it was him from that point."

Stevens asked after her trip to the hospital on the 24th if Sugar came back and spoke with anyone associated with the Italian Inn. And who did you speak with?

"The owner's wife and the owner. I went back with Bryan's uncle Howard. We informed the people that it actually had been him that was at the hospital. We were trying to figure out if they knew any more information about what had happened that night could have led to, you know, to him being in the hospital.

"We weren't sure whether he was hit by a car or assaulted or what had happened. At that point we were trying to gather information as much as possible from them. We thanked them. They were very cooperative, we told them. They asked if there's anything that they can do. They offered us free food for the rest of our life type of thing." Sugar made a joke.

"They talked about the security people, the bouncers that they had hired. Their son was also there and a younger son. I guess he was in charge of the bar side or the Karaoke side. He said that the bouncers were hired on the weekends a lot of people would come for the Karaoke and sometimes things would get out of control.

"We asked them what had happened. So that was the large portion of our conversation trying to get as much information as possible. And at that point the woman went into more detail regarding what had happened that evening and how they were asked to leave. Bryan and another man were asked to leave and the last time she remembered seeing Bryan he was okay. That he had given her his credit card to pay for his drinks and he was sitting on the little cement thing you park your car so your car doesn't go any further. I don't know what it's called. She gave him back his credit card and she said he was fine. That's the first conversation that I had with her with his uncle present."

"What did she tell you at that time if anything about what had occurred with the altercation inside of the Italian Inn involving Bryan?" Stevens asked. I knew from my studies of the Scriptures that drinking was permissible. What harm could come from singing karaoke in the bar portion of a restaurant?

"She told me that first it was verbal. It was no big deal. Then they got a little physical so the bouncers had them removed. But when she mentioned to me about him sitting on the stoop, she said one of his sleeves was torn. I wanted to get more information because it just didn't seem like she was telling me everything. Like she was telling me what I needed to feel comfortable about and not how he ended up in a coma."Stevens asked about whatever had occurred inside. What else did Sugar ask?

"The owner had a very strong Italian accent. I don't know. He said, 'He's a little guy, very little guy but very strong.' That's what he said. So again, that kind of led me to think it was more than just a simple little nothing matter of fight that was going on inside." Sugar testified knocking a homerun for our team.

Stevens asked if she ever had any contact with anyone associated with the Italian Inn after that conversation occurred one or two days after being there on the 24th.

"Yes. I'd say it was Friday. I spoke with the woman who I assumed was the wife. She asked how he was doing and seemed very concerned. I explained he was still in a coma and wasn't doing very well. She started to talk about what happened inside and at that conversation she explained how they were. She started to use the words 'out of control' but at the point the fight was more intense. She had said they were going up and down and some door had been broken inside of the restaurant area. She called Bryan into the office and made him sit in the corner on the floor until he could calm down. I mean it was a totally different story than what I had heard the first time."

"So I was trying to piece together both stories to hopefully get to some answer as to why this had happened. A customer, Andrew, wrote his number on a note and put it on my car at the hospital one evening. He said that he was there when the fight happened at the restaurant. Carl was inside. He said the bouncers were really rough with Bryan. That they didn't have to go that far. He actually said he called 911 from the bar because it was getting out of control," said Sugar. "He said I don't want this going down at my favorite watering hole."

As I read Sugar's deposition, I knew God placed that ambulance just in time to save my life. I knew that I must have been seriously injured sitting in the owner's office. Earlier reports stated that my nose was bleeding. I may have been suffering from some altered mental status and couldn't think clearly.

"Carl said that Bryan must have gone to the bathroom and tried to come back and someone had taken his seat or vice versa but something about an empty seat at the bar. The location of where they were sitting at is what started it." Sugar testified.

Stevens asked if Carl ever said anything about whether or not he had observed anything that might have occurred outside the Italian Inn.

"I believe he mentioned that either Bryan was either laying in the street on the main highway area or that he either took him from the street, or pulled him from the street, or something along those lines. I can't actually recall specifically. At that point I think my focus was just where he was located. His state of mind, what condition he was in. I don't remember the actual details of the fight or anything like that." Sugar told them.

Stevens asked if Carl said who I fought with. Did he say who threw the first punch or punches?

"He mentioned the person sucker punched Bryan so I assume that means the other person hit him first, "said Sugar, our expert witness.

Stevens went on to ask about my time in the hospital and the injuries I sustained. The redundancy of this was such a waste of time. The numerous boxes of medical reports clearly confirmed my injuries. Still, Stevens asked Sugar the obvious questions that only increasingly hurt his own case.

Sugar's testimony was great for our case. However, the police reports proved that I was at the Italian Inn and my van was still parked there. The medical records confirmed my injuries and the witnesses both came forward but Sugar was the straw that stirred the drink tying everything together. I wanted to give her something for the time she did assist me once we reached a settlement. It was hard after all I did for her. She spat in my face and wanted no form of contact after our eight years of marriage together. I gave her flowers and she spat in my face. We even had a child together and I didn't hear anything about her: progress reports in school, holidays, or calling me on Father's Day, my birthday or Christmas. I will reserve my feelings and see what unfolds in our future relationship. Sugar only had herself to blame if I left her out completely. I was always generous with people but her interests were solely on the money.

Peter, my lawsuit attorney, filed a complaint against the Italian Inn. Simultaneously, a Chapter 7 Bankruptcy Petition was filed today to protect my finances by my bankruptcy attorney. I was launching my financial offensive on two fronts just like the U.S. with Iraq and Afghanistan. With God on my side, no weapon formed against me would prosper.

Pete continued to turn up the heat by filing a notification. As a result of the incident, I sustained injuries, lapsing into a coma, unable to eat solid food for three months, and contracting pneumonia. I suffered permanent scarring, missing a front tooth, stitches in my tongue and ear, and numbness to the tip of his tongue. I was incapacitated from work for five months, so I incurred medical bills to include $122,000 at PG County Hospital and $35,000 at National Rehabilitation Hospital.

∞∞∞∞∞

To become a substitute teacher, I had to submit to fingerprinting and a criminal background check. We had to submit to a blood test, I guess for drug testing. A letter came back that the platelet count in my blood test was low. Not having a job with benefits, I again went to a local VA Clinic in Jersey City. Besides convenience, I didn't have to pay the gas or fares to East Orange. My Primary Doctor not only supplied a letter that I could perform the duties of teaching but also a prescription for my high cholesterol.

Peter sent me a copy of the Second Amended Complaint flowing with the personal names of the bouncers and the Italian Inn. The plaintiff was a customer of the Italian Inn and was lawfully on the premises. The named defendants were agents, servants, and/or employees of the Italian Inn. The plaintiff was assaulted and battered by the bouncers acting as agents, servants, and/or employees of the Italian Inn. Bryan was assaulted and battered to the point that he lost consciousness, and continued to be assaulted and battered. While he was unconscious, thereby placing his very life and safety in great jeopardy, the defendants left Mr. Porter there in the roadway in the direct path of traffic again placing his life and safety in grave danger.

The Italian Inn owed to the plaintiff a duty of reasonable care in hiring of their employees as well as provide supervision, management, and training of such individuals, so that the customers of the Italian Inn would not be subjected or exposed to unreasonable risks of physical harm and danger from the activities of such individuals.

Bryan Joseph Porter demands judgment both jointly and severely liable for the personal injuries, emotional and mental distress, permanent and disabling physical injuries, past and future medical expenses, past and future lost earning capacity, incurred by the plaintiff as a direct result of the incident in question. Wherefore, the plaintiff demands judgment against the defendants in the amount of

Three Million Dollars (3,000,000) in compensatory damages and Five Million Dollars (5,000,000) in punitive damages.

Eight Million Dollars (8,000,000) total in recovery. That was a lot of cheddar! Shoot for the moon and land on the stars. If we only get half that amount, it would be four million (4,000,000). For now, I was financially struggling but my life was going to change once I'm awarded the money from the assault, minus a well-deserved third of that for my lawsuit attorney, Peter.

I was transferred to the New Jersey Air National Guard at McGuire Air Force Base. This was an opportunity to get out of aircraft maintenance. Working there only one weekend a month was becoming extremely challenging to my memory, especially staying familiar with the numerous aircraft components and systems. It was easier when I worked full time active duty but as a Guard member just working once a month was becoming more and more difficult after my brain injury. After much prayer, I chose to pick the Aerospace Ground Equipment job. Those guys seem to have it easy on the Flight line. Plus with the training in diesel engines, electrical generation, air conditioning, and heating would guarantee me to find stable employment outside the military. Stable employment had been a constant prayer of mine since I was a child. I made the decision to start studying to take the New York Police exam also. I took two NJ Transit buses to get down to Fort Dix/McGuire one day starting the transfer process. I got off the bus at McGuire's South gate across from the Falcon Courts North gate. Unfortunately, the five minute ride took me an hour to walk across base to the Air National Guard side.

A mandatory appearance came up at the U.S. Treasury Office in Newark one afternoon. Each step was making me closer to freeing myself from the financial walls closing in around me. This would be my last weekend with the 407th Special Operations Wing. The fiscal year was ending and October would start my new year with the Guard. There was no better time than the present. I was proud of my time spent serving in this prestigious unit in the Pennsylvania Air National Guard. They presented me with plaques, certificates, and lifelong memories. As I out-processed, I received my last hug from

Sergeant Lovely. During the weekend, President Bush announced that Iraq was in possession of weapons of mass destruction. After 9/11, American citizens felt vulnerable to more attacks. Our history with Saddam Hussein possessing weapons of mass destruction was a bit unsettling to everyone.

We were beginning to notice that Trè was having some concerns. Shakur and Stacey took him to the Doctors. They explained that since he was in a ball in the womb he wasn't developing the digits in his fingers correctly. This little guy, like his Daddy, was a fighter. For Trè, it started from the womb. Back on the home front, at 5:20 p.m. in the evening on October 2nd, someone mysteriously fired a shot through a Michael's Craft Store in Aspen Hill, Maryland. It missed the cashier but no one was injured. An hour later at 6:30, a 55 year old program analyst was shot and killed in a parking lot of a grocery store in Wheaton, Maryland. On October 3rd, in Rockville someone was killed mowing the grass. Next, someone was killed pumping gas in Aspen Hill, Maryland. A woman got off a bus and sat on a bench and was shot and killed in Norbeck. Then a woman vacuuming her minivan at a gas station was shot and killed. A total of four people were shot and killed within a two hour time span in Montgomery County Maryland in the morning. In the evening, another victim was killed in Washington D.C. Panic quickly spread throughout the region while people watched the news. On October 4th, a 43 year old homemaker was shot and killed at Spotsylvania Mall in Virginia. The increasing number of shootings caused a media circus but school officials reassured parents that children were protected. The media started calling the shooter the 'DC Sniper.'

We celebrated Lil Big Sis's birthday today. While sitting eating cake and ice cream, I reminded everybody about testifying in December for me. This would finally get this stupid supervised visitation removed. Everybody kept their heads down when we talked making the trip. They were all so enthusiastic before ready to help. Now with the fear of the DC Sniper, they were avoiding eye contact.

"You guys don't want to go down and testify?" I asked. It grew even quieter once I asked.

"Well, it's not that we don't want to testify, it's kind of dangerous down there," Mom answered. The others bowed their heads but shook them in agreement and smiled.

"Well, Charity lives down there and she has to go by faith. Fear no evil, God is our Protector," my words of assurance were all falling on deaf ears. No one wanted to travel to the Washington D.C. area while the Sniper was on the loose. The local Media in D.C. were alerting people to stay vigilant and ensuring parents that their children were safe going to school. All measures were being taken to prevent a panic.

The DC Sniper shot a 13 year old boy in the abdomen today on October 7th. As he arrived at Benjamin Tasker Middle School in Bowie, Maryland, he was critically wounded. proving there was no safe ground, not even for the children. On a positive note, U.S. and British forces intensely bombed Afghanistan to hopefully flush out Osama bin Laden and those who have protected him. On October 9th, a 53 year old Civil Engineer was shot dead while pumping gas in Prince William County in Virginia. On the 10th, my background check was finally cleared so I was able to call in and start substitute teaching.

My first responsibility for substituting was to call a telephone number. It was on a first come basis and it was often busy. It turns out that I had to dial my one availability call several times a day. When I finally got through, the call back started at 8:05. My first day was challenging, to say the least. I had forgotten that children today are given a choice whether they are going to cooperate or listen to authority. The pay was $100 per day. Compared to hauling trash at $60 a day, it was true motivation. When I compared the non-stop yelling, the refusal to do any work, the blatant disrespect, and utter chaos to the strenuous, tedious, dirty, element exposed trash hauling of Labor Ready, I just pressed on.

Tragedy continued, on October 11th, a 53 year old businessman was shot dead also pumping gas in Spotsylvania County, Virginia. On October 14th, an FBI Intelligence analyst was shot dead while shopping with her husband at Home Depot in Fairfax County,

Virginia. For the next five days, there were no shootings, and the nation had a moment of peace.

Then, on October 19th, a 37 year old man was shot near a Ponderosa Steakhouse in Ashland, Virginia. In the woods, a four page letter was found requesting ten million dollars and threatening to harm school children. A tactic often used in warfare is called 'shock and awe.' This act of devastation to instill psychological damage is to spread fear and panic. This letter accomplished its ill-fated goal with body bags to match. The police were vigilant. On October 21st, two men were arrested but were found not to be the shooters. A bus driver was shot, the next day, standing on the steps of his bus in Aspen Hill, Maryland. The police released parts of the letter, "Your children are not safe, anywhere, at any time." The driver died later that day from his injuries.

I started reporting for Drill with the Aerospace Ground Equipment Shop (AGE) for New Jersey's Air National Guard. New Jersey had one of the best mass transit systems in the country. A bus dropped me off this time on the Fort Dix side. The whole weekend I spent in-processing to my new Air Refueling Wing. They required me to reenlist for the next six years. With a lifetime of work ahead of me, what choice did I have? I had to appear at a court hearing about my divorce down in Maryland. After our day in court, my divorce attorney treated me to dinner. It was very kind of the General to do. We shared a mutual respect toward each other with our common Air Force background. He told me of a client he had and in this other case he happened to be representing a woman in this divorce case. They were trying to stop the Father from having visitation with his teenage daughter. The Father had even slapped his daughter in the face but the Judge still would not deny his parental right to freely visit her without supervision.

"I told myself, here is a man that has even slapped his daughter and poor Mr. Porter, who never touched his daughter, has to go through supervised visitation," the General said while we ate.

I definitely saw all the irony of the situation. It was something I thought of often. Some women I heard of even took their children to prison to visit their fathers. All these ungodly men received respect from being a father rather than a man of God. We spoke of our next court date coming up. My family was coming to testify and I would bring the letters of character as references.

Thursday after teaching in school I had to drive to the Status Hearing in Maryland. The DC Sniper was arrested with his 17 year old apprentice sleeping in his car at a rest stop off Interstate 70, near Myersville. A total of seventeen people were murdered during their killing spree. His name was John Allen Muhammad. His sniper nest was in the trunk of his car. Truthfully, I was not nervous about the Sniper attacks. Despite all my problems, I kept the peace of God that passes all understanding, will guard your heart and your mind in Christ Jesus. On Friday, Peter and I met and discussed the civil case in greater detail. When I returned home, I teased my Mother and Father that they must have been praying real hard for them to catch that Sniper. Now they wouldn't be afraid to come down and testify at my domestic trial.

McGrady sent his first bill. In just six months, he was already over a thousand dollars. I wondered how much this divorce was going to cost me. I answered the Interrogatories depicting the marital property, bank accounts held, employment history, recent paystubs, etc. The family came down to testify in my Child Abuse Child trail against Sugar. Now I could finally get these supervised visitations dropped. Sugar was allowed to testify first. Her attorney asked her what happened the night between Gabriel and myself. Sugar was such a drama queen. She took about two hours crying and testifying about that one night. Eight years of marriage and she was still hysterical about the one night that I got hurt. How she didn't know if Gabriel was all right. He was bleeding, she said, still crying. Telling the story knowing he had no real injuries she cried wiping her eyes, spinning her tale, manipulating the one incident. The incident happened in about five or ten minutes. How can you testify about it for two hours and not even comment that I was injured that night from their attack? Court was about to adjourn and neither I nor my family had an opportunity to testify. Sugar had used up all the time. Supervised visitation would still be in effect. My medical records, a CT Scan, profile from work, letter from Neurologist, character references, or out-of-town family members never would have an opportunity to speak. Only Sugar's warped perception of the one incident for the past two hours. The Judge asked that I hand in all my paystubs, though. He determined that the Emergency Family Maintenance would be raised to $500 a month and now be officially called Child Support. They gave me instructions to register with the Maryland Child Support Agency. In hindsight, I should have quit the second job before I went to court. Working three jobs to catch up with bills was going to haunt me now in Child Support. It was like being punished for working hard. How could I keep up this pace of maintaining three jobs?

My efforts to spend time with my daughter were never supported by Sugar. My parents asked if they could see her while they were in town. So Sugar said yes, wanting to appear cordial. This is why I wanted the pastors and parents more involved. People behave differently when witnesses are around. This is why Jesus taught to take two witnesses if at first you can't resolve the matter yourselves. If Ruth was alive she would never have let Sugar behave this way without saying something to her. Ruth was a strong outspoken woman who never withheld Sugar from spending time with her Father.

We went to Horn & Horn Smorgasbord in Lanham, Maryland, off Route 450. Mom, Dad, and Lil Big Sis were all making the best of time to spend with Charity. I took Charity to Horn & Horn with Sugar often when we were a family. She liked when I walked her around for the buffet because she had the opportunity to select her food choices. Supervised visitation was still in effect but I wasn't alone with Charity and it satisfied Sugar's desire to say my family was there. And I should still not be alone with my Daughter. It was bittersweet but you have to pick your battles in life. We took plenty of pictures and enjoyed the delicious food that they served.

Next in my busy weekend, I rode the trains Saturday out to Corona, Queens, and took the NY Police Officer's exam. While on the train, I wrote a praise song that gave me further peace. "I lift my hands to you Savior. I give my all to my Creator. I give you my everything, my all. I'm waiting, I'm waiting, I'm waiting. (Pause)Oh my Lord, there's no one quite like you in all the Earth, nor will there ever be. You sent your Word; to come dwell among us; your holy word, a living legacy. That's why I love you, Jesus. Because you've been faithful and true. That's why I praise you! I lift my hands to you! In gratitude."

In my head, I heard the full chorus of a choir singing along in praise. I was in a great state of peace despite being in three different states in the past three days. I didn't feel overly tired and was clearly focused to take this exam. I felt a job with the NYPD would not only lead me to stable employment but also align myself with people that wouldn't sit in silence while I was being attacked. I didn't need people hiding in their prayer closets at my church. What I needed was warriors to stand up with me.

While waiting for the results, I needed a second income that didn't have me working all night like Central Parking. Retail stores were hiring because of the holiday shopping season approaching. So I went to Macy's at Newport Mall in Jersey City. If I worked there I could also get an employee discount and get Charity some nice gifts for Christmas. It didn't take long after filling out the application that I was put on the schedule.

Peter informed me that the Trustee from my bankruptcy case has contacted them, retaining them to represent my Bankruptcy Estate. He wished to discuss it with me before responding and sent more attachments for me to read. I would read it this November's Drill with the New Jersey Air Refueling Wing. We we had our Thanksgiving's lunch. The AGE Shop didn't celebrate it with the entire Squadron so we had less food. People seemed pretty warm to me. Most guys in the Maintenance field had gruff exteriors. If someone mouthed off to you, you just mouthed off back. They wanted to treat me like the new guy in the shop but I was older than most and out ranked half of them. I was the only Black guy in the shop yet still they seemed cordial. The AGE drivers maintain all the support equipment for the aircraft. If you needed anything you ordered it over the radio and the equipment would be dropped off to your parking spot on the Flight line. My old job I was changing from was the 'crew chiefs. 'They serviced, maintained, and repaired the aircrafts. We thought that we were the big shots of the Flight line. There were also the specialists. They, too, thought they were the big shots of the Flight line. The specialists consisted of the hydraulic systems specialist, electricians, flight control specialist, and guidance control specialist. The AGE drivers didn't differentiate who were crew chiefs and who was specialist. They called them all crew chiefs and despised them all, from the Shop Chief down. They felt all the crew chiefs did were break their equipment. And now they had a crew chief in their midst. I had gone from out of the frying pan into the fire. Now there were two strikes against me.

Prince George's County Circuit Court was breathing down a brother's neck and ordered an independent psychological evaluation regarding custody and visitation. The evaluation had to be within 30 days and the fee was $750. When it rained, it poured. Back at home, Mom went to visit her Sister in the Pittsburgh area. She rarely visited her on Thanksgiving. Sometimes my Aunt Clara used to come out to us. She left and didn't leave any food in the house. Shakur was complaining there was no food. I bought my meals regularly to maintain some type of independence and not be a total burden on her. Shakur wasn't working and his girlfriend was here. God allowed me to scrap up enough for us to have a nice Thanksgiving meal. For this, I was grateful, and for life, health, and strength.

After I prepared the food, we all ate and I wanted to make sure we all gave God thanks for this meal and this time. Shakur was angry and said that Thanksgiving was nothing to celebrate. The Pilgrims stole the land from the Indians. They brought disease and death. I differed with him reminding him that although later they stole land, the Original Pilgrims were Christians and after the Indians taught them how to survive through the harsh winter they celebrated the harvest with this meal. He yelled that I didn't know what I was talking about. It seemed I was always yelling. When I talked, I was so loud. Next thing, we were outside again fighting.

It had been a year since our last fight. Again, I didn't last too long just coming out the hospital and breaking my hand against the cast iron fence. I couldn't see him with my contacts out and it took one punch. This time we fought right out in front of the house. We danced around taunting each other taking swings. I had my contacts in so I could dodge his punches. Then he grabbed me and snatched me up over his head like I was a baby doll. As I was suspended over his head like nothing from his sheer strength, he looked up at me like, his eyes saying "Look what I can do." Last year, my hand was broken and I didn't want to punch my brother. This year, I took my fist and came crashing down in his face. It was my statement, "Look what I can do!" Immediately, he body slammed me and I came crashing down to the street. Taking him down with me. My back was to the ground but I was holding on to him ready to line him up with another punch. What ingratitude after feeding him and his girlfriend! Before I could get my next punch off, he quickly took my head snapping it back against the hard street. Again, I was stunned and blacked out. My body remembered its feeble stages. My head was throbbing and temporarily I was paralyzed and helpless. Shakur grabbed me to finish me off but saw how helpless I was and dropped me. Even though he could have hurt me further, I didn't take it that he was thankful for the meal I provided. I called Butch to take me to the VA Hospital but he told me to go to the Medical Center. Later, I scheduled another CT Scan and session with Dr. Weinstein.

Steady work came as a substitute teacher. We had forty-two public schools and five high schools in Jersey City. We kept busy, some days were rewarding but most were unbearable. The attitudes of the children were atrocious. I didn't want to be ungrateful but I was broken inside. Work at Macy's was nicer but the part-time pay was no comparison with teaching. Taking advantage of the employee discount I bought Charity many outfits for Christmas. Like a Baby Phat pink sweat suit, designer jeans, and other fashionable accessories. Dad drove down to the supervised visitation with me. We took many pictures with Charity modeling her outfits. She was so happy, she kept hugging me even though we weren't supposed to touch. Our Monitor didn't mind, in fact, he pulled me to the side and told me that we didn't belong here. But it was part of the Maryland bureaucracy that Sugar was manipulating. In addition to the Christmas presents and bills, there were the round trip gas and tolls for the visitation. It was worth it all just seeing the smile on her face.

When I made it back home I left a note for my Mother joking, "The Warrior has returned." This was the first time I referred to myself this way. I felt like a warrior and I had all the battle scars to prove it. Jokingly, the note was since I stayed on the road and we saw each other only in passing. Joked about having some casualties during my latest adventure. I lost one of my monogrammed gloves from my Air National Guard's Air Refueling Wing. Lost a hat and a nephew. Note to self that "I miss him dearly" I am not sure what that referenced and whether I was just speaking metaphorically. Looking back these were some of the first notes I started writing down for a book, still unaware at this point whether there would be any book. When I left the Washington D.C. area, in 2001, I thought my worst days were behind me and victory in Jesus was near at hand. Little did I know that these days were just the beginning of sorrows.

A letter came from McGrady stating that he sent Sugar's attorney asking for discovery requests that were now overdue. These were the same personal and marital information that I had to submit. Macy's had me working every day, even New Year's Eve. There weren't many customers that day. The Manager came and handed me my W-2 form. Having a Tax business made this completely clear as I was told that this would be my last day. They laid us off so at the last day of the year so they didn't have to include us as employees in the next calendar year. Brilliant! Unfortunately, I would still be paying Child Support based on this additional income.

CHAPTER 2
An Act of God

When I opened my mail, I received a notification that Military Pay was going to start automatically deducting up to $500 of Child Support per month. They were already hitting my teaching salary before I could touch it. The good news was that I also received a letter back from the NYPD congratulating me on passing the written examination. The next steps in the process were passing the Medical Exam and then the Background Check.

I found out that my checking account with Fleet Bank was never suspended. My balance was over $100 dollars. Now I could go down I-95 and see Charity. In the news, the Space Shuttle Columbia disintegrated upon re-entry into Earth's atmosphere. Seven crew members died in the tragedy. Was man meant to travel among the stars? Was this a sign or a simple malfunction? These were my thoughts as I raced down to supervised visitation.

I made it back from DC and all I could think about was the bed. I woke up early that morning around 4:00 a.m. Happy birthday to me. By the time I was ready, I realized that I would never make it to the bus stop in time. I waited for the 5:20 bus. Despite all my intentions and promptness, I wouldn't be given the opportunity to work this birthday. So I visited my cousins on Bergen Avenue only to find out that they were evicted. I wish there was something I could have done for them. It seemed I wasn't the only one having troubles. Satan was out to destroy everybody. Every family was under attack but especially the Christian ones. But greater was He that is in us than he that is in the world.

Joel had snuck off and gotten married. No one was happy with the rush of things. I had warned him that rushing into marriage was a mistake that I made with Sugar. As the man, I should have taken more time and it led to insecurities in her about our relationship. Thursday, I had a 9:30 appointment with Doctor Weinstein. While waiting, I met his secretary from Sierra Leone. I smiled and told her of a friend I worked with at CACI down in Washington D.C. from 'Lion Mountain,' the French translation of Sierra Leone. Davidson taught me how the men of Sierra Leone spoke with strength from their diaphragm. I invited her to sell some of her African cuisine at the concert I was going to have. I told her about my tape ministry and asked if she had a tape player she could listen to it while I was with the Doctor. My interest was more into the gospel getting out than in selling tapes.

Doctor Weinstein asked me to come back to his office. He wanted to know why my lawyer in Maryland kept calling him. This was disconcerting. I informed him about the pending lawsuit that was about to be settled. Doctor Weinstein and I didn't see what my counseling had to do with the case, which rightfully made me more suspicious of everyone. I mentioned how messed up all my family situations were becoming and I could lose custody.

I started taking some nighttime cold medicine in the daytime. It would knock me out but it relieved my congestion. Five days after my happy birthday, Lil Sis had a healthy new addition to her family. My newest nephew Isaac entered the world. I went to the hospital to visit her. When I came in and looked at the little guy, they just brought her dinner in. I knew how most people felt about hospital food so I asked Lil Sis could I eat hers.

"Uh uh," she shook her head saying no. "I just had a baby," she smirked. My male ignorance left me ignorant to how empty she must have felt just going through the miracle of birth. I asked because the food was there, I wasn't hungry. I heard another church member, Edna Cherry, was upstairs so I went to visit her as well. Surprisingly, she was out of her bed and smiling. She was so happy to see me.

"How you doin', Baby?" She said while she hugged me. Although I was a minister, she had children my age and older. "You don't look so good," she said with a stern look switching to her motherly instincts. "Sit down here," she told merit made me laugh how loving Pastor Lanier's members were. She was admitted into the hospital, but she was nurturing me.

"I'm coming down with something," I told her as she made me sit in the visitor's chair.

"Here, eat my dinner," she said, still nurturing me. "My brother is bringing me some real food." I laughed and had a nice visit. I dozed off from the cold medicine. We prayed for each other, and I left to go home.

My bankruptcy attorney confirmed that my civil case was considered property of the bankruptcy estate, with exception to the recovery of lost wages. An estimated wage loss would be calculated so that he can request an exception for that amount. Peter requested me to update him when my 2002 tax return was completed to assist with the calculation. In the meantime, he asked me to keep him informed of my National Guard plans and any other matters pertaining to our case.

Secretary of State Colin Powell delivered a speech to the Congress presented by U.S. Intelligence on weapons of mass destruction making a case for war against Iraq. At first, I had my reservations about going to war with Iraq but once I heard Colin Powell speaking about the weapons of mass destruction in Saddam Hussein's possession, I thought this tyrant must be stopped at all cost. Some of the intelligence depicted mobile bio-weapons labs moving around at night so they wouldn't be able to track them by satellite.

My civil attorney Peter called me with good news. I could really use some good news right about now. He told me that he went to a negotiation meeting with the opposing counsel. Peter was familiar with the number of attorneys for the opposing counsel for such matters. He referred to some unknown persons sitting down at the bargaining table. My attorney was under the impression that they were "structured settlement" negotiators. Structured settlements meant that portions of the recovery would be placed in an escrow account. Portions would be given back in yearly increments to ensure the client didn't fall back into poverty. This was pleasant news to us that they were both ready to settle and my attorney explained that from this point we only had to answer the question of "how much were we settling for?" He told me that the amount being offered to pay me was $470,000 in settlement; with a structured settlement amount of $30,000 to be divided in four annual payments in the near future.

From a possible eight million ($8,000,000), it went down to a mere half a million ($500,000).They were unaware of all the havoc Sugar was causing, making me lose my paralegal job, the recent arrest in Maryland and up in New Jersey, or my bankruptcy woes. If I continued to wait negotiating for higher offers they might find out my mounting legal problems and reduce the half a million offer. Rather than giving my attorney details that might cause this one to quit also, I made the quick decision to move along and accept their first offer. Normally, I would rule against ever accepting the first offer, but Sugar was burning the house down around merit would cost me at least $250,000 but the opposing counsel would be quick to settle rather than find out the collapsing roof around me.

At church on Sunday, I said a special prayer. Tuesday, I had my next domestic hearing in Maryland. This time the courts would remove the unnecessary restrictions of supervised visitation. Charity and I could go back to a normal father and daughter relationship. Sunday night it started snowing heavily. The news reported even as south as Philadelphia. It accumulated up to four inches and grew frigid developing up to New York City. Simultaneously, it started sleeting as far south as Washington D.C. continuing to accumulate through the night. The sleet turned back to snow by the next morning and turned north into a Nor'easter climbing to New York and went as far as Boston. Figured it was good that it snowed Sunday so tomorrow it would be finished because of my court date Tuesday in Maryland. Monday a secondary system formed off the coast of North Carolina moving all the way up the Northeast to Boston. Blizzard warnings were issued and the storm continued until Tuesday the 18th. Needless to say Maryland cancelled all their court hearings and declared a 'State of Emergency.' They didn't have the salt and plowing equipment we had in New Jersey where things were business as usual. It took them days to clear the roads and sidewalks.

Blizzard of 2003 - The President's Day Storm II

The historical record-breaking snowstorm was called the Blizzard of 2003 or the President's Day Storm II.

'Of all the best laid plans of mice and men' this is what the Military referred to as weather hold. Despite all strategic plans nothing could be done until the weather breaks. It was one of the worst snowstorms in decades. It truly was 'an act of God.' Inwardly, I searched for understanding seeing that once again my prayers to restore the relationship with my Daughter had been hindered. The anger of the situation I would wrestle with and meditate on for the understanding of why this would happen to me. A snowstorm so severe this late in the season? Since the courts and schools were closed, I called Reverend Lanier. He said he was going to the hospital to visit with some people. I grabbed my all-weather military gear. It was made of a Gore-Tex material that was waterproof.

Left hospital to visit Minister Jeff where a woman answered the door but seemed not to know his name. I'd been dropping him off for years there. Someone came up and asked 'what was the problem?' Why did people say this? When he found out I was a minister he invited me in and we walked down the hallway to the steps.

"It's funny she didn't recognize his name," I remarked.

"What did you say?" He quickly asked about his Mother.

"I said, I've been dropping him off for a couple of years and the lady didn't seem to recognize his name," I repeated without hesitation standing at the bottom of the steps.

"Well, did you think maybe she doesn't speak any English?" He fired at me.

"No problema, 'yo hablo español' but even if she doesn't speak English, she should recognize the name of a man living upstairs for years," I said in defense of my friend.

"Get out of my house," he turned around and yelled from on top of the steps.

"That man pays rent here and has a right to receive guest," I said in further defense of Jeff.

"Get out of my house," he yelled even louder, pointing at the door. But I didn't budge in response to his yelling. "I'm a Corrections Officer."

"I'm not going anywhere. I'm a Sergeant in the Military, an NYPD recruit, and a paralegal. That man pays rent here and has a right to receive guest." I sensed they were taking advantage of Minister Jeff. As I thought about it, I decided to turn around and leave.

Before I could turn around, all of a sudden this guy came down to the bottom of the stairs and lunged at my waist. My immediate response was to start pounding the crap out of him but there was no force behind his assault. He even began to grown and his legs quivered like he was straining to push me back but I just stood there feeling nothing. Since I didn't physically feel threatened, I didn't hit him. His strength felt child-like, he was so weak.

"Get off me," I told him as the lady who answered the door came back and another young lady entered the room. They both started grabbing him, trying to pull him off my waist. They were all yelling in Spanish. With the three of them, they started to gain some momentum and I was slowly moving back toward the door. "Get off me," I repeated. This time, I was more anxious taking steps backwards. I feared falling backwards on my guitar strapped across my back. As we approached the doorway I reached down and grabbed him snatching him up. The door was open and after I snatched him up in a twisting motion and threw him down. With his hold on me, the full weight of me came down on top of him crashing on the porch.

"Argh," he yelled out in pain as he lay down on the porch. His neighbors ran from across the adjacent house. He laid there in pain, grabbing his leg.

"What happened?" The neighbors asked, running across the porch. "Call the police," they said. "Don't let him go nowhere," they said as the mob blocked the porch area.

"Call the police," I said, "This guy attacked me," I yelled. Minister Roddey came downstairs in his bathrobe. "Jeff, call the Pastor," I said. He said okay and went back upstairs to get his phone.

"This guy wanted to visit him and said something about Mom so I told him to get out," my new assailant was telling his friends.

"Yeah, I was saying how weird it was she didn't know the name of the guy living upstairs for a couple of years," I joined in the story telling.

"And he wouldn't get out, so I jumped on him and started to push him out," he said.

"And soon as you allowed me access to the home I had the right to visit my friend who is renting his room," I threw in my parts of the story as he told the neighborhood mob.

"Yo! Shut up!" One of his friends said to me like I was under arrest.

"No. You shut up. I have every right to speak. He attacked me after he invited me into the home," I said. I was raised under Black Power and I did not let people speak to me like I was a criminal.

"Yeah, we'll see when the cops get here," his big friend said. He was massive, much like the bouncers and that other big guy at Citi-Markets. But I was up for a fight with this guy and I was already eyeing him up where I could hit him in case he moved.

"Well, we'll see. I'm an NYPD Recruit and a Sergeant in the military," I proudly said.

"I don't give a b----," his friend cursed at me. Here I was back in the same situation as with the bouncers and back at Citi-Markets.

I was tired with the violence being confronted directly at me. I started getting angry. This was the day I was supposed to be down in Maryland, having the supervised visitation restrictions removed from me, and restoring the relationship with my daughter. Here I am facing more violence.

"You guys get me sick," said the big Puerto Rican friend staring me down like he wanted to beat me to a bloody pulp. "You act like we owe you something," he said referring to my uniform.

"You do owe us," I told him."You owe us some respect," I demanded from him.

"Here goes, Pastor," Minister Roddey came back and handed me his cell phone.

"Rev, I'm at Minister Roddey's house," I told him.

"Yes, you told me you didn't know where you were going when you left," he reminded me. Why was he going back to square one? Didn't Minister Roddey explain how tense the situation was?

"I stopped by to visit him on the way to Good News. Someone jumped on me when I was trying to visit him and they are threatening me right now," I said upset. I was speaking to the mob as well. Making them think that I was not alone. However, I was always alone.

"Calm down," Reverend Lanier said. "This is like before you are getting all upset and raising your voice," he said not liking the tone of my voice.

"You're right I'm upset. I've just been assaulted again. These people are threatening me on the porch and I need someone to come over right now," I stressed the severity of the circumstance.

"Listen," he said, not liking my tone, "You have to remain calm," Pastor told me. It was easy for him to be calm in his Pastor's Study when I was out in the real world, surrounded by an angry mob of people being threatened again.

"He said 'b---- you' and is threatening me," I repeated his words to Rev. I wanted him to remain calm while experiencing what I was going through.

"You didn't have to repeat it," Rev said. He became so upset to hear that vulgar word he hung the phone up on me. He hung up leaving me to face the situation alone. Minister Roddey was very passive and remained quiet. So I made another phone call.

"Ace! Hey, I'm over at Highland and Kennedy Boulevard. Get some people and come over," I called my cousin. He was confused because I never really called him before. He said there was nobody around. I just wanted the people listening to think somebody was on the way. Pretending like I had back up but pathetically I didn't. Then the police arrived, the lady who answered the door walked right down to them at the curb and started talking with the police. This was the woman who supposedly didn't speak any English. Then the police spoke to the guy lying on the porch who assaulted me. They called an ambulance for him and said his leg was broken. Why was I always the last guy the police talked to? So I explained how he invited me into the home. Once I entered, and remarked how they didn't recognize Jeff's name, he jumped on me. The two women witnessed it and tried to pull him off me and I only defended myself when I felt like I was about to fall back on my guitar. I made it known that I was a Sergeant in the military, a minister, and an NYPD Recruit. Next thing I knew, they were slapping the cuffs on me and shoving me into the police car.

They gently placed my guitar into the back of the police car. The young Officers were initially kind to me. They seemed to believe me and even asked to see my credentials. I took out my military ID card and showed them. But then the older, racist Sergeants arrived. Like the military, they out ranked the young Officers and told them to arrest me.

They drove me to the Precinct on Communipaw Avenue right down the street where I grew up as a child. Never had I been arrested in all those years but society saw me differently now. Even as a military member, even as a minister, I was still a Black man. This was the so-called race card that I was dealt, a victim of assault being the one arrested. If I were already an NYPD Officer, they would have looked at the situation totally differently. I had to align myself with a group of people that had my back. The arresting Officers were young and neutral during the questioning. They explained that since the guy worked for the County as a Corrections Officer. The Patrol Sergeants sided with him like it was a turf war. I told them that my brother-in-law was the Deputy Administrator of the County Correctional Facilities and would come to my aid. When we came in, I couldn't believe how small the inside of the precinct actually was. They put me in a holding cell while I invoked my right to make a phone call.

Waiting in the holding cell, I was literally ear-shy of overhearing everything happening at the front desk. I overheard the names as they supplied them to the Desk Sergeant preparing the arrest documents. The name of my assailant was Alberto Santiago. It sounded vaguely familiar, like he went to my high school.

They yelled out the charges I was facing, 'Interfering with a Police Officer while he was making a lawful arrest.' All this from visiting Minister Jeff on my way to prayer. I tried to focus on the moment and not things that caused pity. My focus determined my reality. I was able to hear what was going on at the front desk. The Police Captain of the Precinct came to my holding cell. They took my wallet. They saw my military ID and saw me in my Gore-Tex all-weather military gear. But all this White Police Captain saw was a Black face. I was guilty and none of my words mattered to him.

"Why'd you do it?" Some old pasty face Police Captain asked me standing in front of my cell. He spoke softly and gave me his cops eyes, convinced of the answer before he even asked the question. Why wasn't I given the benefit of the doubt that there was any truth to my claims?

"Do what?" I asked, staring back in what started to become a staring contest.

"Break into his house?" He smugly said like he or his racist Sergeants were there, staring at me like his eyes was truth serum.

"He invited me into his house once he heard that I was a minister," I told him. He couldn't stop breaking his stare like I was going to change my story. Even to hear I was a minister didn't change his opinion of me. He walked away with his smug smile. He was nothing like the young White Police Officers. Things would be better once they take charge.

They came to the cell and took me out to make my one phone call. I called Butch and told him what happened. He told me he was on his way. Butch was one of the few people I had watching my back. A lot of family talked the talk but when push came to shove, I was all alone like on the porch, like I was at the Italian Inn. When Butch came in, he was wearing his civilian clothes. I didn't know if the police knew him by facial recognition but within moments they recognized him as a high Official of the Hudson County Correctional Facilities was there visiting me. All of a sudden, I had some legitimacy to my story with him present. I wasn't standing alone, but still not enough to drop the charges.

∞∞∞∞∞

Sugar had a deposition with McGrady. Sugar went on and on about how after April of 2000 I was a Jekyll and Hyde. I needed counseling, Charity didn't want to be alone with me. I was telling Charity she would come stay with me. I tried to punch Sugar in the face, and intimidate her. I needed anger management and verbally abused Gabriel.

The General asked if she asked for Gabriel to come live with me in 1999. She answered yes and said because he responded better to the discipline that I used. He asked if Gabriel had ever been violent. She tried to downplay the youth Pastor incident and the teacher at school. He asked who watched Gabriel and Charity when she was at work the summer of 2000. She answered that I was home with the children (but didn't say that I watched them). He asked if she had any qualms about leaving me with Gabriel and Charity after the head injury.

"Were there any untold incidents or mishaps as far as you were concerned in Bryan exercising parental responsibility during that summer?" He asked.

"Could you repeat that?" She stalled.

"Were there any problems during that summer with Bryan being the parent at home with these children?" He repeated.

"Well, he was really not really in charge… I think Gabriel helped him out a lot more than he helped them out. Bryan didn't know that because of his ego."

What happened to Sugar? I knew she didn't love me but a year ago under oath she was more cordial. Still warped but admitted she was never intimated or threatened by me. Now after her unmerited battered women's counseling she was a constant victim and I was a raging lunatic, a Doctor Jekyll and Minister Hyde punching holes in walls and having to rescue Gabriel from me consistently abusing him. If the Grandmothers were still here, Sugar's Mother, Gabriel's Grandmother, and Sugar's Grandmother, they all would attest to this pack of lies that I ever mistreated Sugar or Gabriel. They were my strongest allies but God had called them home. By taking them from me, was it His Mighty hand that led to the events that followed? Were their deaths an 'act of God' that led me down this path? I needed them here and now more than ever.

Good news! Peter forwarded the original Settlement Agreement for my notarized signature. It had to be modified due to my bankruptcy filing. I ran upstairs and showed Mom since she stood by me helping through all of this. Another Application for Compensation came on July 28th. It was informing me of a hearing to pay the Commission of $1,850 for the Chapter 7 Bankruptcy Trustee. I didn't understand all these documents but I did see dollar signs and these dollar signs were draining my pockets. Let me go play my musical instruments for peace of mind. During a great musical practice, Macy's called and said that if I gave them a $15 payment tomorrow and pay $15 by September 9th, they wouldn't release a negative credit rating.

The next day, when I awoke I saw that my appointment was not until 2:30, so I went back to sleep. Later, I called the bankruptcy Trustee and asked did he have any dates for sending my money. Now he said they had to wait for the language for the structured settlement. Once that would happen my creditors would be paid. Then my attorneys would be paid. Hearing all of this, I realized the money wouldn't come in time to make on my past due government card I used this summer. My Commander wouldn't like that.

I dialed my civil attorney to inquire about the structured settlement language. My divorce attorney had sent me a letter. Sugar not only had free legal representation from the battered women's agency but they gave her two attorneys. Ironically, she had no claim that she suffered any abuse and I had that under sworn testimony. My divorce attorney's bill was now up to $5,592.60 and he wanted a $500 payment for the Court reporter to release the deposition. The bills were so overwhelming, I just grew numb at this point.

I traveled over to the East Orange VA Hospital. The Neurologist cleared me. Praise the Lord! He even gave me the results. I wouldn't have to wait the 10 to 30 days. I stopped by the records department and they told me to call next week. I could hand deliver them and in two weeks and thirty days from now I could get my medical approval for the NYPD.

Later, I took the PATH train to Exchange Place. The train's next destination was the World Trade Center. I hadn't been over there since 9/11. Another passenger told me that it still bothered her going there. At Exchange Place, I walked over to the Hudson-Bergen Light Rail. While waiting I read some inspired words by Winston Churchill, "Never, never, never give up!"

I took the Bayonne Flyer light rail to Liberty State Park waiting for a West Side Avenue. Little boys were acting up and everyone was afraid to say something to them. The trend in our country was making new laws where children didn't have to respect authority. They challenge authority constantly. They challenge the teachers in school defiantly. The security guards for the parking lot came over. They boys gave them a little respect, must be the uniform. Then a NJ Transit police pulled up, they respected her. The police had guns and were the only ones they respected. Partly the reason why I wished to become a cop.

One miscalculation I had about substitute teaching was having the summers off. We weren't eligible for unemployment so I had to find some other type of work real quick. So I started working for UPS in Secaucus which was still accessible by mass transit. They started me off unloading trucks on the evening shift. It was back breaking work but it was a little slower than FedEx Ground. Although I was paid on a weekly basis now, my income had dropped immensely and I was still hit with the same amount of Child Support.

Doctor Weinstein called, the Neuropsychological Report was finely finished. I had a great practice session today with the musical instruments. For one of the first times, I was putting together chords on the keyboard like you wouldn't believe. After picking them up, I dropped off some papers with the Newark Post Office and now I was on my way back to Journal Square to the Social Security Office. Steven called me and we were talking about his fight to be with his children. He was fighting for visitation with his estranged wife. I told him about Sugar's attorney and how she was going after my medical settlement money now. Steve said how he had success filing his own motions without an attorney. I told him how my divorce attorney's bill was around $6,000 and we hadn't even been to trial yet. On August 13th, I received a copy of the letter confirming the Settlement Agreement was signed. Great but it wasn't going to be in time to pay off this government card. At National Guard Drill, I received a Letter of Counseling for the non-payment on my Government Credit Card. Grant me the serenity Lord! I need that check now.

Mom and Lil Big Sis were in the house talking. They grew quiet enough to start eavesdropping on my telephone conversation about my medical settlement. Later, I was thinking about going into a recording studio. I was working on my fingering skills but my technique needed work. Over the telephone, the Family Crisis Center called with a telephone interview. Mom and Sis kept talking about the latest news. I had so much drama in my life but no one really cared. When we did try to talk about things they blamed me for everything, leading to arguing at me and disrespecting my thoughts, feelings, and opinions. And I was definitely loud if you got loud with me. Totally antagonistic to everything, I thought or said about my own life. I shouldn't have said this to Sugar and I shouldn't have done that. Everything was always my fault and they didn't even have all the details. Satan was driving a wedge between us and I certainly wasn't helping. I was being nobody's doormat with my personal business. They didn't want to hear any of my advice with their marriages, their children, and their imperfect lives.

Today, Peter sent me a letter confirming his law firm's attorney fees and cost reimbursement he sent to my Bankruptcy Trustee. He claimed he wasn't sure but expected that I should be receiving the final distribution very soon. He strongly encouraged me to communicate with McGrady, my divorce attorney, concerning the manner in which my distribution should be handled to maximize its security. This was a warning shot that Sugar and the Natives were getting restless.

Peter called and told me that my Sister called him and wished to come down with my Mother and discuss with him my settlement. My jaw was paralyzed in awe. This was extremely inappropriate. Even with my limited legal experience, I knew that a lawyer is sworn to confidentiality of a case and could not disclose any details even with family. Why was everyone so concerned with my money? They didn't discuss their financial details with me. I thanked Peter for informing me and let him know that I would handle it on this end.

General McGrady wrote me another letter regarding the $528 owed to the Court Reporter. He felt embarrassed that she sent him three notices and the bill is still unpaid. McGrady was anxious asking me to call him to let him know the status of when I would receive my personal injury funds. The past due government credit card bill came in the mail. The new balance was $1,424. When I went to my National Guard Drill, September 14th now is a day that will live in infamy. My Letter of Counseling was upgraded to a Letter of Reprimand for the non-payment on my Government Credit Card. In 30 days, more punishment would follow. I can't say I haven't been down this road before. I was so consumed in bills that I remained on my second job with UPS, when the school year started. In an attempt to avoid the stress of unloading and loading trucks, I moved over to sorting packages. These guys took the packages off the conveyor belts after reading the zip codes and placing them to their designated belts. Additional pay was given to me after I memorized every zip code and its color coordinated designated conveyor belt. For September, I even received an award for Employee for the Month with Upside was less pay but much more gratification than I was receiving in the Public School System.

Visitation was coming up Saturday but I wouldn't get paid in the School System until the following Monday of the 30th. I had to borrow the money from my Mother even though it was just over the weekend. All she had was the roundtrip money for the Greyhound bus. There was no money for taxis or buses once I arrived in Maryland. They didn't have much of a mass transit system down there. Once I arrived at Union Station in Washington D.C., I had to walk to the Family Crisis Center in Lanham, Maryland. It took me over two hours to reach it by foot. No time for any pity parties if I wanted to see her. Thank God my Mother had the money to loan me for the bus ticket. What inspired me was watching a Civil War Documentary, I borrowed from the library. A newly freed slave walked barefoot from Virginia to New York once he was liberated. If he could do that then I could walk to see my Daughter. Some emotions would come, especially, toward Sugar for putting me through all of this. Gabriel's father was still alive and never tried to see his Son. Two years of this now with never a threat to their safety. It was unconstitutional that all my parental rights were thrown away. I made it to the Supervised Visitation on time. No time to think about myself. It's time to put on a happy face.

When I went in the visitation room, Charity was sitting in there waiting. When I went in smiling and gave her a quick hug, I saw Sugar escaping through the door ensuring that I wasn't following her. She seemed to relish in the attention and drama of it all. Charity was smiling and told me that she had a surprise for me. She even seemed dressed a little nicer. She pulled out a plastic recorder and music notes. It reminded me of when I played clarinet in grammar school. It was reminiscent in its little plastic form. The holes had to be perfectly covered like the clarinet or the sound wouldn't come out right, most kids just squeaked when they played these. Their tiny youthful fingers weren't strong enough to properly cover the holes.

Charity took a deep breath and began playing. It was Beethoven's 'Ode to Joy' and she didn't play it like a little child. She played it skillfully. Every note was crisp, clear, and distinguishable, on a flute-a-phone. This was my child who still, despite the attempts to keep her from me, displayed her inherited musical talent. The emotions were unbearable. I missed her, overwhelmed at her musical talent, hurt because I couldn't even really touch her in my supervised visit. I was proud of the skill she displayed. She took the recorder away from her mouth and just smirked at her accomplishment. My tears bawling down my cheeks were all the applause she needed. They streamed down my face at her note for note rendition.

"You must have been practicing that a lot," I said still choked up, wiping the tears, missing her terribly. All the time lost between us, still seeing our musical connection, like Father, like Daughter. Knowing the amount of practice it took to cover the holes precisely totally capturing the melody.

"Yes," she smiled laughing as she enjoyed the fact that I was wrapped around her little finger.

"That was wonderful, Baby Girl." When I walked back on my two hour walk to Union Station, it was a sweet reminiscing about my little concert. She had to practice really hard for her Daddy. This was the love I needed to keep me going.

CHAPTER 3

THE VIOLATION OF BRYAN PORTER

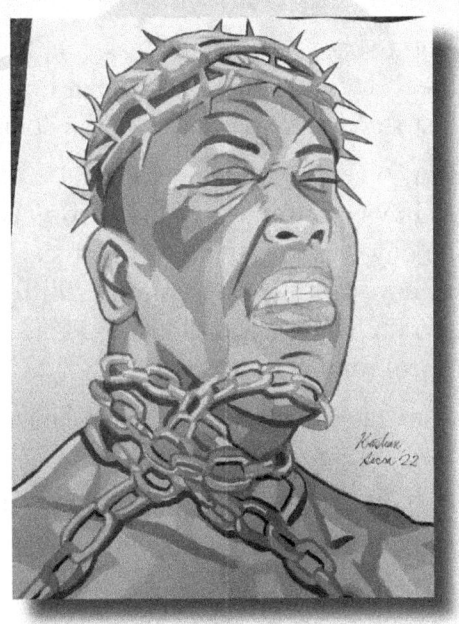

Violated

After an awesome time spent with my daughter, I left Supervised Visitation, still with only the money my Mother loaned me. I walked back from the Visitation Center to New York Avenue to Union Station, Washington D.C. I remembered my daily commute back when I was a paralegal before the coma. Daily I drove down this street, everyday catching light after light. Of course, it went quicker in my car. Still, I had no choice but to walk for two hours to get to the Union Station if I ever wanted to get back to New Jersey. When I reached Union Station, I hopped on the next Greyhound bus back home. I was tired and fell asleep almost all of the way home.

When I finally arrived home, I didn't see anyone else in the house. Upstairs to the third floor, I walked and took a well-deserved hot shower. My four hours of walking for miles can get a man sweaty and grimy with all the cars whizzing by you. Under the hot water, I let the shower blast the dirt and tiredness away. The water was reviving me as I let it rinse off my naked body. Then all of a sudden the door burst open and someone yelled, "A ha!" I was startled. I jumped and attempted to cover myself.

"Oh Bryan, you're back. I thought it was your brother sneaking in somebody up here," she said she was glad that I made it back safely from D.C. She just stood there though with the door wide open.

"Close the door," I yelled, covering myself. I was too tired for this. The glass of the shower doors were frosted so you couldn't clearly see my body. The day was long. The fact that she burst in the door, giving me no privacy, had me very upset. I still felt uncomfortable with her talking to me while I was naked, making me feel violated, yet again. No respect for a grown man.

"You better not raise your voice in my house," she declared, emphasizing that it was her house.

"Get out," I yelled as I stood there butt naked in the shower. There had to be some boundaries and this was one of them. I wanted some alone time and the bathroom was an obvious choice. My mother stormed off and said her last words behind the closed door. I had to move out of here as soon as I get my money.

Mostly all the help I received post-coma came from Momma. She had no ill intentions toward me. She gave me more support than she ever received from her parents. As I grown man, I should not have had to retreat back to her house. However the 'god of this world' was a 'man' hating adversary. The thief came to steal, kill, and to destroy. The destruction of our families started with the attack on all fathers, destroying the whole body by chopping off the head. The rest of the family becomes vulnerable in this spiritual warfare. Then the next logical target is the mother.

Mothers and women were more critical targets of warfare. Spiritual or otherwise, the detriments of war can scar generations. A brutal tactic of the adversary after the destruction of the father was the destruction of the mother. The cruelest, most horrific act of war was the 'rape' or demeaning of women once the soldiers are removed. The definition of rape is a type of assault, normally sexually forced, violating a person without consent. This action may be by physical force, coercion, abuse of authority, or against a person's will or valid consent.

Living in my mother's house was a blessing but paying rent and still being treated like a child made me feel violated. I was being beaten to a pulp like a dog, having my children taken away. My parental rights stripped, I was being assaulted by my stepson and my wife made me feel violated even more. I could easily put a whipping on them but I took the high ground. For that, I had Protective Orders placed on me, arrested, jailed, shackled, and handcuffed. I had lingering Child Abuse charges, lost wages, mounting bills, and supervised visitation. They shackled me and dehumanized me. Stripped of my rights and dignity, I wasn't in the State. I didn't threaten anyone. The shackles were a message of their control and power. Again, I was violated.

October came and the letters of my settlement gave me hope. However, you could sink your teeth better into actual payment than hope of payment. An old saying, you can hope in one hand and fart in the other and see which fills up quicker. I had to do something, my government card remained unpaid. So I sent McGrady a check for $200 because he wanted $500 for the Court Reporter.

When I saw Lil Big Sis and Mom together sitting at the kitchen table, I took the opportunity to confront them about my attorney calling and informing me that they requested to come down and speak with him about my settlement. I questioned what went through their heads, reminding them a lawyer cannot disclose information about his clients without their permission. It was clear that my statement rang a bell in their heads as they sat there still avoiding eye contact with me. They knew there was no way to talk with my lawyer without my authorizing it. They argued with me about so many of my affairs. For this they remained silent. The legal authority was something that they had to recognize.

Another drop in the bucket came in the mail. Another hearing on the Application for Compensation was issued for the firm that represents the Trustee. This one was for Commissions of $12,622 and Expenses of $531. My understanding from all these documents was growing vividly clear. My money was dissipating with every letter before I even was able to touch it.

Another strategic move I made was to pay $550 on the government card. A mistake I learned from the car repossession was to stop looking at the total picture. It could become overwhelming. I looked at payments and payment plans. Lil Big Sis was always so helpful with banking. She helped me cash personal checks so I didn't have to wait for the three day holds.

With substituting, UPS, and my Air National Guard checks, I was able give Mom a little something toward rent. And I do mean a little. I supplied my own food, I was able to send McGrady $325 so thank the Lord the Court Reporter was paid and we would be able to proceed.

This month's supervised visitation came up, I decided to take the Greyhound bus once more. This time, I would walk from the Suitland Train Station on the Blue line of the Metro Train System. This seemed to be a closer walk and I could access the Blue line from Union Station in D.C. to the bus. There was less traffic whizzing by me walking to the Family Crisis Center walking this route. The time seemed to take as long but I am not sure. I wished my daughter knew how much effort I put into seeing her but it would all pay off one day. I had faith God was going to break this bondage and I would be victorious.

All the talk that my money was coming soon led me to hold off working for a while. Gladly, I quit UPS and took few substitute teaching assignments. Around this time, I started concentrating on full-time ministry and a gospel concert. All the years I had been playing bass for Good News, the McGuire AFB Gospel Choir, the Lajes Gospel Choir overseas, the Travis Gospel Choir in California, and Gospel Temple Choirs. I had been a musician, choir director, also praise and worship leader. My friends were even more talented and with them joining me we could have a great night and introduce a lot of people in Jersey City to my growth in music ministry. I played for their choir anniversaries and on third Sunday mornings.

Brother Silvanus Napoleon was a large elderly man who started attending Good News Bible Mission. While I would practice for the concert, often I would stop by his apartment. We would talk a lot about music. Whenever I would stop by, I always asked to go see the gold records mounted on his walls. Commemorating his sons, PM Dawn's record sales of their song 'Set Adrift On Memory Bliss.' One day, I told myself I could achieve a gold record if I worked hard enough. Napoleon credited himself for encouraging 'Kool &The Gang' to form while in they were in their earliest jazz stages. Jersey City was just that rich in musical talent.

My friend Errold, Pastor Lanier's son, worked with me to promote the concert. He was smooth like his father. He believed in me and was a better musician than I was. The songs I selected, I studied note for note. Joel and Alan Berry were going to play on the keyboards. We wanted Deacon Butler on the drums but he had a busy work schedule. Keith Staggers stepped up on the drums and he was a talented drummer. The only problem was that Keith didn't make practices or study the song arrangements. Alan, Joel, and I were trying to take our skills to another level.

Every day, I kept waiting and praying for that check to come along with practicing the songs on the keyboards and the bass guitar. I planned to have three keyboards on a couple of songs. For the rest, I would have two keyboards, me on the bass, and Keith on the drums. I kept asking for volunteers to come and sing with me on all the choir parts while I was still playing the bass for free for them on Sundays. I promised them free refreshments after and started making flyers. Every day, I checked the mail anticipating the check to come.

Errold worked feverishly to help my dream become a reality. My desire after the concert was to play for free in Marion Projects and also at Citi-Markets, ministering the Gospel of Christ before hundreds of people, and spreading the Gospel through our gifts.

I planned to pay him handsomely but he was doing it just because he was my brother. I can't count the amount of hours he put into it for me. His brother Joel was the only other musician who actually put in practice time to work on the musical selections we picked out for the concert. We were in synch for a lot of the chord changes in the songs. No one ever really came forward and practiced for the mass city choir I was trying to get together backing me up. The main song was going to be "We Made It" by Hezekiah Walker. It was written in response to the 9/11 attacks. Hezekiah was from Brooklyn.

"We made it! We survived! When the Enemy came in to take our lives," the song went. These words had even more value since I almost lost my life. Many of the New York Choir identified with loved one lost on 9/11, senseless crimes, and accidents."God lifted a standard . . . no weapon formed shall prosper against us!" How encouraging in the life of a believer. "No weapon formed, would prosper against us," God promised those who believe in Him. (Isaiah 54:17) This powerful promise made through the prophet Isaiah was another song I was practicing to play on the piano by Fred Hammond.' No Weapon Formed Against Me.'

"Determination," Pastor Lanier smiled and said, encouraging Errold and I about our efforts at making this concert a success. I walked up and down Jersey City, trying to make this concert a success. I walked by Universal Full Gospel to leave some flyers, at Reverend Shoemaker's church, St. Mary's Holiness Church, Bread of Heaven Restaurant, and Pastor Daniel's Church to promote the concert. I walked down Pastor Joshua at Cityline Church.

The concert was approaching and the check still hadn't come yet. How was I going to rent the school for the concert? I called Sugar asking if Gabriel and Charity would come to support my concert. She said that she would consider it but I knew there was nothing behind her statement. Ticket sales were pathetic, even volunteers to sing were no shows. Still, I was energized by God's amazing power through the songs I practiced night and day. When I walked to work, I would strut and glide down the streets, practicing choreographies of dance I could see as the music played in my mind. Little did I know with the joy I felt as strutted down the streets, happy for God blessing me with life after death, the whispering would start. The haters would whisper and find their way to my mother's ears. Be careful of your surroundings she would say to me.

We were renting Ferris High School and we needed payment, not faith. I knew God could have sent the answer by now, even if the check was hindered, He could have sent another breakthrough. I would have to ask people for help and they didn't have the faith. Errold and I saw our predicament and the amount was too large for one person. My check was weeks away but I needed it now even though I wasn't meant to have it now. According to Scripture, a brother was born for adversity. Errold was truly my brother and proved that. I asked his father Pastor Lanier for the loan and I would pay him back in a couple of weeks. I told him the lawyer had sent me letters. He asked to see the letter. After I produced them, Rev gave us half of the money. I went to my mother and asked for the other half. She was enjoying her well-earned retirement but I would pay her back in a couple of weeks. She told me "no" and I walked outside. Errold was waiting on the steps and asked what happened. I told him she said no. He went in and told me to stay outside. Errold was charming and soft talking as Rev. He smiled and went in to talk to my mother. He came out with a check from her. It was strange that she didn't loan me the money, her own son, but I was the one who was going to pay it back. I just thanked God for making it happen.

During breakfast, I had coffee with skim milk and two equals, and a toasted everything bagel with veggie cream cheese. A.R. Bernard was teaching on the radio, "Something inside that can change the course of a nation. Naomi left Bethlehem with two sickly sons. Both Sons died. Yet Ruth had determination. She would not turn away; she even worked as a gleaner. Gleaners were the people who came in after the harvest and searched for the scarce leftover food. This was a hard living but Ruth was faithful and someday she eventually became Queen. She was in the lineage of David. She had determination just as Pastor Lanier had spoken about us."

Saturday came and it was the day for the concert. All the work, and I mean it was a lot of back breaking work, came to this. Over a thousand flyers were passed out, all the word of mouth advertising while I played at other peoples church services, all the blocks I walked with Errold, the beauty parlors we visited, the florists, the handbag shops, and barber shops, and all the musical practices with Joel. I still had a vendor coming to sell food. It was all over and the stress was all gone. There were prayer warriors praying on this for months in advance. Brother Napoleon was supposed to have played his conga drums but he was feeling very sick. He was well into his sixties and decided he was not going to the concert. Still, he took the van he was using to make sure we had transportation to Ferris High School.

Napoleon transported all the equipment. Free parking and tickets were $15 at the door. Only Cynthia Hines and Clint Dickerson showed up to sing. Joel came and had this amazing professional two keyboard stand his brothers bought him for concerts. Keith came and my friend Dee brought her son to play the drums a little. The security guards were there. Pastor Lanier dropped by like a proud father. He opened us up in prayer. He left shortly after to go visit his wife in the hospital.

Opening up the concert, I personally thanked him and my mother openly for loaning me the money for making this all possible. My father said that he wouldn't help. He told me, "That's your thing. That's not my thing." His words would haunt me. I found out that he snuck by but no one else saw him, either. Butch was busy and skipped it. Vern, Keith's Uncle, snuck in. His brother Ronnie was vending food and brought his family. Mother Ruth from Gospel Temple came, her daughter Ronda, Mother Terry, Mother Staggers, Mom, Lil Big Sis, and Lil Sis. Errold brought his wife and children. I asked for my children but of course their mother wouldn't encourage them to come. All my family in Jersey City were invited but none of them came. The auditorium sat hundreds so it appeared empty with our small crowd but we filled the place with praise.

I was surprised to see my mother and sisters there. They didn't bring their children or invited any of their friends. I was thankful to see them. That's alright, none of my cousins came or their small children for their free admission. I wonder why God placed me in that position. He had all power and could have that check come anytime

He wanted. As the King's heart is in the hand of the Lord and he turns it wherever He wills."We are the tested. We are not the tester," is a phrase I coined. We are the tested. We cannot choose the test or the time when the test comes, serenity.

After Pastor's prayer, we asked Errold's aunt to come render an A & B selection. We were still setting up with our late 5:30 p.m. start. Aunt Cindy, as we called her, sang professionally with Timothy Wright. Her voice was so powerful and amazing. Next, Clinton came and sang a selection. His vocals were amazing as well. He had a deep rich tone. I was up next. I wasn't as great a singer as they were and being backed by a choir or back-up singers would have helped. But the musical selections we made had so many chord changes and bass lines that it was good. At first, Alan, a professional musician, was unfamiliar with the specific songs we were doing, despite the various audio tapes that I dropped off to him. He was just trying to do me a favor with his busy schedule of events. He had played somewhere earlier that day. Alan was more experienced but it only made sense to have Joel as the lead keyboard because he knew all the chord changes from our practices. Joel was terrific and all who came were amazed. If only each one of them would have brought one other person. If only they could have invited someone else. We gave away free tickets just to fill the seats. I gave some to family members, church members, the National Guard members, and Senior Citizens but no one came. No one from my home church came and supported me. Minister Roddey even bought a ticket just to help even though he had to work. No one from Good News came.

When I was a high school student playing the clarinet, we had our All-City Music Concerts here at Ferris. So afterwards I took the guest and musicians on a brief tour. When Alan saw the facilities, he was impressed. We walked around and looked at the practice rooms they had in the back with pianos where they performed warm-ups before concerts. Everyone saw the potential if we had given a more collaborative effort how different things could have been.

Everyone was encouraged to fix a plate from the food vendor and grab a quick ride. I apologized to the food vendor who didn't make any money. I promised him I was going to take care of him in a couple of weeks. Everyone who came and all the musicians were encouraged to take food plates home with them. My generosity led to rumors of some pending medical settlement. From here on, the wagons were circling and everyone with an agenda or building fund started stepping forward.

An attorney called me from some firm, informing me that I would soon receive a check for $25,000. He thought that they could offer me a banana and I'd be jumping up and down like a little monkey. I asked him about the rest of the money. All I owed in depth was under $10,000 and they were keeping over $333,333. He said that what would remain after my estate was settled would be returned to me. It was driving me crazy.

This was just like the lesson I learned when the car was repossessed. The check came well after the car was repossessed. I had to submit to the will of God. Other than the car, with the concert I had a choice to use either patience or faith. Using faith had me to rely on others. I could have used patience and waited until all funding was there rather than going by faith and using credit cards and spending money before I received it. God didn't force me to make that choice.

Another Notice of Hearing on Application for Compensation came. It informed me of a hearing to pay Peter, my civil lawsuit attorney, a third of the settlement. The Commission was for $166,666 and Expenses for $1,082, an estimated total of $168,000 just on my divorce attorney. I hadn't even received the money and Sugar started the vultures all circling.

Despite all the letters dropping on me, my money still wasn't. I had no money to pay my cell phone bill. I had no money for gas and tolls to make monthly supervised visits. My cell phone was turned off for a while because they had the nerve to ask for payment. I was working two jobs with teaching and the National Guard but both were being deducted by Child Support because I was so far behind. The little left over I offered my mother for rent and nothing left over to live off.

The next letter to hit was delivered by Federal Express marked 'Personal and Confidential.' Could this be the check they were sending? Peter was pleased to announce, because my phone had been disconnected, about his conversation Monday with the bankruptcy Trustee. He was thrilled to ensure me that my check for $25,000 was issued. This amount represented the exemption portion of my distribution. By his estimations, it may take two to three months until I receive my full distribution but my bankruptcy attorney would know better than he did on that matter. Peter reiterated their filing with the Trustee for $167,749, which was well-deserved. He informed me that their law firm incurred an additional cost of approximately $4,000 not submitted for reimbursement. That was kind of them. These funds were realized after expenses were submitted. But to my understanding, the case was not officially settled yet.

Every day, I checked the mail and then finally it happened. Hallelujah! The check came. This would start a new day in my life. I had to suffer through a coma, amnesia, pneumonia, stitches, not being able to walk, family fights, bankruptcy, repossession, police arrests, back biting, etc. I lost a wife, children, career, cars, and church family. It was a long hard road but God saw me through it all. If it had not been for the Lord on my side, where would I be? I would have lost my mind too, a long time ago.

News of my turn of fortune inspired me to focus on what I would do with the rest of my financial settlement. Everyone was happy for me but from this moment on, I would not be able to borrow a penny from anyone anymore. I had to be highly responsible because if I had no one watching my back before, financially no one would be watching it in the future. Among my many visions, I wanted to go into full-time ministry. Among daily prayer, I did a daily devoted amount of Bible study. I wished to continue building upon a teaching ministry I started back in the military. As my studying expanded so would my library of teaching tapes. Also, I dreamed of opening a musical instrument store in the Citi-Markets shopping complex. Music lessons would also be provided. I played the clarinet and the saxophone had its similarities. From my bass guitar playing I had beginner guitar skills. Beginner piano, keyboards, and drum lessons. I planned to provide a studio for this Hip-Hop crowd to work on their beats.

Rev and I talked about joining the Jersey City Minister's Alliance. Pastor Lanier smiled but didn't enjoy the politics of ministry. Rev was committed to daily prayers, visiting the sick in the hospitals, counseling people on a daily basis, and the responsibilities of pasturing a church, in between juggling his finances, caring for the church, and his sick wife. Still like a proud father, he enjoyed my enthusiasm and said he would come with me to their next meeting.

Straight to Citi-Markets I marched. The management offices were located inside with three to four empty stores. One of these stores I claimed to be my music store in the name of Jesus Christ. Confidently, I continued to march into the management office where a met Michael, the Chief Finance Officer. He was a heavy set, well dressed, slightly older Italian man. He was wearing glasses, dressed in neatly pressed dress shirt, silk tie, and patent leather shoes.

"How much for the store?" I asked cockily.

"How much for what? Which store?" Michael responded inquisitively. He must have thought I was referring to one of the smaller stores in the complex.

"For all of it?" I boastfully stated. What I lacked in money, I was rich in faith. Michael smiled at my youthful exuberance and took his glasses off laying them on his desk. Now my education would begin.

"Well," he smiled taking a deep breath in. "The entire shopping complex would cost you two million and that's just the liquid assets you have to keep in on the property." Now I took a deep breath dropping my head in even deeper thought. That type of money was currently beyond me. But if the Ministers Alliance were united we could raise those funds. The community was energized that Citi-Markets was Black owned and brought a lot of job opportunity to this opportunity starved community.

"The owner of Citi-Markets Bob Banks was backed by a corporation that supplied the liquid assets for the shopping complex," he revealed the wizard behind the curtain. Bob Banks was the front man and Citi-Markets was not a true Black owned business. I was in way over my head yet I wasn't discouraged about the two million, just in my faith that I didn't have it yet. I knew the Minister's Alliance wouldn't come together for that purpose and unite our funds but if the unity was there. Together, we could be unstoppable.

"How much for the empty store?" I asked reluctantly accepting my merger role of a musical store owner.

"What do you want to do with the store?" Michael asked.

"I want to sell and rent musical instruments. Provide music lessons and possibly a small recording studio for these young people," I answered him proudly.

"That kind of store doesn't do well in this type of economy," he tried to warn me." I'm going to try and get Dunkin' Donuts in here and a liquor store," he smiled at his ambitious plan.

"I've been working in the Public School System so plan to land some instrumental rentals contracts. I've been playing in the local churches so I would get business there. A Liquor Store won't go well here. Most of the people at the supermarket are church people and those that drink like to buy their liquor on the down low," I tried to share with him. "Not right here where everyone can see them."

"I don't feel that way," he said confidently but he respected my difference of opinion. "The smaller stores yours for a $10,000 deposit. The monthly rent would be $700 per month."

Later that month, I met with Michael again, the CFO, and he told me more on the store plans. To my surprise, he handed back my check back for $10,000. Now the store was secured for me without any money. The blessings were pouring down. I was $10,000 richer with the same entrepreneurial interest as before. Lil Big Sis stopped by Mom's house, so I ran out to ask for a ride. Her sons Double K and Ice pulled up to the house. I called a local city car dealer that sent me a pre-approved auto loan for $25,000. My sister dropped me off on Route 440 to the car dealer on her way home. There were no salesmen around to be found. I waited but finally I gave up, went to the store to buy a plastic bowls to marinate some rib-eye steaks. On the way back home, I ran into Ice, my nephew. I talked to him about working for me and playing college ball. He was looking into joining the Air Force like I did. I didn't want him to go away. But he was looking to see the world and get away.

Immediately, I paid back my mother and Pastor Lanier for loaning me the money for the concert. I had to pay Joel, Alan, Keith, Aunt Cindy, and Clint for their participation in the concert. Errold got the lion share and not enough for all the hard work he put into it. The food vendor was paid for the money he invested putting the food up front and supporting my vision. Believing Peter that the rest of the money would be coming soon, I had a pre-approved auto loan that allowed me some leverage. Part of my true vision was to get these musicians and singers to go minister for free at the Marion Gardens Public Housing area for free. I was hoping the love of God would hit them and my generosity.

Between Errold, the soloists, and the musicians I paid $1,300. The rental of Ferris High School was $1,200, including mandatory School Security. The food vendor supplied his own ingredients. The lasagna was world-class, the fried chicken, string beans, macaroni and cheese were all delicious. Plus he trusted me and waited for payment. We were raised in the church together but he didn't attend weekly. He was more of a brother born for my adversity than a pew full of weekly attending holy rollers. I told Errold to pay him and invite him to the victory 'party.' Most Christians are disturbed by the use of that word. We might have called it a victory dinner but we were going to party that night, as hard as Errold and I worked. We made arrangements at the Sizzler Steakhouse on Friday in the Citi-Markets complex. We had the Minister's Alliance meetings there to generate business. In addition to me, the musicians, Napoleon, Errold and his family came. Alan said he couldn't make it. He had a service to play for that night. Errold passed out the checks and we celebrated the victory. They gave us a group rate per person. All of a sudden Joel's wife walked in. She talked a good game but she didn't support us in the choir or even come to the concert. Now she wanted a free meal. I pulled Errold and Joel aside and told him that we were deducting her meal out of his check. He just smiled because he was just a loving person who didn't want any trouble. But trouble was her middle name.

Alan came in after his church service he was playing for. We passed him a check and he was quite surprised. He would have done it for free he said. I told that I wanted him to do it for pay so he would be on time and make practice rehearsals. Alan was in high demand and had an event he was playing for the day of the concert. Ronnie, the vendor, came with his brother and enjoyed the entree selection. Some other party crashers came who didn't come to the concert. Generously, I paid for their meals but I told them that they were responsible for their own drinks. People already were taking advantage of my kindness. They didn't give us any support for the concert but they crashed the victory dinner.

We sat with Alan and talked about music and how we could have made it an even better experience. I told him that I wanted him to produce and have provided the singers. We could have had a choir with all the talented voices he and Ronda worked with. We talked about David and being the Chief Musician. We talked about commitment and getting drummers who studied the musical arrangements like we did. Alan was impressed with my skills in organizing. We all admitted my playing still needed work. I played very well while working three jobs. In the future, I planned to devote more time to practice and less time to working for others. The check that night at Sizzler's Steakhouse came to around $500. We shared our dreams; it was a great victory celebration in music ministry. That concert and that night were priceless.

The Government credit card still needed my immediate attention. The balance was $1,424, so I paid it right away. Once this was accomplished, I immediately called my Commander informing him. This put me back on his good side. Christmas was coming and I am sure McGrady would appreciate his payment. He had been remarkably patient and hard working on the case. His bill was now up to $7,417.

My main Florist was Brian's wife at Citi-Markets. Her Floral Shop was able to make the arrangements and a delivery Sunday to Gospel Temple, my Mother's Church down the block. She taught me the different flowers as I was putting together different floral arrangements. I had a different arrangement for the Church Mothers and my mother. I had a different arrangement for the Prayer Warriors who had been praying for the concert for the previous months before the concert. Deliveries were delivered simultaneously made to both at

Gospel Temple and Good News Bible where I had my faithful Prayer Warriors, like Mother Ida. I sent my sisters a different arrangement from a different florist so there wouldn't be distracted. Flowers were breathtaking but looked more than they actually cost. I spent about $200 on flowers but I gained the appreciation of a lot of great women.

Great news, Saddam Hussein was captured on December 13, 2003, while hiding in a hole. This ousted dictator was on the run for nine months. People were rejoicing in the streets of both America and Iraq. Saddam had created a lot of enemies while he was in power. However, I still remember President H.W. Bush stating he saw no exit strategy from leaving a stable Government after removing him from office. To date, no 'weapons of mass destruction' were found yet. Still, the capture of Saddam Hussein was hailed as a decisive military victory in American history.

I stopped by the Florist, at Citi-Markets, to create a floral arrangement for Charity's upcoming performance at a winter recital for my daughter. I rented a car to drive down and see Charity in the 2003 Winter Recital of Tchaikovsky's 'March of the Tin Soldiers.' Thank God, I wasn't struggling financially like before. These trips down to Maryland cost me over $100 a trip. I don't wish to sound frugal, but it costs me hundreds of dollars just to see my child every month, on top of the Child Support, and I was only able to spend a couple of hours with her.

Big Brother Mike O'Neill called saying he had been trying to reach me. I apologized and told him how I'd been so busy lately. I mentioned to him that Satan had hindered me. I wished he could have made the concert and jammed with his saxophone. Mike said that the doctors couldn't diagnosis what was allying him. He joked that he thought he was getting old but they said that he had some rare lung disease. God would heal and deliver I reminded him. I shared with him about launching into full-time ministry. I told him with all these past troubles it seemed like the Devil has an all-out attack against me to discourage me. Mike mentioned that the entire body of Christ was under attack. Amen to that!

I shared how the enemy was keeping up confusion in my home. I couldn't even rest there. Last night was the first night I slept in my bed in a long time. He asked what the matter was. "Was it Shakur?"

"No," I answered. I couldn't understand it. I was able to contribute more to rent now and be on time. We joked about the friction sometimes people had with their mothers. One of the most powerful, if not, the most powerful relationships you'll ever have is with your mother. Mike had told me a prophesy about Shakur. I told him that I shared that prophesy with him. Mike reminisced how he played saxophone meeting Jo Mo Kenyatta, the great Liberator of the nation of Kenya.

Later that day, I saw my neighbor shoveling the walkway in front of her house. I walked across the street to the Laundromat that was owned by a man from Kenya. His name was Henry and I was telling him about Mike meeting Jo Mo Kenyatta. He noticed my trach scar and I told him about me being beaten into a coma. I told him about my pictures from the hospital. He asked about the ginger tea he saw me drinking at times while doing my laundry. My ambition was to be the first African-American owned 99 Cent Store in our Community. These guys were Arabs. No disrespect, but we were pushing for Black owned business. Everyone had to take a bus to Journal Square or Newport to find descent shopping. Location, location, location. This store in Citi-Markets wasn't Black owned and the complex rent was too much for my money. My first ambition was still the musical instrument store and then a 99 Cent Store off the Avenue.

While I ate lunch at home, I brewed some ginger tea just how I watched my Mother brew from the root. I teased her that she should start her own cooking show like Martha Stewart. I went upstairs to my bedroom. I grabbed one of the porcelain mugs I liked to collect, some honey and cinnamon. I went downstairs and poured Henry some ginger tea. When I went back to Henry, he didn't want to see the pictures of me in a coma but he did enjoy the tea I brewed. The pictures were of God's testimony and how He delivered me from death's door. Later, I called Rev and he said that he was going to visit his wife in the hospital. I asked if I could go with him, so we agreed to meet at 12:30.

Sugar called me. She never called to exchange pleasantries or let me know how the children were doing. So I just waited for her to ask what she really wanted. She had stated that they were talking to a Navy recruiter and Gabriel was looking to go into the military. Since he was still under 18, they needed my permission.

Bingo there it was. That's what I've been waiting for. Never could she call or encourage the children to call but now she wanted something. I mentioned something to that effect to her. How she wanted support and didn't allow the children to call or attend my concert. I didn't want to make it easy for her to only call at her convenience. I told her to put him on the phone. I teased him right away, "The Air Force wasn't good enough?"

"No," he said. "They wouldn't accept me with a GED." Quickly, I encouraged him that he would make rank faster in the Navy.

"That okay, your Granddad was in the Navy as well, "he chuckled. It seemed to have worked.

This Christmas, I had the opportunity to buy my loved ones some better gifts than last year. When I was active duty in the Air Force, I was able to buy them awesome presents. It felt good to give them nice gifts again. I gave Tia and Charity cell phones. They were AT&T so they were on the same network as Lil Big Sis, Lil Sis, and Mom. So this would give them 'mobile-to-mobile' and unlimited calling between them. I was also trying to encourage them to call Charity and rekindle the closeness we all used to share with her. For AJ, I bought the new Gameboy video game system and some game cartridges. He played a lot with Kyle who I bought a cartridge for Gameboy. For my nephew, Isaac, I bought a remote control helicopter. I bought a pair of diamond earrings and gave one each to Double K and Ice. Now all my nephews were covered.

Previously, I was able to buy some Victoria Secret scented body lotions and body wash for my sisters and mother. They used to market get three items for $20. Now I was able to buy the whole gift set including the scented body lotion, body butter, body wash, and perfume for each of them.

Charity talked with me over the phone. Like I said, Sugar lived for holidays so she encouraged it only during December. When I asked what she wanted this year for Christmas, she said everybody was into white gold when I specified about jewelry. I couldn't find white gold so I bought her a platinum gold chain. For Gabriel, I bought a couple of Eddie Bauer hats, since he was going into the military. I wrote him a message, a military saying that said, "Keep your head covered."

I rented a car and took Charity her presents at the Family Crisis Center for visitation. Again the Monitors remarked how nice we interacted and how we needed to get out of these supervised visitations. I wondered where all their notes were expressing this viewpoint to their employers, the courts. Charity smiled as she opened all her presents. When I handed her the cell phone, her first cell phone, I told her now we could talk more and that her Aunties, Grandmother, and Tia all had the same network allowing them unlimited calling. Gabriel's presents I gave to her. She hugged me. I was so tired of waiting for her to initiate hugging me while they observed me. After visitation, I had some money. This time, I didn't have to rush out. I could go hang in Bethesda, Maryland, where I used to pass time when I was homeless. Now I could eat at Joe's Crab Shack, instead of stare at it. I could go in and order whatever I wanted.

Now I had to rent another car, since I didn't get the pre-approval on the car loan, to attend Charity's Winter Recital. She danced very well for her age group. I handed her flowers after the recital and briefly got the chance to speak with her for five minutes from a four hour trip. She told me they were going out to celebrate and I was off alone to migrate back to New Jersey.

The New Year passed and soon my birthday came up. Charity didn't call me on her new cell phone. Surprisingly, she hadn't been talking to any of the women in our family. I encouraged her Aunties and Grandmother to call. She was only eleven years and they were waiting for her to take the initiative. I took the opportunity for my birthday, to treat myself to one of my favorite past times. I jumped on the light rail train down to Newport Mall and saw a double feature at the movies. Still, it would have been nice to hear from my Daughter but she was at an impressionable age. Like Sugar said, she was a 'Daddy's Girl' and but there was no parental guidance encouraging a healthy relationship with her father anymore.

Saturday came and I traveled to Queens to take the NYPD Medical Exam. There were a lot of candidates. You could feel the energy in the air from all the enthusiastic candidates. When I filled out the questionnaire, I knew that there would be a more intensive inquisition later. I answered 'yes' to 'have you ever been hospitalized for more than thirty days?' and 'yes' to 'have you ever had any broken bones?' Only my nose and hand were broken. I was glad my eye sockets healed and I wasn't walking around with those metal plates in my head. There was no getting around the coma and swelling of the brain in three areas. The gigantic tracheotomy scar on my neck always led to the 'what happened?' speech. The NYPD were very forthcoming about being as truthful as possible about criminal background. They had ways of obtaining the truth and any type of concealment would result in automatic disqualification for candidacy.

The NYPD were updating records in preparation for the upcoming July 2004 class. Their records reflected that I was placed on Medical Review by their Department Physician. The opportunity to clear up the review was being presented so I could move forward in the process. That Neuropsychological Report for Flying Status would help clear me. Another supervised visitation trip came up. Now I could afford to stay overnight in a hotel and have time to think. At the visitation, it came out that Gabriel was not going into the Navy now. He changed his mind.

After supervised visitation with Charity, I drove back to College Park, Maryland. The University of Maryland was where I graduated college. I worked at night and attended college by day. University College had an event center and hotel at the rear of the campus. I would stay at sometimes as an alumnus. There was a music store outside the campus that I often stopped and window shopped dreaming for years. Now I finally had the opportunity to get myself a Christmas present. I had been talking with the owners and getting tips for the music store I planned to open. They custom made their guitar cases. This might become a future business endeavor between us. There was a beautiful Yamaha 5-string electric bass that I had been looking at for a while. The arrangements in Gospel music all predicated on 5-string bass guitars now. The shop also had a rare acoustic Taylor bass guitar with its own case for $2,300. Guitars were expensive enough but most did not come with cases. With an acoustic bass, I could practice anywhere and my skills would grow.

The price was knocked down of the acoustic bass to $1,500. The 5-string Yamaha bass was now $400 with a case thrown in for free, and a couple of guitar stands for $25 each. This might seem lucrative but this was an area I had been participating in for decades. You have to pay to play. The better my playing became the higher the possibilities it might become profitable even playing solely in the church environment.

A bank card came in the mail from Chase Bank and an account number anticipating funds from my settlement. My curiosities were satisfied when I received information that the rest of the settlement money was being transferred to the account they set up for me. Finally, Lil Big Sis helped me with her extensive knowledge in banking. Surprisingly, Sis told me of another smaller bank with a higher rate of yield, and about placing money in Savings accounts for six month and year long timeframes. I dropped $50,000 in one bank and $50,000 in another. She was talking with an investment counselor at her bank. We were going to mutually benefit each other.

I bounced back to the divorce case. McGrady's balance confused me but I wrote him a check for $3,000 anyway. Mom's bailing me out back in 2001 was long overdue so I paid her back and threw in an extra $1,000. She was overjoyed as I handed her a check for $3,600. Since my checkbook was on fire, I wrote a check to Macy's for the new clothes and gifts I bought.

Having Lil Big Sis as a banker was convenient. When I ran out of cash, I just wrote her a check and she would hand me cash. She was like my own walking ATM. My wardrobe had been suffering for the past three years. My working at Macy's gave me some better fashion tips. So I put together a new wardrobe. While shopping some in the Newport Mall someone was selling Prepaid Legal. After my experience with my divorce attorney, this could come in handy receiving a discount on legal fees and references.

The new bank sent me documentation letting me know the day my funds would finally be available. The balance I would be starting with was over $200,000. This was a blessing. But what happened to $470,000 after the structured settlement they promised? The third that Peter's law firm took was understandable, plus their expenses of approximately $167,750, which left $302,250. Were the bankruptcy attorneys taking $82,250 from me? My debts weren't even $20,000 but that wasn't the $82,000 that was missing. Then I remembered the $25,000 exemption I already received. That still left $57,250 unaccounted for. Roughly, $60,000 taken by the bankruptcy attorneys. The commission for the Trustee was only $1,850. The law firm that represented the Trustee submitted commissions for $12,622 and $531 in expenses. The $13,153 still didn't explain the missing $42,247.

These calculations took me years to unravel. Reading all these years of legal documents had me confused. Plus with the constant draining of my funds, I just knew that the $220,000 was low but it was all I had to work with now. And it took years and a lot of hardships to persevere through. A lot of blood, sweat, and tears God brought me through to get to this point. If he wasn't holding my hand and let me pass from death to life, I would not have seen this day. My only regret is that I didn't have the 'wife and kids' to share it with. Technically, I had the wife but she was trying to take the whole pie. She seemed to think she was entitled to half even though we were separated. If I knew that's all she was about she could have stayed away and not even shown up at the hospital. She did a lot but God would have just chosen another vessel.

The churches I fellowshipped with believed in tithing. I was responsible for giving ten percent of my increase back to the church plus an offering. I didn't give it all at once and not to one church. At first, I donated a large portion to Good News, my home church. On the first Sunday, the tithes and offerings went to Pastor Lanier. Members of other churches began approaching me, when I played bass for them, asking if was I donating money to their church. They weren't being greedy. They were active in supporting the needs of their church. These same people who weren't active in supporting me, helping to sing at my concert, purchased a ticket, or bring their taxes. I just smiled and avoided their questions and there were a lot of them coming at me now.

One thing I didn't encounter when I joined the Jersey City Minister's Alliance was that they had monthly dues. Quickly was membership allowed when Reverend Lanier vouched for me. Rev was a humble man but he was a giant in the ministry around the State. The Minister's Alliance had two main objectives: to influence the Mayor's political agenda and to provide outreach to the Community. Influencing the Mayor in helping Ward F, the poverty stricken African-American Community, was 85 percent of the objective of this group. Bishop Ralph Brower was one of the founding members but the current President was Bishop Washington. He was a brilliant Man of God. Every time he opened his mouth, I learned something. He urged the members that when we talked to the Mayor, we had to be seen as a unified group. After meetings, dues were collected and we went to lunch at the Sizzler as we attempted to patronize this struggling Black owned business. This was one of the many businesses brought into existence in the vision of the Alliance to this Citi-Market complex. Business opportunity and employment were revitalized through Federal grants awarded to Ward F.

Next, I dropped off to McGrady the remaining balance of $4,600. All I have been doing was getting beat up by the courts. I didn't have any parental rights established after all this money spent. We never challenged Sugar's representation by this battered women's association when she's never been a victim of abuse. I took care of business down in Maryland and it was back to New Jersey. It was better to focus on a meeting the investment counselor made with my Sister. He offered me an annuity. I invested $3,000 and started a monthly investment of $250. At least I was taking steps into investing in my future. I told Reverend Lanier about my retirement funds. He was proud of me.

Dad took me to go car shopping off Route 46 when he got off work. I became familiar with the area driving home from that paralegal job I had with the Environmental Law firm. My choice was a 2002 Pre-Owned White Jeep Grand Cherokee with 20,000 miles on it for $20,000. After they wrote up the title and tags, it came to $23,000. After I dropped a $10,000 down payment on it, my monthly payments came to $375. When we were done, I treated Dad to a world class meal. Surprised him after dinner with a check for $1,000.

McGrady sent me a letter thanking me for coming to see him and making such a significant payment. There was snow and ice so he appreciated me pushing forward in such increment weather. I was trying to keep everybody on my team happy. God had provided and I was spreading the blessing around. He informed me of a letter from Ms. Playmaker of Charity's dance schedule for a summer program. Again, Sugar never made any calls or attempted to co-parent on any decision. Every time she contacted me through McGrady was costing me $200 an hour. She needed some type of therapy and her church and House of Ruth were lacking in results. She couldn't make a call or attempt to work anything out.

The next day, Mom, my nephews (Ice and Double K), Lil Big Sis, Lil Sis, and all their children came out to the Outback with me. It was one of my favorite restaurants. Those Australian steaks were grilled and seasoned to perfection. That night I showed off my brand new Jeep Grand Cherokee with a sunroof and digital compass in rear view mirror. Everyone was so happy for me seeing how hard things had been the past couple of years. I wished my daughter was with us.

No one knew what to order at this restaurant. They never heard of this restaurant before. I ordered two Blooming Fried Onions, two Aussie Cheese Fries for everyone (French fries smothered with melted cheese, with bacon, and sour cream). The appetizers were so delicious and filling for the ten of us. No one had room for the entrees that were coming. Everybody ate well that evening and they gave us take home containers. I had seen in a Mafia movies how at Christmas they handed out envelopes of cash to everybody. So after dinner I decided to make it Christmas in April, Uncle Bryan style. The smiles from a good meal are different from how the eyes flashed from the sight of cash opening their envelopes. It was a pleasant surprise to all.

For the next couple of days, I shopped around to buy car insurance and got the Grand Cherokee inspected. Shopping around for auto insurance, I settled for All Status Car Insurance for the Grand Cherokee. I had to put a deposit of $1,300 and $168 per month. The bank Lil Big Sis showed me did have a higher rate of yield in their savings account so I transferred $20,000 into it. I had a couple of days left substituting at the school. They saw me go from rags to riches and from brown bag lunches to treating my fellow teachers at lunch. I appreciated the teachers so much. Everybody noticed my rags to riches story and especially pulling up to work in my new Jeep. I gave God all the glory and I appreciated his blessings. Speaking of appreciation, Lil Sis came by one day and dropped me an envelope with some cash. Why on Earth did she think I needed any money now in my life? She said that her income tax just came back and she wanted to give me something. She was always generous around birthdays and Christmas but this was strange. And my Momma didn't raise any fools, I took the money.

I called Sugar and she knew that my settlement money had come. I wanted to spend time and money on Charity. Funny how money finally allowed her to be more cooperative concerning Charity going for an afternoon with me at Dave and Buster's. No Supervised visitation needed, I brought along with me her Cousins: my Nephew Ice and niece Tia. Dave and Buster's was very age appropriate. On the ride back, I talked about Ice about staying in college and working for me but he was really convinced in joining the Air Force. I couldn't talk him out of it and reminded him that I would be down there in Texas at Sheppard AFB as well. We planned to meet up if possible.

McGrady forwarded me a letter from the House of Ruth regarding a summer dance program that Charity had been accepted into. I wondered if they had any victims of domestic violence to represent rather than information that Sugar could have expressed herself. The program would happen between August 1st through August 24th. Sugar wished to exchange visitation dates to allow Charity to participate in this program. All she had to do is call me like an adult and not charge me $200 an hour for the conversation. Everybody wanted a piece of me. I would be away for training in Texas anyway and Sugar knew about this. It was just her manipulating it under the threat of the House of Ruth to ensure her having her way.

My Shop Chief reminded me that a school was coming up and asked was I willing to go away for six months of AGE technical training. This gave me time to start getting my affairs in order. I wrote to McGrady informing him that I would be away until November for any court hearings during that time. A call was made to the Family Crisis Center that I would be away for military duty and unable to attend supervised visitation until I returned. I decided to pay the remaining $11,833 off the car, a choice I would later regret.

Now that I was on the offensive, I called Jeff Ratings, my attorney for Alberto Santiago the Corrections Officer. I wished to retain him to pursue a civil case against Alberto. I had to pay him a $200 retainer fee and explained I would inform him when I returned back from duty. For reasons unknown, I had to pay the Vehicle Transportation Department of Maryland $1,873.19 as interfering with my title search. Everybody had their hands out, it was a relief preparing to leave for my trip Texas. I gave notice to the School and purchased a membership in AAA car service for my long journey, I had to be prepared if I had any mechanical or road service emergencies. This was a great service with free emergency roadside assistance and key lockouts. They gave me a trip booked with detailed maps of the routes I selected traveling to Texas. This peace of mind was great but it cost me $19.99 per month to add to my monthly expenses. I wish they had navigational computers to guide us like they did on the airplanes.

It was time for my annual eye exam. The exam was often free because the eyeglasses and contact lenses cost so much. My eyesight was so poor, I was spending at least $1,000 dollars a year on my vision.

The Government had only given me five travel days to make it to Sheppard's Air Force Base after I packed up and took the NJ Turnpike down I-95 to Maryland. Before I left for Texas, I took my brand new Taylor acoustic bass and hide it upstairs inside Double K's bedroom closet on the fourth floor. It was stuffed inside its case but well hide behind the clothes hanging up in it. I took the Yamaha 5-string with me. On the way down, I explained to Sugar that I was going away to train in Texas for six months. This also meant I would not be able to attend supervised visitations. I asked if I could see Charity and if I could take her shopping before I left. Sugar would not want to withhold anything good from Charity. So she agreed to let me see her since I wouldn't be able to visit for a while. I told her she could come to satisfy her supervision requirements. Surprisingly,

Sugar said no and that meant I would have my second unsupervised visit in four years. Sugar dropped Charity off and I met her at the Greenbelt Mall. Charity seemed a little apprehensive at first. I asked did she need anything and she didn't want me to buy her any clothes or anything. She said no but when I saw how dirty her white sneakers were I told her we were going to buy her some new sneakers. She picked out some sneakers and we bought her an outfit or two. Then we had lunch at the food court. I explained that how I'd be away with the military. We met her mother at the specified time. She gave me a long hug. First time in four years with no monitor watching us. It took a lot of prayer and a lot of money.

"Thank you, Dad. I needed new sneakers," Charity said happily as she got in Sugar's car and rode off. She understood I was going way for a while and wouldn't be able make the supervised visitations. She had my cell phone number and I was only a phone call away.

Driving away, I couldn't understand why she didn't answer her cell phone that I gave her when I called. I reminded her at lunch that her Grandmother, Aunties, and Tia had the same network. They had free mobile to mobile and could talk anytime they wanted. They didn't call Charity even though I encouraged it. She was only eleven years old, too young to take the initiative herself.

After dropping her off, I traveled down to Atlanta. I wondered whether Sugar was allowing her to use it. A little girl's first cell phone, normally she would be so excited and use it a lot. My service plan was different, I was getting hit with roaming charges traveling from state to state. Constantly on the phone with lawyers, ministers, friends or family. This was why I had a different cell phone carrier, still costing me about $150 a month just for my phone. I kept driving down to Atlanta, Georgia, while traveling on government orders the gas, meals, and hotels were chargeable. For these purchases, I made sure I used my government credit card and kept the receipt to file my travel voucher. Tolls and minor out-of-pocket expenses were also reimbursed.

I spent a lot of time on the road today, driving through seven states. A good meal and a nice hotel was the perfect ending to a long day. When I got up in the morning on the road again, I started driving west on Interstate 20. While passing through Alabama, I made a stop in a rest area. They still had Confederate Civil War statues up. I was a Civil War buff so I didn't mind and went to read them. "We defend our State Rights." They displayed the Confederate flags, soldiers, and canons. It was like no one had told them that the war was over. I was alone so I jumped back into my car and got out of there. No more stops in Alabama, kept going until I crossed the mighty Mississippi River. Thought about Gabriel not going into the Navy. I thought it was a big mistake. He needed the discipline and to get away from his Mother. He didn't fare well in academic settings so college was not the answer for him. I prayed for him as I always did.

When I arrived at Sheppard Air Force Base, I drove straight to the lodging office and got myself a room. The rooms were nice at a two star hotel level. The military in their design to cut cost they had you sharing the bathroom with the joining room. The next day, I had to In-Process with the Temporary Duty (TDY) Military Personnel Flight. They were Human Resources for small traveling military personnel. They supplied me with my living quarters, where to report to eat, and where to report for training. Later, after reporting to the Training Squadron at the school for Aerospace Ground Equipment (AGE).

Unfortunately, I had to move out of my luxurious hotel accommodations. Leaving the daily maid service and cable television to suffer in the single barrack rooms of the hard Air Force living. These rooms were nothing like the lodging, the furniture were simple. They had the basic necessities, including a bed, a desk, a mini-frig, a dresser, closet space, and of course a shared bathroom. We had it better than the Army, though. They slept in open bay barracks.

My first day of school was interesting. Our Instructor for Phase One was a Civilian man who knew everything about AGE. His knowledge was extensive but he forgot how to smile. The other Sergeants and I lined up at our classroom door. We waited at a loose position of parade rest. Our young active duty classmates marched in and stood at a position of attention. These Airmen marched with their squadrons from their living quarters to the training barracks. Airmen had to march around the base and couldn't walk freely while in uniform. They were trying to impose military bearing into the new converts.

When the Instructor came and told us Sergeants that we could enter the classroom when he came in. The Airmen had to wait until he told the Class Leader to march them in and they stood at attention at their assigned seats until, the Class Leader gave the order, "Airmen be seated."

Then the students were allowed to sit quietly in their seats without talking until the Instructor gave them permission to. They were supposed to be silent or playing around. This wasn't college or high school. This was the military. Training was our current mission and you were told to be at attention, whether you stand, sit, or speak.

Today's youth was things were different. We feared authority growing up. When I went to Basic Training and Tech School all an Instructor had to do was get in your face and scream at you. They got their message across to you and all the other trainees. These Airmen of today still knew in the back of their minds that you couldn't hit them. They walked away resenting authority. This attitude doesn't flourish well in a military.

During May, I went to the Military Personnel Flight and requested a Housing Allowance waiver to receive the allowance at the 'with dependent rate' based on my home address. I agreed to limited Permanent Change of Station (PCS) entitlements to include without dependent rate Dislocation Allowance (DLA), temporary lodging expense, and per diem. My projected departure date is October 21. What I did understand was that I would receive my entitlement of BAH for housing to help pay my child support. All the BAH would be going to the children and I just had to put the rest from my basic pay. I was getting the DLA on a without dependent rate because I revealed that they didn't live with me. Temporary lodging was still being provided and per diem was a rate that I tried not to go over every day for food. If I save on my per diem, that would be money back in my pocket.

At AGE School training, we learned how to operate, service, and repair a different piece of equipment every week. We learned every component on each piece of equipment. Every electrical diagram, every solenoid that was generated, every electrical relay that was energized. During breaks and down time we had a chance to get to know the new Airmen. I liked them but they were wild, at times challenging, not like we used to be. On breaks when I was an Airman, we all joked around. If the Instructor ripped into anybody we forgot about it and moved on. Now they wanted to bring up everything they didn't like.

Then during instruction, one Airman began to challenge the Instructor like she knew more about electricity than he did. She started arguing with him because she didn't like him. We didn't have time for this crap. Every week, we had a new piece of equipment to learn. Learning every component, every electrical circuit was even more tasking on my memory than the crew chief job that I was running away from. Just with the external power unit, we had to learn principles of electro-magnetic energy and how electricity is generated. We had to learn about alternating current and direct current. What I thought was an easier job was going to be even more hard work. On the aircraft, if you had an electrical problem, you called for an electrician. If you had a hydraulics problem, you called for a hydraulic specialist. In aerospace ground equipment, you were the crew chief and specialist of each piece of equipment.

On orders, we could eat in the Chow Hall but we had to pay at a higher rate because of our per diem money. A lot of us Sergeants liked to go out after we studied. The problem was that there was nothing around us but cows and tumbleweed. The actual town of Wichita Falls was about twenty minutes away from the base. The only place people seemed to go there was Graham's Central Station. It had seven different night clubs under one roof. There was the country music room, the R&B room, the hip hop room (they referred to as the Jungle Room), the classic rock room, etc. When we arrived at Graham's, it was packed. After all, where else could people go?

As a Christian, I didn't feel drinking was a sin. The Catholics, Methodist, Lutherans, Episcopalians, and some Baptists didn't feel that drinking is a sin, either. The Pentecostal circles that I fellowshipped with did teach such things but drunkenness was definitely a sin no matter what denomination you were. "Be not drunk with wine" (Ephesians 5:18).

The news of Glenn Cunningham's death sounded highly suspicious to me, just like when Secretary of Commerce Ron Brown's death. I rented a hotel room in Dallas when I arrived. They had all kinds of restaurants and steakhouses. Life here in Dallas was the big city. It was much faster pace than back at Wichita Falls.

Shopping around, I found a Dentist. One weekend, I was going to schedule having my missing tooth replaced. Finally, after those bouncers knocked it out of my mouth. For a long time, I've been waiting for this. It bothered my self-esteem but I had no benefits to change things. One thing that helped was that I would forget about my smile until I looked at the man in the mirror. Now I had the money to get it fixed. Now I could do a lot of things. I could buy myself a television out of the Base Exchange and ordered cable.

One day during training, the Senior Master Sergeant of the TDY Military Personnel Flight sent me a message to report to her at once. At lunch time, I drove over to see what the matter was. She called me into her office and closed the door behind me.

"First," she wanted to let me know, "your ex-wife has been calling down here." She shook her head in dismay, "that wife of yours, you better watch out for her." I smiled, little did she know. "She and her lawyer wanted to know how much you were getting for BAH (or Quarters)."

"She wants to know how much and wants more money in child support." Then she was at a loss for words, her mouth was open in astonishment thinking of what to say next.

"I met a lot of women," pausing, "You better be careful with this one." I explained that we had filed for divorce and had our separate attorneys. She didn't have legal access to my personal information like she wished to. I explained that when my wages dropped they wouldn't lower my child support but if I found a quarter in the street they wanted to raise it. I assured the Senior Master Sergeant that I was having my Child Support automatically deducted from my pay.

Meanwhile back at training, the younger troops were getting restless. Some weren't assimilating into military life too well. They kept getting in trouble getting caught drinking underage or caught having sex on the football field. Acting more like they were in college than in the military. We told them to wait until they finished training and go to their permanent change of station (PCS) before they started partying but they didn't take advice too well. Some took our tips on keeping a good crease in our uniform, and keeping a spit shine and high gloss on your boots.

One weekend my Nephew was graduating from Base Training at Lackland Air Force Base down by San Antonio, Texas. Despite the fact that I was already in the state of Texas. I misjudged the time it took to travel from Wichita Falls to the southern part of Texas. It took almost six hours to travel. By the time I finally arrived at Lackland their Base Liberty was over and the window for visitation had passed. I left a message for Ice on his cell phone.

Double K's birthday came up so I gave him a call. After we talked, I wrote McGrady a letter expressing my desire that Gabriel's inclusion on the Child Support be addressed as he was no longer a minor child. I wished for that decision to reflect his receiving of a GED in February, him working, and reaching his eighteenth birthday. I wished for an emergency motion to be filed in time for unsupervised visitation of Charity for this upcoming Thanksgiving, Christmas, and New Year's. I referred to using a basis of my 'parenting time' a term Steven had used in family courts in New Jersey. I was denied parenting time for the past three years which alienates a child and she was unable to visit her grandparents who were also out-of-state. Due to the dates at hand, time was of the essence and I asked for a prompt response which would be greatly appreciated.

When I called Mom, she said the neighbor cemented part of his backyard so he wouldn't have so much to mow. She wasn't getting much help mowing the lawn at her age. I offered to have half of her backyard cemented and she called me back with an estimate of $450. I was only too glad to send it to her. Dad was two car payments behind so I had to help him and sent him $800.

After a hard week learning to repair diesel engines, I drove to Dallas. On the two hour one way trip, I would sing songs and call people on my free nights and weekends. Texas had some of the best steakhouses, especially, Dallas. An incoming call came from Lil Sis. She told me of an opportunity that she was getting from her job to make a home loan. She needed a couple of thousand dollars to make the closing on a house. I told her that I would send her a check. She never asked me for help in anything before, she was very independent. I was more than happy to help get a home.

Someone called me and said that someone was using my mother's credit to allow their car to be repossessed. Butch was raised to be respectful and protective. He loved my mother and thought it was wrong for her credit to be ruined by co-signing. Immediately, I called the person and about the car repossession. They admitted they were behind in bills and saw no way out. So, I asked how much they needed. They asked for more than just the past due car notes. I told them after reluctance of their other bills that I was only giving them money for car note. They wanted me to write a blank check so they could pay the bills as they saw fit. As I saw fit, I had to be firm that I only was giving them money to pay for the past due car payments. They weren't very happy to be told how to do it. It didn't stop them from taking my money. It showed nothing but attitude, no appreciation.

It was time for the monthly expenses, including cable bill, AAA, auto insurance, Child Support, dry cleaning of my uniforms, food, my cell phone, Charity's cell phone, and other expenses. Thankfully, I was blessed to pay my car note off and for the moment I had no rent but my monthly expenses were around $1,500 a month. While I was writing checks, I sent McGrady the latest $500 he asked for Sugar's lawyer, sending him letters instead of talking to me. Some of my fellow Sergeants and I went to Graham's to blow off some steam after training.

Coming back from Graham's Central Station, I took out my military ID card as I approached the front gate. Air Force bases are gated and closed off to the public. When entering, a person must show proper identification or have someone sign them in. Military

ID must be shown to access the Air Base. Headlights are dimmed to not blind the Armed Security Police at the Gate. As I approached the gate, I dimmed my headlights, skimmed through my wallet for my Military ID, as I rolled to a stop in the same motion. When I handed the Military Police my ID, he then told me to pull over to the side. I moved over and waited for him to approach the vehicle. He came forward and asked me if I had been drinking. I didn't want to lie so I told him that I had a little. I was told to park my car over by the front gate, and then the Military Police arrested me. During the whole situation, I was in denial. They drove me to the holding cell and then called my First Sergeant. While I was waiting, they made me blow into a breathalyzer. The First Sergeant came and drove me to my dorm room at the barracks. On the trip there, I apologized and told him I didn't have that much to drink. When he dropped me off, I thanked him but he got out the car and walked me to my room. He lectured me about being a responsible NCO and told me to report tomorrow to the MPF.

When I reported to the Military Personnel Flight the next day as ordered. The Senior Master Sergeant had me waiting outside for what felt like forever. A young Airmen was there because he received a fine for throwing up in the grass. He was underage and in big trouble. It seemed the town of Wichita Falls was profiting off of us Military men. The Senior Master Sergeant called me into her office and lectured me. She pointed out some good points. If I had to wake up at 05:00 a.m., why was I out drinking until midnight? After she said it to me, it made a lot more sense. I felt like a failure, not only in trouble with the military but also a poor witness of Christ. I prayed for God to forgive me. As a punishment, I lost my base driving privileges. For the rest of my time there I had to rent a bicycle from MWR.

Most of my weekends, I stayed off base where I drove freely. One day, Errold gave me a call, he had bad news that a dear friend and church member, Vera Taylor had passed away. I thanked him for letting me know and ordered a Peace Lilly arrangement for her funeral. It was seemed like every time I left for the military campaigns someone died.

Butch called me about purchasing a new computer from a new company called Dell. They specialized in laptop computers and Butch enjoyed helping people with computers so I sent him a check for $800. Rick James sadly passed away this month. This coming weekend, I scheduled to have my missing tooth replaced. The cost was well over a thousand dollars but worth it as well. Finally, I would be able to smile again. I sent yet another check to McGrady for $500 for the month of August. I sent a check paying $135 to AT&T Wireless and new bill for $100 for Charity's phone. We talked a couple of times but not much. She still hadn't been talking to Tia, her Grand Mother, or my Sisters.

Coming back Sunday, I heard the latest song from Marvin Sapp. His music ministry really moved me. I didn't even know it was Marvin from the introduction of the song. The rhythmic guitar chords captured my attention. Then the distinguishable voice of Marvin drew me in. The name of the song was 'I Believe.' The bass kicked in stronger toward the end and the choir harmoniously. "I believe what he told me. I believe your word is true. I believe in His promises. I believe your word is true."

My military orders were coming to an end so I was officially subpoenaed to appear November 1st at 10:00 a.m. I had to produce any and all records, including hours of work, dates of employment, rate of pay, overtime payment, W-2 forms, pay studs, all benefits offered by the employment, and any pension 401K retirement or saving plan, and any change or gum I found on the ground.

After out-processing Sheppard Air Force Base, I had about three travel days to get back to New Jersey. My Orders were expired October 26 and I was taking the scenic route. After I drove up from Wichita Falls, Texas, I made sure I stopped in Memphis, Tennessee to sample some of their world famous barbeque. Looking through my out-processing folder, I saw notes documenting Sugar's calls about my pay. There were other notes about the night I received that DWI. The MP stated that I was so drunk that I handed him a credit card. I just accidentally grabbed the wrong card. Then I read the blood alcohol reading from the breathalyzer. It was 0.02, far below the legal limit showing I wasn't intoxicated. This is why they didn't include a reading in my counseling statement. Regardless Sheppard took my base driving privileges away.

Finally, I arrived back at McGuire Air Force Base, New Jersey. I had to report to the Refueling Wing's Military Personnel Flight to in-process back into my Duty Squadron. As I reported and signed in, I was told by the Duty Sergeant that I had to report to the Military Personnel Flight Commander (MPF). My eyes were wide open with shock and astonishment. Normally, you just signed in making sure that you made it safely and during the time your orders were authorized. Speaking with the MPF Commander was highly unusual. Curiously, I walked back to the MPF Commander still a bit bewildered not understanding why this Commander wished to talk with me. Was this about me losing my driving privilege down at Sheppard?

The closed door indicated the MPF Commander was a woman and a full bird Colonel. When the door was closed for an Officer you had to knock and wait to be called in. If they were seated at their desk, you had to march to them, stand at the position of attention, render a salute, and say "Sir/Ma'am," your name, rank, and "reports as ordered." This set the pace of the situation, you were ordered there, not asked. After stating the reporting statement, your mouth stayed closed. It wasn't a two way conversation but one thing for sure, this was a serious matter. So I knocked on the door and waited.

Next, I waited until I was verbally told to enter. "Come in," she said. I opened the door and walked directly to her desk, made a facing movement toward her popping a salute, and stated, "Ma'am, Sergeant Porter reports as ordered." Then I stood there with my hand saluted at the position of attention.

"As you were," she ordered. I dropped my hands and stood at the position of attention. "At ease," she stated allowing me to stand at more relaxed state but not too relaxed. I did stand attentively and patiently. This was a full bird Colonel, a silver eagle. She was one rank under a General. Lieutenant Colonels wore a silver oak leaf on their shoulders and the next rank under a full bird colonel. This was a powerful woman and I was at her mercy for the moment. "Your wife or ex-wife called and said that you were not paying your child support for your special needs child."

"My child has special needs and I don't even know it?" I said in despair. I dropped to my knees and sat in the chair. The pain of never being with my child and knowing so little about her cut me so deep. It was like one of those Sanford and Son moments."Elizabeth, I'm coming to join you honey," I said and felt like I was having a heart attack. I broke posture without the Colonel's permission.

The Colonel could tell that I was so distraught that she became consoling. Then I smiled and thought to myself that she has high cholesterol. "Ma'am, I have my Earning Statements in the car showing my child support payments." The Colonel told me to go retrieve my LES statements from my vehicle. LES statements were military paystubs. When I returned, she saw that the child support payments were being deducted out of my checks on a regular monthly basis. This cleared me of any impropriety and the Colonel wished me well. My orders expired October 26th, so I traveled back to Jersey City.

∞∞∞∞∞∞∞

Back home I checked my piles of mail. A cell phone bill came on the 20th with a balance of over one hundred dollars. If only there were a cell phone company that had unlimited calling. Paying every minute with all these hidden fees, nighttime fees, and roaming charges was killing me. A new petition from Sugar's lawyer claimed I owed $3,240 in emergency family maintenance. This was before Child Support back in 2001. My income today was totally different, Sugar's actions made me lose time at work, decrease in salary, imprisonment, and loss of employment.

This woman was unrelenting. I brought this matter to Judge Loveless in a Motion when he smirked and laughed at me. How could I make family maintenance payments based on income she made me lose, on a job she made me lose, placing me into homelessness, and forcing me to relocate back to New Jersey?

One letter from McGrady reminded me that a reset hearing was going to be held on Thursday for the divorce proceedings. McGrady asked me to show up about 8:00 a.m. to review my case. Now the

General wished me to make anticipated payments and $1,000 should do it for now. When will it stop? Sugar never looked at the money she was taking away from me through this legal process. It would be money that she was taking away from herself, money that she was taking away from the children. She cloaked in her free legal undeserved representation. She was driving the wedge between us in her greed for more, and would definitely, receive as little as I possibly could now.

I took the Yamaha 5-string with me to Texas but I missed my Taylor acoustic bass. I had so many plans to improve my playing. Up the stairs I climbed to the fourth floor. I couldn't wait to run my fingers all over my baby. I peeked through the clothes hanging and saw the case. It brought a smile to my face as I grabbed it. To my horror, when I opened the case, the bass guitar was missing. I asked everyone who stayed in the house but my brother hadn't been around lately.

Most nights, I stayed away from my mother's house. I slept at Gary's or in a hotel. I would ride down to McGuire and get me a room for $25. Citi-Markets was now named Extra. It was owned by Spanish people. It felt like God had judged them for what they'd done to me when that cop arrested me. I heard that a lot of employees were stealing. Their spokesperson, Banks, was charging Nets tickets and luxury items against the store's account. One night, I was tired and slept over my mother's. She woke me up in the morning and said that my brother was downstairs and wanted to talk to me. He began talking and apologizing to me. Shakur admitted to hocking my bass guitar at a pawn shop.

"I was desperate and needed the money," he told me.

"I don't care. I have been searching for a bass like that my whole life," I yelled out. I told him that it was the most expensive bass I've ever owned. That bass was worth over $2,000. "How much did you get for it?" I asked.

"$50," he answered with his head held low. I asked where and he told me the pawn shop on Newark Avenue. When I went down there, I asked them about the bass. I told them that I was selling a case for a Taylor acoustic bass if they were interested. They seemed to know of a person who would be interested. Then I revealed that I was the original owner of the bass and the transaction was illegal. It was stolen from me while I was away on military duty. Then she called my bluff and asked for the name of the person who stole it. If it was stolen, then she would have to report it to the police. If I pushed the issue, I would have to give them Baby Bro's name and he would be arrested. Painfully, I had to drop the pursuit of my stolen bass guitar. It was like losing another child.

On November 4th, President Bush successfully won his re-election campaign over Senator John Kerry. President Bush was still justifying his actions for imposing the war with both Iraq and Afghanistan. The capture of Saddam Hussein was a positive for his administration but Osama bin-Laden was still at large. The fact that no actual weapons of mass destruction were found was still a sour note for Bush. Some people from the campaign were questioning Iraq's having any participation in the 9/11 attacks that prompted these wars.

When I came back, I stopped by the Library to visit one of my friends from church. Her name was Barbra and she was catching me up on all the happenings while I was away. Edna Cherry's name came up and I told her how she feed me when I visited her in the hospital. I told her how I couldn't wait to talk with her now that I'm back. My friend Barbra looked me straight faced and said that 'Edna Cherry was dead.' I corrected her not to say that. Vera had passed away, Edna Cherry's wasn't dead, and I smiled as I corrected her. Her eyes told me more than her words did as she was trying to break the news.

"Brother Porter," she paused. "Edna Cherry is dead," she said earnestly. I didn't know what to say or how to react. Slowly, I walked away to my car and just started weeping. I would never have the opportunity to say goodbye. Not until we met again in Heaven would I have the chance to see Edna's smiling face. The tears were streaming down my face as I drove down the street. It took the whole week to finish mourning her. When my Cousin Al-Hajj died while I was stationed overseas, I couldn't attend the funeral. It had me lingering emotionally, the mind needs closure. McGrady sent me a letter requesting dates of availability to come down to Maryland and be deposed by Ms. Playmaker. This was her second request to provide her this information. And by the way, he said, "I asked you to send me $1,000 in the prior letter. As always I look forward to seeing you." Christmas was coming in the McGrady house and Bryan was his Santa Claus.

I'm sure he looked forward to seeing me and looked forward even more to seeing my money. These were now for anticipated funds and billing me for letters requesting 'anticipated funds' not for actual work product. My florist started with a small store when I left, now her husband Brian had the small store with handbags, hats, and jewelry. His wife took a larger store with a larger inventory of flowers and floral arrangements. The Orderly Room of my Squadron called me that my orders were ready for the next thirty-one days. They put me on orders to keep me fresh on my newly acquired training from Aerospace Ground Equipment School. The training was called Seasoning training. I would keep my skills up and my military pay would be substantially larger than my civilian pay. I would be responsible for my food and housing but it was still a good deal.

Life was so much easier driving around the base with a vehicle. The MPF gave me my Personnel folder to transport to my Shop Chief. From my Special Ops days, I learned to check my folder and take all unfavorable information out. I read things about my supposed DUI. I just reached for the wrong card. The breathalyzer results were under the legal limits. Still, I should have used better judgment in my liberty in Christ. The consequences from this were from my own fault.

The District Court of Prince George's County ordered that I appear in a Show Cause Order in person before the court on December 15th. This would be after my Seasoning training at McGuire so I saw no conflict of interest. I finished Seasoning training with my Air National Guard unit. Life was easier with me driving and all. My Shop Chief and Master Sergeant Grant questioned me on what happened with losing my driving privileges down at Sheppard. I was trained to service more equipment for our shop. Our KC-135 aircraft served as flying gas stations and were on a vigorous flying schedule. Our equipment was old and highly used. My work initiative kept opening doors for me. Several members of my shop were full-time Air Guard members who worked on a daily basis. During my time, I completed another Security Clearance Application this November. This went easier than when I applied in 2001 with the Pennsylvania Air Guard. The three year difference of living in seven different locations within a year. I was trying to remember and locate a person to verify each location. Furnishing their addresses and telephone numbers was excruciating. Surprisingly, my life was getting less complicated.

A billing statement for my government card came today with a balance of $1,318. Ironically, it was the same amount of my monthly expenses. Your life gets detailed when you are going through a divorce and have to account for every penny. Thank God, I could pay this and no more past due statements for me. Lil Sis had already moved down to South Jersey so I went to visit her after working at McGuire one evening. I drove her around showing her how to navigate to Route 130, Sunset Road, and the Burlington Mall. There was a famous place called 'Gaetano's' and I treated her to a cheese steak. It was stuffed with so much meat and cheese that the one 12 inch filled her, her boyfriend, and three children, and they still had leftovers. I was able to finish mine.

December came and I decided to move my cell phone carrier over to Cingular Wireless. There were no unlimited plans yet. However, Cingular was offering free nights and weekends starting after 7:00 p.m. The hard lesson about the seven o'clock free evenings is that it didn't count for calls started before then. One had to hang up and reinitiate the call to get the discount. I didn't realize their policy until months of overcharges starting calls close to 7:00 p.m. and speaking aimlessly. My orders were finished and I decided to take a leave of absence from teaching. I decided to take time to concentrate on my divorce and ministry. I had to have faith in God. Besides, I was constantly on the road and unable to work consistently in the school system anyway.

I sent a check for a $1,000 payment to McGrady. Lil Sis let me drive Tia, AJ, and Isaac down to this year's 2004 Winter Recital of the 'March of the Tin Soldiers' to watch Charity dance. After the recital,

I took plenty of pictures of Charity and Tia, hoping they'd rekindle their sisterly bond. I presented Charity with her bouquet of flowers. This time, Sugar gave us ten minutes, instead of five, to spend with my daughter after a four hour trip. We were leaving the area, I drove them to Union Station in Washington D.C. The Christmas lights decorations looked amazing amongst the columns and architecture. We jumped out to take some more pictures. The cousins didn't mind the road trip to see Charity and with some burgers and fries for the home trip we were all happy campers. Of course, the trip cost me money but it was worth it all in the long run. I invested in my family.

For Christmas, I received a letter with a copy of a Motion for Emergency Relief that was filed on my behalf. Then he enclosed an updated billing statement. How nice of him, just about every day I was receiving a new letter. Most lawyers had a cap on their salary but I was McGrady's cash cow. I felt like a virgin on Prom Night. Another letter from McGrady came the next day, informing me a copy of a Notice of Deposition for me dated for January 27th.

I bought everyone some nice presents and for myself a pair of diamond earrings. Both ears were pierced. I bought my nephew Kyle a keyboard. He played mine on occasion, so maybe he would catch my musical bug. When in uniform, I had to take out my earrings and when I was at church, too, which was daily. I sent a check for $3,320 to McGrady through UPS Next Day Air costing $25 dollars. To insure the cashier's check, it cost an additional $11.55 with additional delivery confirmation costing $2, for a total of $36.15. But I wanted The General to have his money before the New Year. It would cost me less than driving down there to deliver it. Later, I received a billing statement from McGrady, acknowledging three payments totaling $6,117. My balance now was $40.

This year for New Year's 2005, I booked a hotel room around Newark airport. The hotels out there were cheaper. I made a date for the new year and expected the start of newer stronger relationships this year. My date stood me up and Lil Sis called me with an emergency down in Willingboro. It was not how I expected this year to start. Butch dropped everything and drove down there with me. On the way down, I talked to him about trading in the Grand Cherokee with all the mileage I had put on it. Lil Big Sis called Butch to tell him that Lil Sis car had some minor property damage and some vehicle trouble. All that mattered to me was she and her kids were safe. Her unemployed boyfriend needed a ride back to Jersey City. The closer we came to Jersey City, we heard that he had let the air out of all her tires. I drove him back with us and tried to enjoy the evening. She was safe the kids were safe. The next day, I drove back and fixed all four of her tires, with her being a single working mother her car was a priority. It was an all-day project jacking each tire and taking them individually to the servicing station. Using these primitive tools and the rust on lug nuts made it challenging. A simple project took all day. She came out to check the progress and thanked me. She reminded me so much of my mother. I spent a couple of tanks of gas driving up and down the Turnpike and a lot of elbow grease.

I was thinking about all the mileage I placed on the Grand Cherokee while traveling to *Texas* and *back*, plus all the *weekend trips* to Dallas, and the *supervised visitation trips* and *recitals*. It would be in my best interest to trade this vehicle in. My birthday came up and people asked me what I wanted. What I wanted was the gift of time, so I asked Gary and my sisters to go out to dinner with me at a Portuguese restaurant called Spain's. Dad and I would often go there and enjoy an appetizer. Butch had to work so Gary and Lil Sis both worked in New York. So we meet them at Newark Penn Station. After dinner, I drove Lil Sis home to South Jersey. A couple of days after my birthday, Butch took me to a car dealer. It was time to get Bryan a new birthday present. However, a vehicle wasn't just a present, it was an investment. My mother taught me that a car was just like a member of the family. When it broke down, you had to fix it.

SUVs were catching my eye and the Cadillac EXT was the granddaddy of them all. I wasn't going to blow all my money on one. I had been eyeing the Chevrolet Avalanche. It had a similar design and was at half the purchase price. The vehicle price for a 2005 Avalanche was $43,485.

The vehicle was fully loaded with a retractable sun-roof, heated seats, electric windows, electric doors, cruise control, CD player, airbag deployment, a year subscription to Satellite radio, and a one year subscription to On-Star. The On-Star subscription included automatic notification of airbag deployment, stolen vehicle tracking, emergency road service, remote door unlock, remote horn & lights, and remote vehicle diagnostics. With the On-Star, you had hands free, and voice activated phone calling. You could receive calls with the press of a button. I never had all these features in a vehicle before.

The Dealer Incentive Program cost me $2,500, minus the $16,633 they were giving me for the trade in on the Grand Cherokee. This made the value of the vehicle at $26,852. They added $1,611 for the State sales tax. With a documentary fee, vehicle registration, and title fees, the overall price moved it up $2,150. So I was buying the Avalanche for $29,000. I put a down payment for $2,500, leaving me a balance of $26,500.

Butch had more experience with car dealers than me but I didn't get the color of the vehicle I wanted. After I purchased the Avalanche, I took Butch, Gary, and Dad out to Casa Dante's on Newark Avenue for a victory dinner. On the television show, 'Everybody Loves Raymond,' they talked about a dish called steak pizziola. I was raised on fine Italian cuisine but I never heard of this dish before. It pleased me that Casa Dante's served it. Butch wouldn't let me treat him and he had treated me over the years. I thought it was odd but he made a handsome salary. I just wanted to show my appreciation. Later that month, the Annuity Lil Big Sis helped me invest into was at $3,083. Oh yeah, baby! I mean, hallelujah!

McGrady sent me reminders of the upcoming Deposition, so I chose to leave on Wednesday. He sent me a bill that now his balance was $400 for January. I was actively apartment hunting, looking for a place to live. I worked out with Mom that I would use her house as an office, rent upstairs, and start giving music lessons. I was sleeping upstairs while trying to open the music store. Thursday came and the deposition in Hyattsville, Maryland. After a good night at the hotel, I met McGrady and we reported to our conference room. Sugar showed up with two of her House of Ruth lawyers. Most of the time, the General just read his newspaper. They asked if I ever spanked Gabriel. My answer was that I have spanked Gabriel until Sugar and

I agreed to stop disciplining him that way. Then I added that Sugar was the last one to spank him when he hit the Youth Pastor. She sat there cold and expressionless now that her stories were no longer one-sided.

Playmaker asked about my work history but mostly about my money. How much of my settlement money did I still have? Then they wanted to know every purchase I made over $200. So I mentioned all the jewelry I bought for Charity. The diamond earrings I bought for Ice, Double K, and myself. The thousand dollars I gave to each of my parents. What presents did I buy my mother, my father, my sisters, and my brother? How much was each present? How much did I spend on AJ's Gameboy? How much on Kyle's and Isaac's presents? What did I buy Trè? How much did I spend on Ice and Double K? When I answered the questions, I answered truthfully. "I have always been generous with my family."

Playmaker asked whether that was my attorney sitting next to me. "For now," I answered sarcastically. The General raised his eyebrows and gently put down his newspaper. Then she asked how much was I paying him. He answered $200 per hour. She sarcastically commented that was a lot of money to read the paper. My estimation for the day cost me at least a thousand dollars of reading his paper. It was robbery to pay that much but it finally felt nice not to be alone. She didn't ask how much was I spending on Charity on top of the Child Support. How much supervised visitation was costing me per trip? The thousands of dollars this divorce was costing me. McGrady couldn't help reminding me of January's balance. What about the $6,117 I just paid him last month? He was acting like I avoided paying him.

February came and I still kept apartment hunting. The General mailed me a letter thanking me for my recent payment of $400, which cleared my account. The crafty old fox made sure to note that, even though I had a zero balance, the deposition in Hyattsville was ten days ago, plus preparation for, was an additional 8.5 hours. What preparation? He sat there with his mouth closed while I answered every question and he read his paper. Billing from McGrady came, and for one month in January, it was up to $1,700. The deposition of January 27th was $1,000 alone. Just a couple of phone calls and letters did the rest.

He further hinted that he needed time to prepare for the settlement conference coming up the 17th of February. God only knows how much time he would charge to prepare for a case he'd been working on for the past four years. How much preparation did he need? He assumed that the conference would probably be two hours. The good news continued, after thanking me for my payment, preparation for the conference, and the divorce trial was quickly approaching. Even more time would be needed to properly prepare. Again, what has he been doing for the past four years with no new circumstances that he wasn't prepared yet? Finally, he came out and asked for an additional legal fee retainer of $1,500 for anticipated time. Anticipated time? He starts out that I owe him a thousand for the deposition and prep. Now he wants an additional $1,500 for anticipated time and preparation. This was ridiculous. Like Biggie said, "Mo' money, mo' problems."

Shakur wanted to make amends by helping me. Reverend Lanier told me how important it was to show forgiveness. He offered to keep the truck cleaned and polished for me when I came around. I would throw him a couple of dollars for it. Maintaining a new vehicle was interesting: buying car wax, car mitts, window wipes, and Armor All for the tires and interior. The time was a new constraint plus it gave my brother and I an opportunity to mend. I asked how was Tré. He said that his legs needed to be placed in a leg brace to help him walk straight.

I received a new letter from McGrady dated February 9th, regarding an email I sent him on the 7th on my concerns about the status of the case and his representation. He mentioned that previously I expressed the same concerns about the quality of his work. He was frank to say at this time a military expression can be made that I have 'lost confidence' in him. His reference to a military term I felt was more a Freudian slip to the General's rank and authority. He expressed that I should not be placed in such a position and a 'change of counsel' may be the appropriate action. It sounded like he was actually doing me a favor. Then he decided to comment on some of his concerns. What audacity for this guy after four years and charging me over $10,000 preparing for this case to now try and jump ship before it was completed? I knew the Bar Association would never allow him to withdraw from my case after all the time and money I invested but having a threatened attorney would be even more to my disadvantage. Like all my other problems, this had to be managed carefully, not reacted to in emotion or anger.

Then he started whining about me voluntarily filing for bankruptcy when my domestic case was moving forward. How did my filing for bankruptcy delay the court's finding in letting me visit with my daughter unsupervised? How does a financial legal matter affect the ability to parent with the lack of any violent action denying it? It didn't stop McGrady from padding my bill answering letters and filing motions during all that time. Then he commented on me being away for military duty from May to October 2004. Again, he still billed me and filed motions for visitation as I requested.

Then he attacked my request to file an injunction to prevent Charity from attending afterschool dance or engagements that weren't supporting the role of me being an active father in her life. Their whole proposed Order and visitation schedule was designed to be offset for any dance function Sugar wanted to schedule. I didn't ask if that would be successful in filing against. Most lawyers know they teach you in law school to present an argument. All Sugar's claims maybe unsuccessful but at least her free lawyers were filing her request. To have me go to anger management, batterer's counseling, parenting seminars, and alcohol abuse programs. I'm paying his butt and he wants to now argue whether they would grant it.

Then he went into joint custody and the unlikelihood of me winning it. He used this in an attack against me, suggesting that our approach should be more aggressive, which would never result in joint custody. Even though joint custody became moot, I was expressing aggressiveness toward supervised visitation, which was granted with no legal cause and enforced for four years uncontested. And the verbal abuse and alcohol abuse allegations were never challenged in four years and over $10,000 in legal bills. I rarely drank alcohol our entire marriage. We never kept it in the house. I went years without having a drink and had witnesses that would prove it. My marriage was deteriorating as well as my relationship with my divorce attorney.

He continued to lick his wounds to my suggestion of being proactive and not reactive. He said that our interpretations of 'aggressive representation' were very different. He stated that he thoroughly researched my case with regard to Sugar's claim to a marital share of my personal injury monies. He suggested that he gave candid opinions that I may not like. I expressed that if I don't like what he's saying, I'm going to let him know. He is the one with the problem that I have the power as the client. Then after he finished sobbing about telling me his displeasures, I told the truth that he was legally bound to continue our case and I knew it. It was my decision if we continue and I would not release him, as much as he suggested. I had invested too much into this racehorse and I was going to jump on his back and ride his butt to the finish line. The Bible expressed in Romans to be 'men in business.'

McGrady kept threatening to quit if I give in to anger and fire him. How much would it cost to pay a new attorney to prepare for four years of legal history to catch up with? The responsible thing was to pray and try to work with him to get the best results for rebuilding the awkward relationship with my daughter. Being responsible didn't mean not reminding him that he worked for me and that part gave the General plenty of trouble. He had the nerve to request $1,500 for anticipated time and preparation when I was up to date with all my payments.

Taking off work to concentrate on my divorce was my primary focus but I had other important things to be concerned about. For one, I needed to find my own place to live. Having my bass stolen confirmed that it was time to move out of Mom's house. If the music store worked out, I could give her rent for the top floor and use it as an office for the ministry and tax business as well. This would give her a source of income also and not allow other people living upstairs which caused her concern.

Riding around South Jersey, I would stop in to see Lil Sis and Curtis. I bought Lil Sis a lawn mower for her house. It was a gas mower I chose to teach her son AJ about gas motors, spark plugs, throttles and things he would need to know in the future. At the nearby Burlington Mall, walking through, I saw the newest flip phone they called the Razor. Its sleek breakthrough design was thin in comparison to the older generation of cell phones. Thin like a razor blade and the flip fold-up design made us 'James Bond' generation feel we were spies saving the world. The Sales Representative had an earpiece that was flashing a blue light. Never before have I seen anything like. It looked like something out of Sci-Fi movie. This new technology was called 'Bluetooth' and was one of the first wireless accessories patented to only work with the Razor. My mind said that I had to have this right now. The cost of this new technology was $800 but the Service Woman said they gave her the Bluetooth for free. She said that I could buy hers for $100. The Razor itself cost me $400 with the monthly cell phone service came to $269. It was costly but walking around with this Bluetooth was trendsetting.

My monthly expenses kept going up but now I had a cool new phone. Everybody noticed God's blessing with the Bluetooth and the Razor. Are material possessions a blessing? In the parking lots of Extra, I blasted my Christian music and telling everybody about Jesus. Some of my family members thought I was crazy but I had to tell everyone how good God was to me. My family should have understood, remembering me in the coma. Up and down the NJ Turnpike I drove searching for an apartment down South Jersey. After dark, I was ready to find a hotel for the night. I saw the no vacancy sign but I never thought it couldn't hurt to ask the front office. Maybe they still were offering a single room. After a check with the front office and a quick pulled off, as soon as I pulled out, a Sayreville Cop pulled me over. He asked me to step out the Avalanche and place my hands on the hood. When I asked why, he repeated himself but wouldn't answer. He told me to spread my legs and began to start patting me down on my right leg squeezing my genitals once he came up the top. Immediately, I reacted taking my hands off the hood, turning around with my mouth open in shock and gave him the death stare. He must have felt awkward and just laughed in what I assumed was an accident. He asked that I turn around and I was fuming but did it. I placed my hands back on the hood of my Avalanche. He started patting me down on the left leg from the bottom going all the way up until he squeezed my genitals on that side, too. Immediately, I spun around and this time I started stepping toward him. This was worth going to jail punching him in the face. There is a time for to pray and this wasn't one for it.

"What?" He said, raising his hands like he made an innocent mistake. "Haven't you ever been frisked before?" He asked smirking slightly embarrassed.

"Not like that," I objected. He acted as if the police had every right to physically grab your balls, as if you weren't human, as if they could violate you. From my stance, he understood that this search was over and if he tried anything further, I was going to bash him right in the face. He told me that hotel was a spot known for drug trafficking and he watched me drive in and leave quickly.

I told him that I was checking for a vacant room. We were at an impasse with our conversation since it started off on bad terms. He still looked at me with the cop eyes searching for truth and not seeing it on my Black face. I told him I was in the military and they constantly tested me for drugs. Then he started to notice the Department of Defense Decals on my windshield for the Military Police and my military uniforms hanging up in the windows of my truck. He started seeing me more as a military man and eventually decided to leave me alone. This matter was far from over. I was going to get a lawyer and sue the Sayreville Police as soon as possible. Maybe this was why God kept allowing these things to happen to me. With my paralegal background He wouldn't allow much more that I could bear. I could fight these injustices so with that it became an honor. From there, I would start encouraging people that God would judge racial injustice and would bring it to light. I prayed to receive more support from my elders in the church.

I felt like I was starting to come down with a cold. Slept a couple of nights at McGuire Lodging hotel for $25 a night. There I searched on the internet for apartments in the area. After much prayer I found a beautiful quiet furnished apartment off Route 70 in Browns Mills by Presidential Lakes housing complex. This studio apartment was furnished with a maple wood bedroom set with a matching maple dresser, desk, and couch. The room was enormous with my own private bathroom. The kitchen and living room I shared with the owner and another room that was empty at the moment. The owner was an African lawyer from Newark who was also an Officer in the Army National Guard. Being a fellow military man helped open the door and we were both Christians. The rent was $400 every two weeks, $800 per month with utilities included. My monthly living expenses kept climbing, now I paid well over $2,000.

The kitchen had an amazing amount of cabinet space that I shared. The living room was spacious with a pool table. We had a man-made pond in front of our white house. We were deep in the back underdeveloped woods that military bases love to build themselves around, directly on Route 70 deep in the wooded areas. There were no cities, there were no neighbors, no stores, there was no litter, but I had plenty of peace.

In the comfort of my new home, I called McGrady. It was important that I speak to him with respect and listen to his wounded ego. However, I told him how I didn't appreciate these unnecessary distractions during a pending divorce. No one stopped him from voicing his opinions but I certainly have a right to voice mine being the client. I let him understand that I knew that the power to terminate his representation rested upon me. If that was my intention, I would let him know. I do not wish to see any more letters with him asking me every week before a hearing if I wanted to replace him, and then billing me for the letter.

While in Browns Mills, I would start writing my memoirs for a book. I felt God's call to write several books as I went deep into study. I prayed, studied, and practiced my instruments. The only job I kept was my monthly Air National Guard drills that went straight to Child Support. Actually, it never bothered me to pay child support because the money should be going toward my children. Gabriel was over 18, out of school now, and working from what I heard. Still, I was paying for him as well.

On February 17th, the Settlement Conference came up so I rode down to Maryland. Sugar's attorneys were like ravenous wolves, ripping and clawing at my finances. God had blessed me for my suffering in the hospital but now I was in all out warfare with the

Adversary. And Sugar was his most powerful instrument against me. All the money I spent on legal services could have gone toward her or the children. Still, I could spend more on the children if I was ever permitted to spend time with them. But she would rather gamble because she felt entitled to half of everything. The wolves at the House of Ruth smelled blood. I felt violated as they tried to take all of my blessing by force through the court. The Devourer was lurking even though God promised to rebuke him, like the children of Israel I had to battle to possess the land.

At the Conference, Ms. Playmaker referred to the Emergency Family Maintenance back in 2001 that I was unable to pay. I filed a motion back when Sugar made me lose my job, and my ability to earn income, forcing me to relocate out the State. I waited five months to receive unemployment and Judge Loveless should have reduced the payment that was based on my salary or lack of it. Judge Loveless, who always smirked and belittled me, just ordered me to pay Sugar $3,240 now. Sugar and her lawyers were hugging each other, clapping, and giggling. They were already receiving monthly Child Support from me. Now I had to give her this and any loose change I found in my pockets. I had to leave her a check before I left the building.

McGrady again had a heated exchanged afterwards when I was surprised at the Judge's decision. The General kept repeating that he didn't understand what I was saying, like I wasn't speaking English. I repeated that I filed a motion and gave him the dates before he came on the case. Again, he smiled arrogantly at me and said he didn't understand what I was saying. He was a lawyer. I was a paralegal. How can he not understand that a motion to amend the emergency family maintenance was filed on a certain date? It would be more a question of not being able to hear rather than not understanding. I explained it was before he came on the case and he chuckled that he didn't understand what I was saying. Then I realized that he wouldn't acknowledge me. I wasn't going to let him abandon this case even though I wanted to fire him on the spot. I wrote Sugar a check for the money and drove back home to a long trip to Browns Mills, New Jersey.

On the ride back, all I had to think about was how everybody was feeding off me like a pack of wolves. They kept pawing at me. I had to pay for the attorney fees for the day, the Child Support, the Emergency Family Maintenance, the hotel fees, the toll charges, the gas, and meals. The trip down there was an extra $200. My monthly expenses were now $2,037, not including visitations, court appearances, and dance recitals that superseded everything in Sugar's world. I kept everything in prayer. They tried to break me before but God wouldn't let them. Back in the hospital, when I was laid in the bed and I couldn't walk, I knew God would deliver me. They lied to me and tried to imprison me but God delivered. They tried to destroy my character and my testimony but God continued to grant me the victory and favor. It was not because of me being good, but because He was God alone and true to His promises.

On February 23rd, McGrady wrote me a letter informing me that he prepared and filed my Answer to Sugar's Second Amended Complaint for Absolute Divorce. He drafted the proposed Court Order as the Judge directed, and would send me a copy of the final. He reminded me that I had to pay Sugar an $8,000 monetary award within the next two to three weeks. Paying her must have worried him because he asked me to have his payment of his legal fees deposited into an escrow account as soon as possible. The next day, another bill of $1,050 came from McGrady for the month of February, for services provided of three letters, one call, one court appearance, and dictating a Consent Order. The balance due now was $2,750, including a past due of $1,700. McGrady sent me a letter not even twenty days ago that my balance was clear. Now I had to deal with this and more of his arrogance. I was battling not only Sugar but also my $200 an hour divorce attorney daily and there were still other matters going on in my life. The Devil is a liar.

March 4th came, I had to pay $400 for two weeks of rent. While driving near Columbus, I was pulled over by a Police Officer. This time, I made sure I wasn't speeding. After pulling me over and finding my license and registration were good, the Officer gave me a ticket for things hanging from the rear view mirror. They called it Obstruction of Vision and a second ticket for the Unsafe Operation of a Motor Vehicle. All I could do was remain calm, pray, and remove the air fresheners from my rear view mirror. McGrady wrote me on March 11th that he received another proposed Court Order following the hearing. I should review this again regarding a visitation schedule, something Sugar still was trying to manipulate. He said that there were other things about the Order that he took issue with. The Motion stated that Sugar wanted sole legal and physical custody of Charity. I wanted joint but even visitation was becoming a huge obstacle. The motion was worded that I could not remove Charity from the State or country without prior permission from the Plaintiff. Who would want to take their child away from their school and home? That type of thinking was so warped and is a desperate cry for the real counseling that Sugar needed. Although, it reeked from the guilty conscious she felt from pushing me away, not letting me see my child. Never had I attempted, threatened to kidnap, or take her away. Sugar's perception was warped and I did tell her God would straighten her out one day. This she wrote used in the courts as a threat while the church at HC remained willfully ignorant to it. All this while her church HC kept burying their heads in the sand from her allegations from four years ago. To this day, they still cried ignorance instead of trying to find out what was going on. Paul wrote to "be not ignorant." Was this is the acceptable behavior of a Christian woman? Sugar was born and raised in the church.

They wished to arrange the language that my visitation shall not interfere with any of Charity's scheduled dance training/intensive or activities in the event of any conflict that Charity's dance schedule would supersede any of my visitation rights, including holidays, birthdays, funerals, emergencies, family events, parenting time, anything was subject to any dance activity that came up. No matter how big or how small the event. Well, they were only trying to document what they were ingraining into my daughter for all these years. Her dancing should take priority over her relationship with her father and her father's family. One day when she stops dancing, the effects of this would be detrimental to our relationship.

All exchanges for visitation were scheduled to take place at Sugar's home. This is from a woman who used to have a mental breakdown from me knowing their physical address where they lived at. I was treated like a stalker or something. Another attempt to financially dump all the responsibility on me trumped that emotion. Eight hour visitations were to start next month until July 1st. After July 1st, I was granted every other weekend. Holidays were placed on a schedule of odd and even basis. This was the beginning on a somewhat fair visitation schedule that can be revoked any time Sugar scheduled a dance activity whenever she felt like it. Still for Sugar, progress was being made and my lawyer was working to remove most of that language. Finally, I was moving past five years of supervised visitations. To remove it from Charity's mind was another thing entirely. All Charity cared about now was dancing. Seeing me didn't really matter right now. There was no one in her life to encourage her to have a healthy relationship with her father. It used to really hurt but she couldn't tell that she was being manipulated by her mother. I wonder if Sugar would have chosen dance over spending time with her father not knowing how much time they would have together in life before his premature death.

Sugar wanted it ordered that I maintain life insurance with a death benefit in the amount of $250,000 or greater. Charity would be the designed beneficiary and Sugar the Trustee. Not if I could help it. It was different to want something for your child and being forced to do it. I wonder how much life insurance Sugar was ordered to maintain on herself. My current life insurance policy was $400,000 anyway.

The proposed order documented that I should have 'appropriate sleeping accommodations' to include a separate bed and no more than one child of similar age and gender to share a bed with Charity, as if I needed to be reminded these specifications. Sugar was the one who slept with Gabriel on occasion. One winter night in particular because it was cold. He was sixteen and when I spoke to them about it of course they saw no problem with it. It was definitely the preverbal pot calling the kettle black. But the kicker was that it was ordered that I shall pay Sugar a monetary award of $8,000 within fourteen days. Why?

I just paid her $3,240 in Family Maintenance. What was going on here? Why do I have to give her $8,000? Just within the state traveling back and forth to Jersey City was costing me an extra $200 in gas a week now with the eight-cylinder power of the Chevy

Avalanche. With trips to Maryland, I was spending a thousand dollars a month in gas traveling back and forth right now. For the moment, all I could commit to was my military drills for work. After March's Air Guard drill, I decided to drive by and check on Lil Sis and the kids. I wondered if I should go see Curtis first, he was off on the weekends and lived in the same town. I was still wearing my uniform when I stopped by Lil Sis's house. One of my Cousins had come down from Jersey City. He was there with some other friends. I asked where was Lil Sis and they told me upstairs. When I went upstairs to say hi, she was busy straightening up her house, folding laundry, and placing clothes in draws. She looked distracted and obviously was concentrating on cleaning her home rather than hanging out downstairs. When I went down and sat, my Cousin Q asked could he borrow the truck for a minute. So I tossed him the keys and sat with the others while he took off. They offered me a beer and some other things they were smoking. I grabbed a beer but turned down the herb and sat with them joking around. I kept noticing how Lil Sis never came down with all the guests in her house. I had a couple more drinks, waiting for Q to come back while I started getting tired. I had Drill the next day and had to get up around five o'clock in the morning. My Cousin Q still wasn't back and it was almost 9:30 at night. I stopped drinking and he finally came back. After handing me the keys, I was planning to get something from the liquor store before it closed. My plans were to stock my mini-bar at home and get a little air before I drove home to Browns Mills. It was almost ten o'clock and the liquor stores were about to close. Q finally came back and Lil Sis came downstairs with a bag full of trash.

"I'm going to the liquor store. Do you want anything?" I asked her standing up trying to get motivated.

"I don't think you need to be drinking anymore," she told me.

"I didn't ask you if I should be drinking anymore. I asked if you want something," I gave her back in sibling sarcasm to my little sister. I had stopped drinking, I was tired, and this was for my house. I didn't feel I had to explain myself to her.

"Get out of my house," she yelled, pointing her finger at the door. Her guests all got quiet and jumped up trying to see what was happening.

"Are you going to kick me out the house I helped you get?" I asked back in my even louder shocked voice. My Cousin Q grabbed and pushed me outside of the house. Lil Sis started running at me and yelling while her guest tried to hold her back.

"You don't need to grab me," I told Q.

"I know but it's best to just get away from them. You know how they are. You know how they are when they get mad at you," Q was referring to the other cousins around Lil Sis's age.

"I helped her get this house and she treats me like this? I should have gone to my friend's house. I'm going home," I hugged him. "Love you, man." The other guest came out the house and gave me a hug. Everyone was in shock because things were so quiet and just out of nowhere the yelling came.

"Love you too, Cuz," Q hugged me and I got in my truck and drove off with a heavy heart. Why did people that I loved treat me this way? I loaned her money for that house. I drove her around, teaching her how to get around. I bought her things, like the lawn mower, and helped her. I chased her no good boyfriend away.

I've been beaten and left for dead but these women in my life knew how to hurt me deep to my heart. I knew I should have stopped by Curtis's house. None of this would have ever happened if I just went over to see him. I never should have gone to her house. I should have pulled over and stopped at the diner to get some coffee but I just wanted to get home. My heart felt so broken. Emotionally, I was carrying a lot of baggage from my mother and sisters. I just started crying like a baby. It was hard to see. I should have pulled over at that diner but after that point it was just trees and the dark country roads. The only lights came from the headlights or from the oncoming traffic. The back roads of Browns Mills started looking unfamiliar to me. So I sped up and continued driving but I didn't see any markers identifying what county road I was on. After driving miles into it, I pulled over and made a nature call. Nothing was looked familiar so I decided to back track the way I came and do a

U-turn. All of a sudden, I saw headlights approaching me. It was the MPs, Military Police, and they got out of their vehicle. Turned out I was on government property in the bivouac of Fort Dix.

I explained to the MP's that lived in Browns Mills and I must have taken a wrong turn. The MP asked me if I'd been drinking. My eyes were red from crying and I told them I had some drinks earlier. Next thing, I was in the back of their vehicle. How could I get into this again? I should have stopped for coffee at the diner. I wasn't used to driving around here. I haven't been living here for a month yet. The MPs had no crime to fight and no cases to crack. Life on a military post could be very boring with all the law and order. If they could catch you speeding or drinking and driving, they were on it. And by speeding, I mean doing 28 in a 25 mile per hour zone.

They gave me a breathalyzer to test my blood alcohol. Then they put me in a jail cell. Eventually, the First Sergeant came to pick me up. The only good thing about being in my uniform was that I was already dressed for work. When I went to Drill Sunday, I was called into the Shop Chief's office and all the Master Sergeants were in there as well. They were chewing me out and it was well deserved. I was explaining how I just got lost back in Browns Mills and rode onto a bivouac. They understood the area and the possibility of the mistake. They also understood about drinking and driving. They told me that I blew a 0.08, which was the legal limit in New Jersey. This being the second DWI brought to their attention made them feel that I had an alcohol problem. What a poor witness for Christ I was to allow myself to be put in this situation. I told him that my sister threw me out of her house and I was just hurt that's why I got lost. Master Sergeant Granite told me that she threw me out because I was an alcoholic. I shook my head and from that point on, I just remained silent. They recommended that I see the Chaplain.

I was at war with the Adversary and I was giving him areas to attack me in. And attack he did, this was going to be detrimental to my military career and to my chances of making the NYPD. It cost me about $400 to get my Avalanche from the impound yard. By Wednesday, March's bill came from McGrady, well at least half of March, up to the 15th. This month was only $250 so far. The balance now came to $3,000, which he wanted right away, like I didn't have other bills. I had to pay my rent for the next two weeks that would take me up to the 31st. I paid the cell phone bill, AAA, the car insurance, my car note, the cable bill, my ever growing gas bill for the Avalanche, and food. The checks for the month came to $2,300.

One day, a frozen meat distributor came to the door. When I was stationed out at Travis Air Force Base, I ordered frozen food before. This distributor had a wider selection of seafood. I particularly liked the lobster tails, shrimp, and salmon. He was particularly fond of the Sea bass they caught in Chile. He said they grew larger and tastier out there than anywhere else in the world. I found it amazing how God did wonders like that. The Sales Representative boasted how their seafood was 'flash frozen,' that they were cleaned and frozen immediately on the ship to ensure maximum freshness and flavor. We had a large freezer in the house, so I filled it up.

Using the Dell laptop that Butch helped me buy was coming in handy. I was able to use a legal services computer disk to help me file an action in the Special Civil Court against Alberto F. for filing those false criminal charges against me. Now I was finally on the offensive. I didn't want Alberto F. to forget about me or tell lies on those who spread the gospel of peace. The charges were filed maliciously and were baseless. As a result, I was falsely arrested and prosecuted. I suffered due to Defendant's actions. The maximum I could sue for was $15,000 in damages with the small claims court. Now I would see how he would sweat this out. As I mentioned to McGrady, some things that were filed weren't always to win, as he should have known. Sometimes it was just to present an argument. Maybe if I was successful, I could raise the consciousness of these Police Officers who came and refused to document my statement. My credentials showed that I was a person of integrity and my testimony should have been considered. It was protected by the Constitution and a jury of my peers should have decided based on proper police work. The police aren't authorized to pick and choose which parts they want to include on their reports. This type of racism, however, so slight have a reprehensible effect in due process.

The embarrassment of getting myself into this position forced me to seek out an immediate legal defense. The Chief of Maintenance told me that his brother got caught with a DWI and blew a 0.08 and the lawyer hired an expert witness to challenge the calibration of the breathalyzer. Prepaid Legal made life easy. I called telling them the type of lawyer I needed and they gave me three references. M & W Attorneys at Law agreed to represent me for the flat fee of $770 for the first appearance and $300 for each additional appearance after that. A hearing date was scheduled for June 6th at the Fort Dix U.S. District Court. Flat fees were going to be a blessing rather than these hourly rates my divorce attorney was killing me with. I prayed long and hard for God to forgive me. Some people would blame the whole incident and all my troubles on alcohol. There was no alcohol when Sugar and Gabriel attacked me, when I fought Shakur, when I was shopping and arrested at Citi-Markets, and when I was praying for the sick and attacked at Minister Jeff's house. The Scriptures were clear that God said he would make enmity, hostility, between God's seed and Satan's. I had to use better wisdom by not giving the Enemy areas to attack me.

When I drove up to Jersey City, I would minister in the parking lots of Extra Supermarkets, formerly Citi-Markets. I was blasting my Christian music and telling people about God's goodness to me. My aspirations were still on opening the instrumental music store but it would have to happen more by faith because the money was running low. My Florist moved into a bigger store in the complex. Business must be well. She was able to display a larger number of floral arrangements. Her husband Brian took her smaller store. He was selling hats, handbags, watches, and urban books. He was a Christian, had a good family, a good husband, and a good father. He was a schoolteacher and we had a lot in common.

The Red Beta Fish that I bought my mother had died shortly after. I bought a blue one for myself. This time, I asked more questions to keep him alive. I thought that it only needed the roots of the plant in the vase. She told me that they needed some protein, too. This time, I bought some fish food for beta fish. She taught me also that they needed spring water and ten per cent of their old water.

Shakur was in trouble with the law again. Life on the streets was hard enough but God especially didn't care for my family to roam it. It seemed like the police arrested him just because they saw him out there. My cousins were all calling me to find out was I 'going to do the right thing' and bail him out. I never knew they had my cell phone number before. No one ever really called just to talk or say hi. Now everyone wanted to know what I was doing with my money. Who bailed me out when I was arrested? At least I was innocent. Who did the right thing for me?

The tape ministry actually started from a Bible Study I began at McGuire back in the early 1990s with Steve Buchay and Ron Butler. Sales weren't virtually non-existent but it kept me in intensive study making them. Enjoying my new residence, I would see two birds fly in every morning to our man-made pond. The owner, who periodically stayed, told me that they came every morning. They were male and female he taught me with his African perspective on life. One day, I was feeding them and I noticed how big these ducks were. There was a lot of delicious meat on these ducks. Then it was revealed to me that these were geese and not ducks. I was such a city boy. One day, God guided me to another park to show me His creation. There was a lake in the park and God spoke to me for the March 31st divorce case. The vultures were still circling. Shakur called while I was in Maryland needing to get a ride out of town quickly to stay with Lil Sis for a while down in South Jersey. I told him I was in Maryland then I thought about it. I called Double K asking him to drop off his Uncle at Curtis' second job at Newark Airport. Curtis lived in the same town as Lil Sis anyway. I called Curtis and he told me what time he got off work. God always makes a way.

Once I returned and went back in Jersey City I opened up some mail. A letter dated March 29, 2005, from McGrady about a response to his letter of March 22nd addressing his need to communicate with me about the opportunity to visit my daughter this coming weekend. The dates of visitation were initiated by Ms. Playmaker. He asked that she please call him at her earliest convenience with her client's position on visitation for this weekend, pursuant to what was agreed upon.

He documented speaking to me yesterday and understood that there are still telephone problems between the two parties. He documented that specifically Mr. Porter has been denied the opportunity to speak with his daughter on numerous occasions and that the number is either blocked or active measures have been taken to deny access to your client's residence. It was expressed that all I wanted was to continue a healthy relationship with my daughter and that blocking telephone calls was extremely counter-productive. Therefore, he strongly advised for her client to not only allow Mr. Porter access to his daughter but also encourage it as well. This would be in the best interest of Charity also. Then the General socked it to them. If this matter stayed unresolved by April, he would need them to please supplement the production of documents, in accordance with Maryland Rules. He landed a hard blow that he has received very little information in regard to financial matters at the time of separation and subsequent thereto. Consequently, I asked that you please be prepared to supplement your production of documents in accordance with the Maryland Rules.

The letter was generated to articulate the problems I was experiencing communicating with my daughter. It was written to let me know what he was doing about the matter, as I had started expressing some concern about our aggressiveness. And he slammed Playmaker with their lack of compliance to the visitation schedule that they composed. Now their failure to respond was forcing them to supplement more documents. I wasn't sure of the legal jargon but it was a slam dunk.

Ms. Playmaker never contacted us about visitation. News reached me that I missed picking up Charity for my first unsupervised visitation. No one informed me of this. All Sugar had to do was call me and confirm like she used to do with supervised visitations. After a conversation with McGrady, he wrote Ms. Playmaker that according to the draft Court Order that she proposed, I was entitled to an unsupervised visitation last weekend. However, I was of the belief that the entire Agreement was being challenged and did not realize that visitation was expected. McGrady pointed out that he was unfortunately out of town and unable to advise me on the matter.

Please convey to Mrs. Porter the reason Mr. Porter did not show for this visitation.

For clarification, he wished Ms. Playmaker to confirm that while they continued to work on certain aspects of the proposed Court Order that both parties would recognize the validity of the visitation schedule and therefore Mr. Porter may initiate visitation once again beginning the weekend after Easter.

Who knew after four years of supervised visitation that Sugar would be so accommodating all of a sudden? I have not completed the anger management programs, the alcohol abuse programs, the batterer's counseling, and the parenting seminars. All of a sudden, I wasn't dangerous and could enjoy the company of my daughter with this dangling carrot of visitation so that she would have access to my settlement money, not to mention all the arguments and shouting matches with my family members over how much of my money Sugar could get. I shared with them what McGrady said but they knew more than him about it. Why did it matter? I never got so upset about their affairs. It was still my money.

I met the prettiest girl at a bank in Willingboro. Her name was Monica and she had this amazing haircut. She had the prettiest chocolate skin with the hourglass proportions that defied gravity. My concentration was solely on rebuilding my relationship with my daughter but I wanted to get to know Monica better. As I spoke to her, she helped me with my bank account. It didn't hurt when she saw all the zeros in it. I was physically attracted to her and she was a Christian as well. It seemed we shared a lot in common in our faith. She boasted about being a Prince George's Mason or female equivalent (Eastern Star). That had me questionable, but as I said, I wanted to get to know her. I asked what her favorite flower was and she taught me about the Calla Lilly, a pretty white petal flower with inner yellow stamen, the inner pollen producing part.

With all on my mind, I made the decision to pay the Avalanche off. Being able to trade-in the Grand Prix made me feel it was almost like an investment. There was a saying that the minute you drove a car off the lot it started to depreciate. The balance left on the truck was $26,492, so I wrote a check. On the 1st of April, I sent a check to McGrady for $2,000. Shortly after, I received a letter from him thanking me and appreciating my diligence in keeping my bill current. Next, I wrote a check for my rent of $400 for another two weeks taking me to April 14th. On Monday, I signed a client fee agreement with M & W to represent me at the U.S. District Court on Fort Dix and gave them a check. The agreement specified that the firm would make all necessary court appearances, research, investigations, correspondence, preparation, and drafting of pleadings and other legal documents, and represent me properly. All this for a flat fee of $770 for the first appearance and $300 for each additional. The flat fee did account for the 25 percent discount from Prepaid Legal. After the first appearance, any other appearance was referred to as an anticipated costs included but not limited to postage, photocopies, court cost, filing fees, telephone toll calls, and other expenses. If I failed to comply with the stipulations of this agreement, the Firm may request the Court for permission to withdraw representation.

We had a late snowfall in April that year. When I went downstairs in the morning, everything was covered in the beautiful white clean snow. I ran back upstairs and grabbed my digital camera. The cars and the old barn by the man made pond. The fields were blanketed with the pretty white snow and I took the most beautiful pictures. When I went back downstairs, it was amazing. The sun was shining bright in the sky and by noon every trace of snow was completely melted. It's as if God was playing a trick on me, showing me His handiwork. If I hadn't had the pictures, no one would have believed it snowed that morning. I took the photos to the pharmacy to be developed. Photography was becoming a hobby now. I had the time and finances to do it. It was starting to become an expensive hobby with double prints and compact disc I was buying.

For clarification, Ms. Playmaker never contacted us back. All their talk about visitation was lie. On Friday the 8th, I sent another check for $500 to McGrady. The next day, April's bill from McGrady came and for the month of April was $800. My payments on the 1st and 8th left a remaining balance of $1,300. I had Drill this weekend and to no surprise I was told that I would have to see the Commander tomorrow. I may get the DWI charges dropped in the civilian Court but the Military had adopted a zero tolerance policy for that type of behavior. Saturday was a normal day driving around the flight line servicing all the electrical power units with jet fuel. Sunday I was ordered to the Orderly Room with my Shop Chief. Embarrassingly I reported to the new Commander and called to attention. They read a Letter of Reprimand from the Maintenance Commander about the DWI received on 13 March 2005 being unacceptable. As a member of the 66th Air Refueling Wing, I must display a positive image at all times. My driving privileges would now be suspended on base for a year. I was still able to drive on the flight line to perform my job but not my civilian vehicle. My Commander had been aware of problems in my personal life. I was referred to numerous self-help support groups as well as the Chaplain.

Easter came and past, Sugar still didn't contact us about visitation. I started spending more weekends with Curtis and Annie's house now that I moved to South Jersey. They saw that I was hurting over a lot of family issues both from my mother, siblings, to Sugar, and missing Charity. I told Curtis I should have just came over his house instead of Lil Sis that night. I would have been safe there with him. They never blow up at me, never argued, and never had a problem. I always loved and respected from a friendship over 30 years. Curtis didn't go to church but had an abiding faith in God. He was the most Christ-like loving person I knew.

We were talking about all the gas I was spending driving back and forth to Jersey City. He rode back and forth on the weekdays working two jobs up North Jersey. I shared how the gas was costing me over $100 a week. Curtis suggested selling me his 4 cylinder blue Pontiac Sunbird. He was looking to buy a newer car so he sold it for $400.

Next, I wrote the monthly bills of $2,100 with the added cost of $200 in gas bills. My car insurance didn't go up that much because the Pontiac was so old. The light powder blue paint was fading. My newest hobby of photography was starting to become expensive. I kept thinking about going back to teaching before the academic year ended so I could use it on my resume as a leave of absence.

I ripped across South Jersey on the back country roads. Around Fort Dix, I was pulled over by the police for speeding in my Avalanche by Vincetown. It seemed better to just pay the ticket than to try and fight this one. You had to learn how to pick your battles. Vincetown was a virtual speed trap. I noticed this florist nearby the courthouse. I bought some beautiful ceramic flowering pots I saw. From each of my florists, I learned a little something. This florist taught me about ordering flowers from around the world. The Calla Lilies from Holland bloomed richer than any other place in this world. I took my flowering pots and left.

The deadline to file taxes was coming soon. Last year, I was still able to make approximately $24,000 but I had to claim $1,744 just in taxable interest income from my banking accounts. After the Federal income tax withdrawal was subtracted, I still owed $389 in Federal taxes so I sent them a check. As the Bible says, "Render to Caesar what is Caesar's." Don't start none, won't be none.

I wrote a check today paying the rent for two more weeks taking me to April 28th. I was bleeding bills paying off the truck. I spent over $32,000 just in the month of April. This made me decide to move back to Jersey City. I arranged to store some of the lobster tails, shrimp, and salmon in Butch's freezer as I planned on moving. I offered him to help himself to anything but he wasn't really looking for anything but helping me. The weekly cost of traveling back in forth was over $200 a week. I was going to have to make the Avalanche my weekend vehicle. I saw that I wouldn't have enough the capital to invest in a music store. One trip up, I ran out of gas and made it to Woodbridge Mall. Butch had to come bail me out because I was low on funds. I was waiting for some money to be released from a certificate of deposit account.

As a veteran, I got my peddler's license. I bought some ice coolers and tried to sell ice water and cold drinks on the corner of Virginia Avenue and Martin Luther King Drive. It was the Light Rail train station stop. Many people were stuck waiting for the next train. Humorously, I would witness to them and sell my beverages. My trademark line was, "Jesus is free, and Salvation is free. But the sodas are $1.00! The water is $1! Get your drinks here, get 'em right here. Keep that money in the Community." If people weren't buying they were laughing. I would play some Christian music as well.

May 1st came and McGrady's bill for the period of March 15 – May 1st. It brought the balance to $1,300. My main focus was on the civil trial against Alberto F. in Jersey City. Cruising in the Chevy was normal around seventy miles per hour. The motor was so quiet I hardly noticed before I knew it I would be at eighty miles per hour with little effort. In Mansfield Township, the police pulled me over. Next, I was getting a speeding ticket for $389 paid to the Mansfield Courthouse and three points on my license. I dropped off some things on Butch's backyard when no one was home. They lived in a safe neighborhood or so I thought. Butch said when he came that he saw some relatives of mine smiling and loading their cars with my bags. He told them that he was going to tell on them they just laughed and pulled off. Everybody thought I had so much taking from me wasn't stealing. No one knew the bills that I had.

The car Lil Sis drove broke down. She was a hard working single Mom getting up at four o'clock in the morning to get to work in New York City. Shakur was actually helping dropping Tia off to school because the school bus wouldn't come for her. She had problems in school back in Jersey City and I wanted her to finish the G.E.D. Program she was in. Pastor Lanier had been sharing with me struggles he had with his mother and in-laws. He took the opportunity to teach me that even when they hurt him he, like Jesus, showed them love. I drove my Pontiac Sunbird over to Lil Sis so my brother could drop her off in the morning and keep Tia in school.

During May, I moved everything back up too Jersey City. Monica said she wasn't really interested in me one time when she got mad. One time was enough for me now with women. I had placed some clothes back into my mother's house but I kept most of my things in the back seats and bed of my pick-up truck. Some nights, I stayed at my Cousin Sonya's apartment. Some nights, Pastor Lanier allowed me to sleep in the church Annex. A brother named Will, who re-dedicated his life, was staying there. Some nights, I slept in the truck. For special weekends, I rented a hotel where I could keep my food and beverages cold and to cut down on buying ice and iron my clothes for Sunday's service. Shakur moved back to my Mom's house. I only went by to check my mail there. Ironically, she didn't seem to have the same frustrations with him living there.

On the 11th of May, I received a letter on Hudson County letterhead. Enclosed were two copies of a Motion, a Brief, and supporting documents, along with proposed Order regarding the case of: **Bryan Porter vs. Alberto F. Santiago. NOTICE OF MOTION** it read in bold letters. Then it read **TAKE NOTICE;** and noticed I did. Take notice that the undersigned will apply to the above blah blah blah for an Order to Dismiss Plaintiff's Complaint. Further reading allowed me ten days to object in writing after the date I was served this motion. The lawyer I paid in this matter didn't inform me of my options to sue Hudson County. My focus was upon Santiago himself but the divorce and visitation had me distracted, not to mention the paralyzing legal bills. The daily letters from my divorce attorney. My family conflicts over my money. Life was hard enough. Despite my impression that I had a lawsuit, I looked up the statutes after the trial.

My name appeared first, so I was the Plaintiff but it was taking my rights away, yet again, and any liability of the careless way these Officers treated me handling my case, never taking even my statement or account, arresting me on fraudulent testimony, and now covering their tracks with not even an apologetic tone. I was consumed by my divorce trial to pay attention to the statues of limitations of this case. The clock was ticking away while I was away on military orders. All I knew was that Alberto F. was still represented by the County and I was fighting and funding this case alone.

Section 2A:14-2 defined Actions for injuries caused by wrongful act, appointment of guardian ad litem. The State gave me two years to file a claim for my injuries. They may have a clause because of military duty. Then I read the police statement that was in the original filing was back in 2003.

I stated that Alberto's mother, Ms. Santiago, couldn't speak enough English to recognize the name of the Minister living upstairs or be able to form the word 'no.' She shook her head in disgust and just shut the door as I walked away. The police report read 'that she states that she answered the door seeing an individual.' This corroborated my account. She further states 'that she answered and spoke to Mr. Porter, that she believed the individual was not at home, at which time, Mr. Porter tried to enter the hallway of the two-family home. At which time, Alberto F., the son, came in and did state to Mr. Porter that he was not allowed into the house and the tenant was not upstairs. At which time, Mr. Porter did insist on passing Ms. Santiago. At which time, Mr. Alberto F. Santiago, a Hudson County Corrections Officer, did identify himself as a Corrections Officer and Mr. Porter was not allowed in the home. At which time, Mr. Porter did push Mr. Santiago. Both Mr. Santiago and the actor (Mr. Porter) did fall to the hallway floor. At which time, Mr. Santiago heard a loud pop in his right leg around the ankle region. Mr. Porter did back off from Mr. Santiago and the Police were called.'

'Once the Officers were at the scene the Medical Center arrived. They did administer first aid to Mr. Santiago and from the EMTs they stated that Mr. Santiago may have a broken lower leg. Santiago was transported to Christ Hospital for treatment. Mr. Porter was then placed under arrest by the Officers for Criminal Trespassing and Aggravated Assault on a Police Officer. The Officers notified the West Sergeants and also the West Detectives. The Officers did notify the Hudson County Corrections that an Officer was involved in an off-duty incident on said date.'

How not surprising was this? With all the Officers that arrived on the scene, they took the lying statements of Santiago and the statement of his lying Momma. And not one unbiased Officer wrote down my statement of the incident. They failed to mention that Minister Jeff was at home, he was upstairs and had the right to have guest. All these racist cops saw was a Black face. Even with me identifying myself as a military member, a licensed minister with the state, and an NYPD Recruit. Cops are paid to be unbiased and they are mandated to write their reports with all the facts presented. I am blessed that the God I serve did protect me, with all odds against me, and without my account even being documented, it took a mostly all-White Grand Jury to be color blind and to not appreciate waiting for an interpreter. I believed my account not even knowing my credentials. What a Mighty God I serve! When everybody else was too busy to come to court and support me, while his whole lying family showed up, including his lying Momma, I felt alone and abandoned but as Pastor Lanier reminded us with his favorite poem of 'Footsteps. 'When the person looked back and saw at times only one set of footprints in the sand. God responded that 'those were times I was carrying you.'

The gifts kept coming, the next letter of the same date regarding **Bryan Porter vs Alberto F. Santiago** advised that the undersigned represents the interest of Defendants, Alberto F. Santiago and the County of Hudson in connection with the above referenced matter. I asked the County Clerk to kindly accept this letter brief for Defendant's motion to dismiss Plaintiff's Complaint.

At least this letter addressed my counter-claim against Santiago filed in the Jersey City Municipal Court for simple assault. The charges were consolidated and disposed of by the Jersey City Municipal Court on or about May 7, 2004, while I was distracted getting ready for Texas. On or about March 18, 2005, Plaintiff filed an action in the Special Civil Part alleging false arrest and malicious prosecution against Defendant. Specifically, the Plaintiff stated that Defendant was responsible for filing criminal charges arising out of an incident that occurred in 2003. A copy of the Jersey City Police Report was filed. They stated after a thorough review of the records of the Hudson County Law Department failed to show that a Motion of Claim was filed on behalf of me, the Plaintiff.

The perceived threat that I had a right to sue Hudson County for supporting Santiago prompted them to continue providing him with free legal defense. It was absurd that, with all my mounting legal bills, their high powered lawyer dropped an atom bomb on me and I was fighting against City Hall. My legal computer disk was not equipped for this battle. I was in no position to bleed more time and money into this. I prayed daily but 'Vengeance is mine says the Lord. I will repay.'

Not staying at my mother's house would allow me to not have to change of address yet again. My main diet was eating the rest of the seafood I kept in the cooler and cooked on the George Forman Grill. Daily, I tried to sell drinks. I asked Pastor if I could use the empty refrigerator in the Annex to keep them ice cold overnight. After morning prayer, I would load them all up in my cooler and hit the streets. I claimed that corner to start vending beverages. I dropped off to my father some shrimp, a lobster tail, some salmon, and the

Chilean bass to take home. I dropped off some in my mother's freezer for her. Mom called and had a very serious tone in her voice.

"What is this food you left in the freezer for me?" She asked. I told her that I left some shrimp, a lobster tail, some salmon, and the Chilean bass."I only have one lobster tail, one salmon, and only a little bit of shrimp. What's that other thing?"

"It's called Chilean Sea Bass, Ma," I said slowly in disgust. All my mother ever ate was Whitings and Porgies. Everyone started complaining about the gifts I gave them lately. Now they were never good enough or too small in quantity. I was getting tired of this money and how everyone was changing. Biggie was right, "Mo' money, mo' problems."

"There's only one of everything," she continued."What if I want to have some for Kyle?" Kyle was my nephew, Lil Big Sis's baby son. Mom would babysit and cook for him all the time."What if I have some dinner guest? I heard you gave Butch a bunch of them." I wonder where she could have heard that from. No, I wasn't wondering. It was Lil Big Sis with her distorted facts.

"First of all, you're welcome," I said reminding her of the tone of this conversation and for the gift she just received. "Those are luxury items if you want to treat yourself to a gourmet meal. If you want to treat everyone to a dinner, go ahead and do so. I'm not feeding all your friends. Butch is only holding some things for me since I moved." And with that, I ended yet another awkward conversation. Speaking of fish, they made wonderful meals but poor traveling companions. For the most part, I would leave Blue Fish in the Avalanche. I would take him out when I went to visit people. Every now and then on a hard turn, I would forget and hear the vase flip over. The water splashing on the carpet.

"Hold on little buddy. I'm coming," I'd encourage him with my heart beating out my chest. I would pull over and there usually still be some residual water in his vase. I would poor some room temperature spring water from the bottles in my truck bed. It was a hard summer for Blue Fish and me. But we were surviving. Praise the Lord!

For my friend, Monica, I ordered the Calla Lilies from Holland. The florist from Vincetown told me that from there they bloom like nowhere else in the world. Surprisingly, they were only $1.50 per stem per dozen. They were so beautiful I had to order a dozen for my mother as well. I dropped off Monica the lovely white flowers I arranged with yellow baby's breath to highlight the yellow centers of the flower and floral greens. The others I gave to my mother, wishing to share God's miracle which flowers screamed to me in their beauty.

When I went to check my mail, I saw Mom in the kitchen and she smiled when I gave her the Calla Lilies. She said in the softest kindest voice, "Please, next time could I just have the money?" With all the emotional pain I still had, I was planning of showing her some love. The hurt just overwhelmed me from out of nowhere. None of the sons I knew were able to fly flowers from around the world to their mothers. It was so much like my relationship with Sugar.

"Money, money, money, that's all I hear from you. God made something beautiful and I wanted you to have it. I had those flown in from Holland for you. It only cost about $15. Next time, I'll just give you money if that's all you want." I walked away. This is why I only came around to check my mail.

Opening my mail, a letter came reminding me to renew my annual Prepaid Legal. Getting lawyers at flat rates would have changed this whole interaction with McGrady. The man had received well over $10,000 and was still crying everyday like he was being taken advantage of. I received a letter from my attorney from M & W summoning me to appear at the Magistrate Court of Fort Dix. The June 6th court date had been rescheduled. Good news came. I passed my Medical Exam and now it was the final stage of the Background Process to enter the Police Academy. My Blue Fish was so beautiful with his matching blue marble stone and blue ribbon on the vase. Everywhere I took my traveling companion people were both tickled and fascinated. Whenever I asked someone to babysit, they were more than anxious to. I asked Joel and he felt honored to watch him.

A friend I met while I lived in Browns Mills had been inviting me to Philadelphia to her Open Mic Night on Thursdays. I would bring my acoustic guitar and strum some chords. My guitar playing was basic but my singing showed potential. Shakur went with me once. We often got out late; when I drove back I grew too tired to make it to Jersey City. Lil Sis's house was close so I stopped by to crash over there but she wasn't in. Shakur let me in and I fell asleep on the couch. In the morning, Lil Sis was upset that Shakur let me stay over the house without her being there. This was the straw that broke the camel's back for me. She personally left that message as he dropped her off at the bus stop at 4:30 with my car. I showed a lot of love with her kicking me out of her house before. She didn't even know the repercussions of the DWI that I suffered from that night. She never showed any kind of gratitude or appreciation for me letting her use my car, helping her get that house, getting to work in the morning, or doing her grocery shopping after work. I had warned Shakur this day was coming. He still got so angry at me for taking *my* car back. All of his protest didn't matter, it was my car. If I let them continually take me for granted, I would equally be at fault.

I called Pastor Lanier to ask for his prayers. I let him know after showing love that I was tired of them using me and treating me the way they did. While I was talking, I spend off in the Sunbird still having keys. Pastor was listening to me. He could tell by my voice that I was clearly upset. He asked how I was going to move two cars at once. I didn't understand the question because I was constantly moving, deprived of oxygen. I told him, "I don't know. I'll leapfrog it," I told him as I was improvising. My answer to him sound unclear but to me it made all the sense in the world, as I stopped the car and double timed it back to the house. At the house, I jumped in the truck and drove the Avalanche, passing the Pontiac for a quarter mile. I jogged back to the Pontiac and drove it past the Avalanche a quarter mile. I guess my creativity spawned from my military ingenuity. Many times I didn't put in perspective how my actions looked to the average person. Little to my knowledge, the Willingboro Police was watching my bizarre behavior of me moving two vehicles looking highly suspicious. While talking with Rev on the phone the sirens fired up behind me and I told Rev that I'd talk with him later. When the police pulled me over, they asked to see my driver's license, registration, and insurance for both vehicles. I explained my argument with my Sister and why I was moving my car away from her house. The police came back and told me that my vehicles were registered and everything was proper but a speeding ticket was showing not paid and they were going to have to detain me and drive me to Court in Vincetown. There were several people waiting to pay their fines before a Judge. The Judge gave a lot of people the opportunity to pay the court cost and avoid the points on their license which coincidentally came to the same price as the fine. When I went before the Judge, he saw that I previously paid my ticket and told that was an unfortunate clerical error. Truly it was just more confusion from the Enemy. After waiting hours in the Courthouse of Vincentown, the police drove me back to Willingboro to get my vehicles. After that, I dropped off the Sunbird over at Curtis house.

Eventually, I brought both vehicles up to Jersey City. I picked up Blue Fish from Joel. He was such a loving person. We were not only musically connected but also shared admiring God's creative handiwork in the beauty of music, sunsets, and animals. Joel went and researched on the internet that beta fish needed protein. So he went in the backyard and dug up a worm. God's circle of life was amazing. Joel didn't want me to take Blue Fish but I missed my 'little traveling companion.' We were connected, we were both homeless.

Every morning, I was up at five o'clock. I would be at my corner preaching Jesus and selling my waters. People were supportive. The heat from the sun caused me to go through a lot of ice to keep things cold. As much as I was making, I had to pour back into it. Generally, I wasn't making much but I took it as claiming my territory. That corner was going to be mine and I would expand from cold beverages to include hot coffee and candy. After the morning rush every day, I talked to Brian and his Wife, the florist. Another store in the complex sold movies and CDs. She saw me carrying Blue Fish one day and she became a great babysitter while I was ministering in the parking lot. The direct sunlight was not good in the truck and could overheat his water.

I made the decision to cash in the $3,000 I had in my retirement fund. It wouldn't be enough money to pay off all my bills but it would help. Pastor Lanier wasn't happy that I was cashing in my 401K but I had to survive my present first. Besides, I paid my tithe and offering so I was sowing into my future that way. I called M & W to try to get representation to sue the Sayreville Police for the cop squeezing my genitals twice. The receptionist told me to hold and an attorney came on who I explained the situation to. He became terribly defensive of the cop.

"Excuse me, are you a police officer?" He sarcastically interrupted my telling of the story.

"What?" I objected in shock.

"Are you a lawyer or police officer to know what they are allowed to do?" He said in further defensive of the cop stopping me, frisking me, squeezing my genitals twice without probable cause.

"I'm a paralegal but you don't have to be a lawyer to know that the police do not have the right to squeeze your privates," I said with an equal amount of sarcasm. What a jerk!

"You don't know what the cop was looking for and if he had probable cause," he continued in his insolent tone.

"I know he didn't have a legal right to stop me or to search me like that," my tone continued to reflect the hurt and anger I felt. Another lawyer got on the telephone in this fruitless conversation.

"Hello, this is Mark and I am an attorney. First of all, I want to apologize for what happened to you and thank you for your service in our military," he led with.

"Thank you," I said. Certainly, I didn't expect to be attacked calling a lawyer that I was going to have to pay.

"I hear what you are saying and it definitely was not right what happened but I don't think that you would be successful in fighting this matter in court. It would cost too much money. It would be too hard to prove the damages it caused and simply not worth pursuing," he said. I thanked him his advice and decided there were too many barns burning to continue.

Before having my Lasik's treatment, I had to stop wearing my contacts to let my eyes breath. The problem was that I couldn't see a thing. It seemed foolish to buy expensive eyeglasses for three days so I just roughed it. One day, while in the Post Office, I was trying to write on an envelope. So, I was squinting and burying my face to see the letter. Out the corner of my eye, I saw two little old ladies pointing and grinning at me. I heard one of them talking.

"Look he can't see a thing," she said as they kept laughing. "He can't see us," it happened to be my mother and sister Lawrence from Church. Laughing, I just shook my head at them. Just see me in a couple of days. I'll have 20/20 vision. Who will be laughing then?

Soon June's bill came for $600. This made my balance to McGrady $1,900. June came and I decided to give myself the greatest present, the gift of sight. It was becoming time to order more contact lenses but I had been researching the latest in Lasik technology. I wasn't about to let anyone experiment with my eyesight so I looked at optometrist for how many successful procedures they performed. Of course, the New York Optometrist had the superior numbers. My optometrist performed over a thousand procedures. So, I scheduled myself to have a bilateral Lasik procedure for $3,200. The money in three years would pay for itself, I was spending a thousand dollars a year in eye exam, glasses, and contact lenses. They asked that someone pick me up so I arranged that Gary come since he worked in Manhattan. I didn't really plan to wait for Gary but they wanted me to supply them with a name.

When I arrived at the Optometrist Office, they asked if I had anybody coming to pick me up. I arranged for Gary to meet me at the Sushi restaurant around the corner once he got off work. I couldn't see what all the fuss was about, pardon the pun. They heavily sedated me for the treatment. Though sedated, I could still feel the laser was hot as it cut my cornea, and then I passed out. After the treatment, they bandaged both eyes and told me my vision would return 24 to 48 hours from now. Now I understood why some people elected to do one eye at a time. Even more so, I understood why they felt it necessary to have someone pick you up. They bandaged both eyes with gauze and gave me black glasses to protect me from the UV lights of the sun. They told me that I may have sensitivity to the sun light for a while. When they woke me up, they asked again because who was picking me up because they were about to close. Now I was blind and they were putting me out in the street. They gave me drops to numb my eyes because they were cut from the laser. They also gave me more sedatives for the pain. I asked them to call Gary again and I talked with him. He was still at work so reminded him to pick me up at the sushi restaurant at the corner downstairs. His office was nearby and he said that he was on the way. They gave me a cane, black glasses, and asked again who was coming to get me. I asked if I could get some assistance to the Sushi restaurant downstairs and around the corner. When I arrived there, I asked the hostess (who didn't speak much English) if an African-American man come by to meet someone. She said 'yes' and he left. Why would Gary leave me like that?

The disappointment I felt was so extreme. It seemed I had no one reliable to depend on. The tears instantly rolled down my cheek. The saltiness caused a burning sensation. Temporarily blinded, I now had to escape from New York and travel all the way back to Jersey City. My emotions went from anxiety to despair. Then I focused, God would direct my path. My God and my faith would make it possible. Through God, all things were possible.

As I left the restaurant, with my walking cane, I used the wall to keep me from the street. I walked toward the corner and subway. As I approached the corner, I pulled down my bandage and peeked out. The burning sensation increased and I saw a blurry image of where the subway was. I called out asking for someone to help guide me down the subway stairs. People were reluctant to help anyone here in the New York. There were a lot of scam artists and beggars. God finally touched someone's heart seeing my bandages, black sunglasses, and a cane to help lead me down into the subway to catch the Number 1 train. Once down there, he turned me toward the direction of the train. "I see," said the blind man. Actually, I couldn't see but the NY Metro Train System had an audible announcement for each train route and each train stop. I thanked the Good Samaritan as I stepped on the train. I thanked God, knowing I was safe in His arms. I was confident He would guide me back to Jersey City. With God's favor and people's help, I managed to get on the train. People graciously stepped aside while I swayed my cane back and forth. Ask and you shall receive. So I asked the people on the train to let me know when we arrive at the Times Square stop. The good people of New York all called out the stop and made sure I got off. You could feel the love and it made me feel safe. For God is love. People offered their seats to me. I asked them to direct me to 34th Street and they were glad to oblige. From 34th Street, people helped me to the PATH Trains for New Jersey. God kept sending people who saw my cane, shades, and bandages to help me on the train. I was so grateful to my God that even though I was blind, through Him, I could see. Once at Journal Square, someone helped me to a taxi where I drove to my mother's house. There, I took my painkillers and rested on the couch. I was told that I wouldn't be able to see until 24 hours later and should keep the bandages on.

The Devil never gives up, even though I was blinded laying on the couch my mother somehow got into an argument with me. I could have kept my mouth shut and laid on the couch but I always had to say something back, which is something Reverend Lanier kept getting on me about. I read in the book of James that 'a man who could bridle his own tongue could conquer a whole city.' Unfortunately, I was not that man yet, although I was striving to be.

It was late, so I took off my bandages and thank God I could see. It wasn't 24 hours yet but the burning sensation had subsided. I could escape this constant fussing that I fueled giving my constant loud feedback. My mother used to be my greatest prayer partner. How did our relationship deteriorate like this? In 2001, she was writing about my character as a son and now she said there was no difference between my brother and me.

At my Cousin Sonya's house, I could crash on her couch in peace. I got up and left the house walking down the street. There was a group of teenage girls who were acting wildly. They ran up to me, trying to touch me and include me in their crazy shenanigans. I was very prudent against women touching me both from the ministry and in the school system. There was a Police Officer not even 20 feet from us at the Light Rail train stop. I yelled for him and told the Officer how I just left an argument from my mother's house to have these teenage girls harassing me. The girls went away and the Officer told me to get out of here before he arrested me. It was so frustrating with these Police Officers felt like they could talk to any Black men and could easily throw us in jail at any whim.

I started to object in protest and declare my rights. These off-duty cops were collecting overtime, ensuring that traffic stopped for the new Light Rail train. At any other community, they would take some initiative. I was the victim. Instead of talking with those girls, they threatened to arrest me. They told me I was a troublemaker that I just came out of the house arguing. The Devil was busy but greater was He that was within me than he that is in the world. I kept my mouth shut and walked away. I went to my cousin's house and had some peace at her house. I would fall off to sleep and wake up in the wee hours of the morning. Energetic, I walked back to get my car parked at my mother's. Since the coma, I thrived on four hours of sleep per night. I would drive to the Path-Mark off Route 440 or the one on Grand Street. I would use their rest room for my morning grooming.

Next day, I called Gary and asked what happened. I was disappointed, explained how I was completely blind, but God helped me home. I felt I had no one that I could rely on. Gary told me that he came to the sushi place and the lady told him I just left. I shouldn't have listened to her. I could depend on my friend. The next couple of days, I vended from my street corner. At prayers, I told Reverend Lanier my testimony how, I once was lost but now I see. God brought me safely home from New York after my Lasik procedure. Pastor was happy for me and fascinated by the procedure. He had plenty of questions thinking about getting it done himself. I stayed a couple of nights down in the church with Will. We made sure the sanctuary stayed vacuumed and clean. I normally kept my television in the truck and brought it in the Annex. I supplied the food seeing that Will and I ate well. He was glad when I stayed over. I tried to give him some piano lessons from the keyboard I carried with all the other things I carried with me.

When Pastor Lanier came to his Office, we ran out like schoolboys and seeing what were the main objectives for the day. Setting the trash out, move things for the food pantry, or anything of that nature. I was in the Pastor's Study first and then Will came over later. As we all were talking, it turned out that Will didn't lock the door to the Annex. Someone came in to tell us that the door was wide open. I raced over on to discover that my 5 string bass guitar, printer and a couple of cell phones were stolen that quick. Our church was right across the street from a housing project, there were a lot of good people, but there were always one bad apple that spoiled the whole bunch. I called the Police and filled out a report but little could be done.

I didn't see this as a theft committed from an individual but part of continued attacks from the Adversary. I didn't feel like a victim but I acknowledged where all the attacks were originating from. Being violated by law enforcement felt no different how I felt my parental rights were being violated by Sugar and the court system. Joint custody was lost and visitation was still being denied. Forget being a veteran, I didn't have the rights of most Americans but life itself was still a gift from God. I didn't need to wake up on a hospital bed again. If God wasn't the center of my life I would have never been able to endure all the hardness; but endure I shall. As a good soldier in Jesus Christ (2 Timothy 2:3).

The money seemed to be changing most of my family dynamics. People thought I had so much that they just took things. To them, it wasn't stealing. Others kept out of what was happening it seemed unless they were talking about me. I was fighting a losing battle against my wife and now my own $200 an hour divorce attorney. My finances were depleting and were almost out, none of my business ventures were taking off. I still had little to no time with my daughter and it had been over four years now. Areas of my Christian walk needed to be re-examined. These episodes of drinking and driving were a blemish on my walk with Christ and possibly would jeopardize my NYPD career. My guitars and cell phones were stolen right out of the church.

The Lord kept encouraging me that the battle was not mine but the battle belonged to the Lord. Under the Old Testament, I learned this prayer that "If a thief were caught stealing he had to repay it back sevenfold (seven times)" (Proverbs 6:31). Satan would have to repay back all the time he stole from me with my daughter, repay all the legal fees, all the money and guitars stolen, the business opportunities lost until he learned not to bother this child of God anymore. I prayed for this and kept it in routine supplication.

Now the money was dwindling down, I moved back to Jersey City but not into my mother's house. Sometimes, when I slept in my truck off Route 440 in the parking lots of K-Mart and Path-Mark. K-Mart was having a 40 percent off every purchase in the store. Mommy and Charity's birthdays were coming up soon. I thought it prudent to take advantage of the sale. I bought my mother and Charity necklaces and earrings with their birthstones in 14 karat gold. They were born in the same month. My hope was for my mother to leave the ruby jewelry to Charity in her will. I bought her other gold jewelry that she could give to her other granddaughter or daughters. Both of my sisters were born in October but I was surprised they had two different birthstones, tourmaline for Lil Big Sis and opal for Lil Sis. My niece, Tia, had the same birth month as me. January's birthstone was the red-like garnet stone. After buying the ruby jewelry, I was disappointed that my birthstone wasn't as lustrous as the ruby. The garnet stone was considered a great gift for friendship and trust.

One of my cousins was having her wedding this weekend. My father was officiating the ceremony. My surprise gift was to play the wedding march for her as she walked down the aisle. My extensive family never came to my concerts or my church. They never really knew of my musical talents. I offered to help my father with his officiating but his nerves would not allow it. Pastor Lanier handled a whole staff when it came to ceremonies. It was an honor but Dad didn't wish for any help.

Lil Sis was coming up for the wedding. She was very close with this cousin. Lil Sis told me she wanted to start paying me back the money I'd loaned her last year for her house. I laughed because even though I needed the money, I never planned to ask for it back. She was a hard working single mother. All I wanted was a little appreciation.

That Saturday, I came to my mother's house and she sat down at the dining room table to write me a check. While she was writing the check, she started fussing at me like she was talking to one of her children. I'm not sure if she still had issues with me taking my car back or whatever her problem was. I'm not sure if she thought the fact she was paying me money empowered her but I started straightening her out that it was money owed.

"Hold up. Who are you talking to? Nobody asked you to pay me back, so don't be talking to me like that, like I owe you money or something," I said back in my sarcastic loud voice. My mother raced downstairs, burst into the room, and did what she always did.

"Okay, Bryan get out," she said like I wasn't even her son. I had been beaten into a coma, punched, and stabbed in the face but their emotional scars cut me deeper than physical beating I took. They always made me feel like I wasn't one of them, especially if it came to me or any of her other children. "Get out," she kept yelling and started pushing me. I should be used to this treatment. It's why I joined the military. With everything I was going through, it hurt too much. I just reacted and refused to get out.

"Why do I always have to get out?" I cried out. "You don't even ask what happened. You always just kick me out all the time."

"Don't be yelling at my mother like that," Lil Sis said and started lunging at me like she did in her house. This time, there were no friends between us, so I tossed her little butt on the couch in the living room. She started swinging and punching like we could trade blows with me in a fist fight. I never punched my sisters though but you did have to defend yourself. Mom tried to grab her and continued to yell at me even louder for not listening to her. This was like the childhood fights when people fight because they know it's going to get broken up.

"I told you to get out of my house," mother grew even angrier placing all the blame on me. She was able to get in between us pushing Lil Sis away, but never once yelling at her to stop. Lil Sis ran into the kitchen. I started walking toward the hallway and heard her going through the draw with all the kitchen knives. My mother was in the hallway still yelling at me. Every situation would have been handled if I just listened and did what she told me, like an obedient but violated dog. I asked her why she never said anything to her other children. Why didn't she tell Lil Sis to stop or sit down?

"Because I told you to get out," Mom kept yelling. Lil Sis found the biggest butcher knife she could find. She started marching from the kitchen down the hallway. It angered me even more that my mother continued to yell at me and it didn't bother her that Lil Sis was coming at me with a butcher knife. I told her that she had a knife and her answer was for me to still get out.

"I promise you, if she comes at me with that knife, she'll be making a trip to the hospital," I pointed with my eyebrows arched. This was fulfilling a promise that I made to myself as a teenager. If anyone ever came at me with a weapon, they would be going to the hospital. That would send a message to everybody.

The apples didn't fall far from the tree. If my mother could have still whipped on me, she would have. She knew I meant what I said and turned around and grabbed the butcher knife. Lil Sis didn't give it up without a fight. They tussled a little for it and finally my mother was able to rip it from her arms. Still, she had the nerve to keep charging me. As she lunged at me, I took her and shoved her to the ground, while she was down there I gave her a well-placed kick in the butt. She stopped coming after me after that, so I walked out the house. They kept yelling and I yelled back to call the police. I called the 911 on my phone and they made me call another number because it was a non-emergency.

I expected the police to come to the scene and to tell them my rights. They should be the peacemakers we paid them to be. They couldn't just eject me from the house while I was invited in and then verbally attack and threaten by someone who didn't live there. Just because I was a man, I still had rights if I wasn't hitting or threatening anyone. The police would take the threat of her coming at me with a butcher knife as a serious threat and give her a good talking to.

The police pulled up in a couple of cars. The first face I saw was the female cop that had me arrested for not filing my claim. She recognized me and yelled, "Oh no, I'm getting out of here," she turned around while the other Officers came. I was sitting on the steps of our neighbor's house.

"What's going on here? Someone called the police," the Officer asked. About four Officers walked up to me.

"Yeah, I called them," I started telling them how I was here to get the money my sister owed me when she started yelling and my mother told me to get out the house. I stood up and was talking with my hands. It was clear that I was highly upset.

"Calm down, calm down," they told me. Weren't they listening? How could you be calm when the people you love hurt you like this?

"Calm down! Sit!" Some muscle bound cop yelled in a threatening manner. So much for calling the cops.

"Yeah calm down," yelled his bulky Black sidekick. He wasn't as tall or muscular as the other Officer but he had me beat in stature. He had the same threatening tone and wild look in his eyes.

"Don't tell me to be calm. How can you be calm when your loved ones just attacked you?" My words just infuriated the cops more. I could overhear my mother talking to the police in a calm soothing voice. It fueled my rage that she could be just yelling at me a couple of minutes ago and talked all softly to the police.

"He's never been the same since he got out of the hospital," she told the cops. Her words would haunt me for years to come as they echoed in my mind. She often mocked me in the house and it was her true sentiment. She blamed me and my 'brain injury.' I could hear her mocking tone. It didn't matter that my sister was coming at me with a butcher knife.

The Officer talking to my mother walked back to me. Was he ready to take my statement unbiased? "How you feeling?" He asked.

"How would you feel after your mother and sister just attacked you?" I asked still hurting emotionally.

"Your mother and sister attacked you?" He asked.

"Well, not my mother, she just yelled for me to get out of the house. My sister came at me with the knife," I said.

"Did she cut you?"

"No," I answered. She cut me emotionally, however, deeper than any knife could ever pierce my heart.

"What happened to the knife?"

"I don't remember," I couldn't remember if she had the knife when she hit the ground.

"Then what happened?"

"She jumped at me, so I pushed her to the ground and I put my foot up her butt," I blurted out. Obviously, I was still mad. I was a vented with my emotions. People judge but they didn't live what I was constantly going through.

"Where do you work?"He asked.

"I'm a Sergeant with the Air National Guard," I told him.

"Let me see some ID," he said. I stood up and reached into my pockets. I didn't feel my wallet in either pocket.

"I can't find it. Maybe it's in one of my cars," I told them. They started smiling. "There, right over there," I pointed at the parking lot.

"Oh that's all right, Serge," he said and started saluting me. The other four Officers just laughed at me while he mocked me. Here I was being mocked and berated only after one little conversation with my mother. I'm glad they didn't have more time with her. An ambulance pulled up and I saw what this was quickly turning into. Good thing I was a paralegal and knew my legal rights.

"I refuse any medical attention," I boldly told them declaring my rights. But why would I be given my medical rights when everything else was being violated?

"Okay Serge," the Officer kept mocking me, laughing and saluting. They forced me in the ambulance and drove me to the Medical Center. As we drove, I had to remember the times I was in the hospital, the jail, or sleeping in my car. 'I will fear no evil, for thou are with me.' The Lord would deliver me out of this as he did everything else. The police escorted me out of the ambulance into a waiting room. Security came and stood by the door as the police left. Soon, there were six Security people telling me to take off my clothes. Even though I knew God would deliver me, I was still angry. One thing after another kept happening to me.

"I refuse any medical attention," I declared once again. Once again, as a Black man, as a Veteran, and as a person, my rights were totally ignored.

"Take your clothes off, please," the Security Officer asked in a room full of six security people.

"I'm a Sergeant in the Military. I was Special Ops and you don't have enough people in here," I answered in anger to mess with their heads. They looked at each other for a moment nervously but then I took off my clothes and slipped on the hospital gown. They immediately strapped me down to the hospital bed like I was a dog.

They rolled me back to an isolated room. Unable to move, I laid there unable to pray. Filled with emotion and pain, I just cried. A short little Nurse came in to ask me a list of questions. I answered them all as truthfully as I could. Do you have a history of mental illness? I answered no. Are you a danger to yourself, others, or to property? I answered no. Do you wish to harm yourself? I answered no. Do you wish to do others harm? My eyes lit up remembering what just happened to me and how I was lying there strapped to a bed.

"That's a difficult question to answer right now," I told her in disgust. I bet the computer geek that thought of these questions wasn't just told off by his mother, threatened with a butcher knife by his sister, and mocked by the police. It made me furious to be apprehended after refusing medical attention. "I'm not going to answer that," I said in protest.

"Well I'm not going to untie you until you do," the cocky little Nurse told me as she walked away. As I lay there, I was in emotional agony. The restrictiveness having your arms and legs tied down with arthritis was both painful and stressful. It became clear that I was going to miss the wedding. I wasn't going to be there to play 'Here Comes the Bride' as she marched down the aisle. This was supposed to be a joyous occasion. I was receiving some money back that I loaned out. This was how my love was repaid back. Lil Sis comes after me with a butcher knife and I get detained by the police and placed in the hospital. With a heavy heart, I laid there. This was about their female anger using the police to lash out. Then God sent an angel, her name was Phyllis, a sister from our church. She worked at the hospital and saw me tied to the bed.

"Minister Porter," she cried out in astonishment with her mouth wide open.

"Call Pastor," I pleaded. God was answering my tears. I laid there tied to the bed like an animal. It reminded me how they tied me down overnight when I came out of a coma. God delivered me then and God would deliver me now. But it was nighttime in my life and emotionally I was drained. Lying there, I kept hearing my mother's words, "He hasn't been the same since he's come out the hospital." She had the whole police force disrespecting and laughing at me.

"Rev," I cried out as Pastor Lanier eventually came, seeing me tied to the bed. He looked bewildered but he was a warrior. He had seen a lot. I told him what happened. He remained silent. I told him my mother's words to the police. 'How I never been the same.' Nothing was wrong about coming at me with a butcher's knife. I had been telling him about my deteriorating relationship with my Mom. Yet another reason why I chose not to live there anymore. I just went to check my mail. Today, I just went to pick up a check. He looked puzzled for a moment but he did what he always did. He started praying and gently caressing my head. My heart was too heavy to pray but it says that the Holy Spirit will make intercession with groans that cannot be expressed/uttered (Romans 8:26). The tears from my broken spirit and contrite heart were expressed through my tears. The cocky little Nurse came by and was touched. She untied me and I whispered, 'thank you.' I never did answer her question the way she wanted. Certainly, the concept and timing of some of these questions need to be reconsidered.

Just the presence of this man of God allowed me to receive this morsel of kindness. After Rev left, they moved me to the Psych Ward. I called Butch to come help me. Everybody else was at the wedding. No one was caring about me. They fed me and I talked to this African Doctor. It had been hours and I was able to tell the story much more calmly. I explained about the traumatic brain injury and how my mother said that I wasn't the same anymore, and how she still yelled at me to get out even though my Sister was coming at me with a butcher knife. I told him the humiliating treatment by the police and me telling them that I refused any medical attention.

He smiled and revealed that there was no medical reason to keep me. As I put on my pants, I reached in my back pockets. There I found my Military ID Card. I wondered if that cop would have acted differently but I seriously doubted it, especially when my own mother told the police there's something wrong with me. God released me and I could give no one else the credit for this victory in my life. The Medical Center was right next to the Light Rail train. I jumped on and it took me right back to Virginia and Martin Luther King Drive where my vehicles were parked. As I jumped in my Avalanche, I saw Butch in Extra's parking lot. He was honking his horn excitedly. He was happy for me that I was released but wouldn't come down to help me. We talked on the telephone later. Butch called me almost every night before he went to bed. He had a large home and wanted me to stay in his basement for a while but we didn't think my sister wanted it.

The reception was being held at the Masonic Lodge on Oxford Avenue. As I walked in, I saw the faces of my sister and my mother all grinning and laughing while they left me to be humiliated, tied down like an dog, and confined to a Mental Ward. They lost their smiles as our eyes met. They were neither happy to see me nor happy I was out. However, this was my cousin's wedding. It was neither the time nor the place. I walked to her table and apologized that I missed the ceremony. She asked what happened and I just told her that I was tied up for the moment. Despite the irony, I found nothing amusing about the matter. I wished them God's blessing on their marriage. And as quickly as I came, I made my exit. My Cousin Bill was outside and asked why I missed the wedding. I gave him the short version of the story. He just smiled and shook his head. Most of the family respected me as a cool headed, calm, and rational person who was going to church and doing the right thing. We spoke more in our silence and I just left to go find a peaceful spot to find a space to park and rest for the night. What doesn't kill us makes us stronger. Yet through all the heartbreak and madness, God showed me His deliverance from a Psych Ward, from the police, from more lies, and from butcher knives.

My heart was still heavy, though. Family meant the world to me and mine was in peril. Even where I slept that night wasn't peaceful. I slept in a dark point at the K-Mart on Route 440. It had a spacious dimly lit parking lot. Even 18 wheeler trucks parked there overnight as I hid myself behind them.

While deep into my sleep, I heard an explosion, as I was shocked back to consciousness. My eyes opened, I saw a car wrapped around a tree. It had burst into flames just 300 feet in front of me. The fire engulfed the car against the darkness of black night sky. There was little hope for the driver inside. It seemed young people liked to race on this quiet stretch of Route 440 at night. Jumping from a deep sleep to witnessing a fatal accident, the shock I experienced continued by sirens racing toward me while a small crowd was developing. Hearing the sirens of the fire department, the police, and the ambulance approaching made me flee the scene. It was in the wee hours of the night as I slipped away under the cover of darkness. One thing was certain, this night couldn't get any worse because it was almost over. Though weeping endures for the night, joy comes in the morning. I parked in another dark spot to get more sleep, waiting to see what the next day might bring. It was an unpopulated spot under the Pulaski Skyway. A thunderstorm started as it cracked the night sky. If lightening couldn't strike twice, it hit a transformer on a light post. Again, the firefighters and police sirens blew up another spot for me. Can't a brother just get some sleep?

CHAPTER 4
Seeing Things More Clearly

T hings were becoming increasingly clearer to me now, even more than back in 2001, when the House of Ruth took Sugar's Battered Woman's case against me. At first, I thought it could have been Ruth, Sugar's mother, who left her money to divorce me and strip me of my parental rights. It couldn't be. Ruth loved me and expressed to Sugar not to divorce me. Why would a battered woman's organization even take her case, making every effort to keep me away from my child as someone who never physically assaulted or abused his wife or children? Why would they keep a loving father away from his child? They knew how many Black fathers were absent from their children's lives. Why did they have so much hate inside them to keep me from my child with no physical violence or abuse? It was even established in the deposition through years of marital counseling that Sugar never even alleged any type of verbal, physical, or alcohol abuse.

It was now becoming even clearer to me. This wasn't just a personal fight as it should have been. This was just as much a spiritual fight to be in the life of my child. Certain women, especially from the House of Ruth, brought whatever bias from any violent or abusive relationship they ever heard a man perpetrate. Even people who were supposed to be on my side had to be reminded when they spoke of some other man's violence toward their wife or child. "That wasn't me. What does that have to do with my situation?" I often had to ask, Why should I be penalized or punished because of what other men did?

All the strikes were against me in the courts. I was presumed guilty and had to prove myself innocent. God would show Himself Mighty and Strong because this was a rebellion against Him, as well. It was a rebellion against God's Sovereign rule just like the men of Benjamin fought against it. They were rebelling for the freedom to do anything they pleased, even to commit unspeakable wickedness rather than be ruled by the Law of God. Fathers have little to no rights in their own children's lives today. If a woman suggests she was verbally abused it can never be proven and some feel it can't be challenged. Most will say that's the way it should be until it's their son who is accused, until it's their loved one. I never verbally abused Sugar. It never was mentioned in all the years of counseling and the Saints that knew it had no dog in this fight. They kept their mouths shut and out of it. The Bible speaks that you are guilty not only in what you do but what you allow. The Scriptures first called for a husband to bring his rebellious wife before the elders. Forget the Israelites that lost their lives for righteousness. She didn't state any of these lies running to my bedside at hospital, or would dare repeat them in front of our families, both hers as well as mine.

I felt led to share this testimony, that I warned my mother and family ever since I came out of the coma. I reminded them all God's revelation to them that I would 'live and not die, and declare the works of the Lord.' Despite me reminding them, they stopped seeing me as someone that was still an overcomer despite all the odds against me. On the contrary, they began to mock me. They began to tell me that God wasn't with me. That God wasn't speaking to me. They mocked me that I had 'brain injury' and they said it in a hurtful despising tone. It wasn't said in love and it whispered to whoever would receive it. Not all my family would believe it but confusion was being spread. My middle name was Joseph and I had faith. I was a dreamer and I dreamed big. They liked to play it safe. They were dream killers. Inwardly, they said to themselves, let us destroy this dreamer and let us see what becomes of his dreams.

Many capitalized on my faults. I acknowledge my faults and they were many. But God never uses perfect vessels to carry His perfect message. Anyone who pointed a finger at me had four fingers pointing back at them. What about their imperfections? What about their many faults? Who were they to judge me? Why were my liberties in Christ so questioned? If they only knew about other clergy and their liberties or their sins. But 'He who was without sin let them cast the first stone.' All I had to do was to ask for forgiveness and God was faithful and just to forgive. How could anyone judge me? God was going to deliver me out of all my trials. If others lacked the patience to wait, I would wait on the Lord. My faith would not waiver.

At the next Minister's Alliance meeting, Mayor Healy was coming. This was truly a positive gesture of him to reach out to us. Bishop Washington had us gather early to remind us to stay united. If the Mayor sensed that we were divided, he would dismiss our petitions. It was a challenge to keep a room full of pastors and ministers to stay focused without drifting to their own personal agendas that benefited their individual congregations or politics.

Bishop Washington asked the Mayor about the latest developments that benefited our Community. A special emphasis was placed on the latest developments in employment. The Mayor was glad to let us know that he was going to hire more police officers. The Mayor was a retired judge. This was never a popular advancement in the Black Community. The newly hired Officers were scarcely from our Community it just meant more frivolous arrest. I took the opportunity to address Mayor Healy with perspective of my recent experience with the Jersey City Police Department.

"Mayor Healy, some of us don't really feel that more police are an answer in improving our Community but rather training the Officers to respect the people and especially the men of our Community." My comment was greatly supported by the Minister's Alliance but Mayor Healy looked confounded why we weren't as excited as he was with his startling revelation. Then some pastor addressed how he had some union construction worker denied work and they reminded the Mayor on the stipulations the Federal funding placed on workers hire specifically from Ward F where the construction was. Then another pastor started advocating for a union construction worker from his congregation. Then it went from an Alliance to a room full of individual pastor's each trying to get jobs for just their members. Bishop Washington shook his head and told me this is when we lose our power when the Mayor can come and see that we are not unified.

Afterward, I stopped by to see if I had any mail. I was glad the mailbox was outside. A letter from McGrady dated June 15th told of Ms. Playmaker's office delivering hundreds of pages of documents regarding Sugar's updated financial documents. She was finally releasing things that were requested back in 2001. He commented on my instructions of allowing me to help review them and me denying yet another deposition of Mrs. Porter that he quoted me saying were a 'waste of money.' He told me that if he found some documents that would cause him to issue subpoenas then he would do it. If he could find documents, it meant he was ignoring my instructions to not search them. He sarcastically asked if I read his letter of June 1st because on the telephone conversation of the 9th, I revealed I hadn't read it yet.

He said that he enclosed a bill as of June 15th. He reminded me that he hadn't received any payments since I was last in Maryland around my deposition. He stated that he 'must insist' on full payment no later than Monday, June 27, 2005. He warned me if he wasn't paid by the 27th, he would be compelled to file a Motion to Withdraw. He said that I 'berated' his competency to his staff almost every time I called. He told me that this could be the opportunity that I had been looking for. Then he again issued me the ultimatum to pay him by June 27th. That if I wish to replace him, I needed to indicate so in writing. All I'll be doing on the 27th is celebrating my father's birthday.

This guy had some nerve. If I wanted to fire him, I didn't need his permission in a letter to do so. It's obvious I hadn't desired to replace him or I would have done it already. The General just wants to document again his displeasure about the comment I made that "for now he represents me" and bills me for the time of writing these insulting letters.

He further reminded me of the bill needing to be paid, regardless. He expressed an interest in continuing to represent me and blurted out "even in the face of my criticisms on almost every telephone call to the office." He reminded me that it wouldn't be an economic hardship for me having testified that I still had approximately $70,000 remaining from my personal injury settlement. He was referring to the deposition back in January, like I didn't have a mountain of bills eating me up.

What is he talking about? My deposition was back in February. I paid him January, February, and just paid him $2,000 on April 1st and $500 on April 8th. This has been the first time I have ever gone past thirty days for a payment. His insolence insults my intelligence but I had to handle this puppy with kid gloves for about one more month.

If I didn't have a couple of weeks before the final divorce hearing, I might have replaced him. However, I invested too much money in all his years of "preparation" for this case to get rid of him now. It was better to keep him rather than to find a new lawyer and pay them to come up to speed for five years of preparation. Besides his child-like whining, there was no way an ethics board would allow him to withdraw from the case this late in the process. This is even without further payment but I will pretend with him that I don't know that. Then he gave June's bill dated the 15th from McGrady, which was only $200, but with the past due balance, which made it a total of $2,100.

He had the audacity to say that 'he wanted to continue to represent me,' like he had a choice. I gave him no ethical reason to withdraw from my case. His subliminal suggestions of me writing a letter to terminate him would only happen when and if I desired it. For now, I will pray very hard and wait. Paying him after he gave an ultimatum of the 27th would empower him to continue this daily harassment of writing me letters, billing me to write them, and demanding payment. I still had a greedy ex-wife fighting for her pay day in Court.

The Jersey City Police Department was going to pay a hefty price for forcing me into an ambulance when I refused medical attention. 'Consent' was not given and my legal rights, my human rights, and citizen rights were violated. Prayer led to me finding an attorney downtown. It felt so gratifying for someone to finally listen to me. Church people were sympathetic but left it to just another sad story. Finally, there was someone with the intelligence to realize how "I" had the legal right to refuse medical attention. When I emotionally told him how they forced me to take off all my clothes and strapped me to a gurney, he looked confident that our case was strong. We could sue the City for millions. I could see what I thought was a bad experience God would turn into a blessing.

One day, I was driving up from prayer and I came across Aunt Cindy. She really was Errold's and Joel's Aunt but I called myself a member of the family. I had known her ever since I was a child. As I pulled the Avalanche over, I was honored to offer this 'woman of God,' this songbird, a ride. She was one of the greatest, most anointed Gospel singers I ever heard.

"You need a ride, Aunt Cindy?" She saw me and recognized me. I was glad I had recently seen her at one of the District meetings at Church. I went out of my way to greet her all the time.

"If you don't mind," she hesitated. "I'm going all the way up West New York," she warned me. West New York was a small city right next to Weehawken and Union City.

"No problem," I smiled. She stepped up into my pick-up truck. "It would be my honor." Aunt Cindy knew me from a little boy. She knew my mother and father. Pastor Lanier was her brother-in-law, and she knew I adored her. I could tell from her out-fit that she was a homemaker making house calls.

"Why is such an anointed Singer still working? You should only be singing for the Lord. Thanks again for singing at my concert back then." She giggled of me appreciating her gift.

"No problem. I enjoyed myself. It was nice," she said with her soft voice. She sound so much like her sister, my Pastor's wife.

"Well, I wish we had more people come. That's why I wanted to be titled 'Bryan Porter and Friends.' I wasn't sure you were coming but if I would have put you as top billing we could have packed the place out." She kept smiling, flattered by my comment. Then, it came to me. "Maybe we should do another one with you as the top billing and Michelle White. Maybe people will come out then." The idea of this excited me. Their names would surely draw people out. It reached the address in West New York and she stepped out of the Avalanche.

"Well, I'll think about it," she said. "Thank you for the ride," she smiled as she left.

In my spare time, I started to do a personal background check on Ms. Playmaker. It often baffled me how Sugar could qualify for a battered women's agency when I never touched her. We never argued, I never even yelled at her or berated her. Then it came to no surprise that Ms. Playmaker lived off London Lane in Bowie. Sugar had a friend who also lived in that same housing complex. It fell all along Sugar's pattern, like the Principal at Charity's school, the CFO at work, the Dance Choreographer at HC, and the female Pastor at HC. How she charmed up to people of presumed power who she manipulated with her one-sided drama to get sympathy, free legal support, and promotions. People who should have been wise enough to know there were two sides to every one-sided story. People she gave unrestricted access to my very own daughter while I went through supervised visitations for years. There is even scripture warning not to even receive an accusation against an elder of the church.

A call came from J.G. Wentworth, informing me that he was going to need my wife to sign some paperwork since I was still legally married. I reassured him that we were already in divorce negotiations and she had no rights to my structured settlement. He wasn't sure so I told him that I would have my divorce attorney relay that information to him if he wanted. Now I was going to have to pay McGrady on time if I wanted his cooperation.

My attorney from M & W called and explained that the state's legal limit was 0.08 on the DUI charge, so he planned to challenge the reading. He presented that if I paid $1,000 for an expert to challenge to the breathalyzer and the Judge would drop the DWI charge and reduce it to a Reckless Driving charge. I was so happy. Prayer was great but God provided the money. It was a shame that money was a vehicle to resolve matters than all the years of responsible driving history. I authorized my lawyer to hire the expert witness.

I wondered why I hadn't heard from my attorney about our case. He wasn't returning any of my calls lately. A letter came Tuesday. Guess from whom? That's right, McGrady. I called to let him know that I did not want him to review the latest documents since he already repeatedly determined the stature the Judge would use to rule on the case. He repeatedly told me this and documented through thousands of dollars of trial preparation. Sugar had no hidden assets to discover. Joint custody was moot since I lived out of the state, as he pointed out. I was trying to keep the cost down of what was already an expensive divorce. Most of my remaining money was mostly in my structured settlement. I called Greedy McGrady explaining that I was trying to send him more money, even though I didn't appreciate his constant threats. My funds from J.G. Wentworth were in the process of getting released and I needed him to speak with their attorney if he wished to expedite the payment of his funds. He needed to verify that Sugar had no legal right to my structured settlement and did not need to sign off them.

Then came Dad's birthday. I was looking forward in celebrating it with him tonight. Maybe I'll take him to the Priory Jazz Club off West Market Street in Newark. McGrady's latest tirade was about the telephone call he received from me on Friday. He didn't appreciate me reiterating that I didn't wish for him to review the 'hundreds of new documents.' They were documents about the same old things that Sugar submitted and charging me hundreds of dollars to do it. He repeated my words that, 'I did not want to pay him to review these documents' and my wish to have a relative come by to pick them up was inappropriate. The request may have been but instead of him understanding my desire to keep down the escalating cost of a fierce divorce battle. He was frustrated that his ability to continually charge me was being limited. Instead of offering me a reasonable flat rate or another option, his only desire was to withdraw from the case, which he constantly suggested daily. He often said, "That's not the way I work." He informed me that we had reached an 'impasse' regarding his continued representation. An impasse means a stalemate, a gridlock, or a standoff. I didn't see it as an impasse. God gave me the wisdom that as long as I didn't give him the written documentation to dismiss him, he was legally bound to represent me until we underwent the rigorous process to properly end it. Finally, I was forced to remind him that he had a legal obligation to continue my representation until I release him and I had no intention of doing so. With that disclosure came a great silence over the telephone, and with that our conversation ended.

He stated that I had not responded to his letters of June 15th and June 22nd. The letter of the 15th also echoed his deadline of payment and on the 22nd I called him. He raised interesting points that he had to answer Ms. Playmaker's request for my bank statements, retirement documents, and my military documents, which should include my current points earned in the National Guard. This was the type of work I was hoping he stayed focused on. It had nothing to do with reviewing Sugar's stacks of meaningless job searches that led to nowhere but her being unemployed.

He threatened again to withdraw. He said that he followed up with the telephone calls with me pertaining to procedural matters. He said that I indicated a couple of months previous that I had at least $70,000 in my testimony but now I indicated that his fee was contingent upon success in me obtaining my structured settlement without the signature of Mrs. Porter. He told me that he made a call to your New Jersey lawyer as I requested, which I mentioned in my June 22nd letter. Then he scolded me for not providing him with an address and phone number of J.G. Wentworth. Therefore, he couldn't do anything until I provided him with this information.

So it goes without saying that he made his childish threat to withdraw from the case again. Then he told me how important my case was in respects to custody, visitation, and monetary award. He told me that I should retain the services of another lawyer for this matter. He pointed out if I represented myself that he thought it was not a good idea. If I did wish to I had to file with the Clerk of the Circuit Court in writing. Now God said that my people perish from a lack of knowledge. I was so grateful I possessed the knowledge that he could not withdraw unless he filed and they would not grant it as long as I was working with him like I was.

Moving on, July birthdays were coming up. When I looked for the bag of jewelry I hid in my mother's house of everyone's birthstone, the bag was missing. Charity and Mom would never get the ruby necklaces and earrings I bought for them. No one knew how my things were missing, all I knew was that the bag didn't grow legs and run away. How could the jewelry be missing but there were no break-ins into the house? The 4th of July was coming up. By this time, I wasn't allowed in my mother's house anymore. I can't even remember why, but I didn't care. I was a grown man supporting myself. I didn't have to run back to her and groveling at her feet. From my ministering at the parking lot of Extra, people respected me ministering the gospel. For the 4th, I decided to barbeque some food and pass it out. Preparing your own food was always cheaper than eating out. If you know what you were doing, it was tastier, too. I had to eat and cooking a little extra was a blessing. Anyone around me was able to eat also. I wasn't spending the high amounts that I had to pay McGrady. The $50 could go to feed me for weeks and not make a dent in my divorce bills. It was strange to the neighbors that I was barbequing in the front down the street instead of at my mother's house. They just took this as just more bizarre behavior from the guy playing his loud church music in the parking lot and talking about Jesus.

I danced and praised God openly, blasting my Christian music. I was seeing things more clearly. Literally, I once was blind but now I see. Remembering when my life hung by threads but God spared me. Little did all these people around me value such a powerful life changing event. I remembered lying on that hospital bed when I couldn't even walk. I forgot all my present troubles and yelled out the Gospel of Jesus Christ. I forgot about my custody battles, my divorce case, my court cases, my homelessness, thefts, and all my other problems.

At a distance, I saw people watching me, judging me. People who should have shared rejoicing in victory with me. It reminded me of David when his wife Michal, the daughter of Saul, watched him from her window, seeing him leaping and dancing praising the Lord as the 'Ark of Covenant' entered the city. Michal was King Saul's daughter given to David as a prize for defeating the Giant Goliath. Michal grew up spoiled and pampered. She despised David in her heart for praising God with his whole heart. Unlike Michal, David's life was anything but pampered and spoiled. He was delivered from a peasant's life to now a King of Israel. Throughout the journey, he slept in caves, fought lions, bears, a giant, and 'tens of thousands.' The struggle was more intense, so his praise reflected that. I had family that couldn't relate, some Christians that couldn't relate, and some neighbors.

Then Charity's birthday came and it would be another one I would miss. This time, when I called, I actually was able to talk with her. I promised we would celebrate it the next time I saw her. She talked about how much she loved chocolate. So, I promised her a chocolate cake. It still bothered me I wouldn't be able to give her the ruby jewelry I bought for her. It bothered me about a lot of things. A lot of nights, I stayed in the church annex. At the church, Will enjoyed the leftover barbeque and the television. I taught him a song on my keyboard and sang some worship songs with him.

All week, I was excited in anticipation of an outdoor ministry at the housing projects across the street from our church. Saturday came and I needed all my microphone stands, microphones, amplifiers, and both vehicles to move them. Earlier, I saw my Cousin Q who asked could he use the blue Sunbird this weekend. I told him after I was finished using it for this outdoor ministry. They let me use the church but no one supported the service. I had to pay a keyboard player to play with me. He had one hand but played better than most people with two. I played the bass guitar and Will was there to support me. We played the songs I practiced for the concert I had before at Ferris. My vision was to have the skilled musicians and talented singers come minister the gospel for free after the ticketed concert. I forget how I was able to move all the equipment there in two vehicles. Moving them back after ministering was physically exhausting. When I saw

Q later, I told him to take the car to Sonya's. He told me that he was busy and Shakur could move it there for him. I was reluctant but I tossed him the keys anyway. Shakur hadn't talked much since South Jersey. After a day, I found out the car was missing and it was obvious that Shakur stole it. By Monday, I was telling Gary about it and said he could find out about it. He smiled and called Lil Sis to get some information. It was a shame that he had a closer relationship to my own little sister than I did but this was how it was.

He asked how she was doing and then he asked about my brother. Lil Sis told him that my brother had gotten arrested over the weekend. So, I went to the Jersey City Police to ask about my car being impounded. I reported the car stolen but they told me since I gave him the keys he didn't steal it. Instead, they referred to it as a 'Unlawful Taking.' They searched my license plates and couldn't find the car. Then they searched my brother's name that previously was out on bail for over a year now. I posted bail but was never paid back. The police told me that he was arrested down in South Jersey. No car was reported confiscated in the Police Report. My car was still missing. Good thing I had another key once I finally found it. God help the person that's driving it, though. Prayer won't be my first reaction if I catch them. Gary's call also let us find out that Lil Sis was moving back into my mother's house from South Jersey.

The next day, it was Mom's birthday. I wasn't going to broker any peace now that the ruby jewelry I bought for her was stolen. More and more, I clearly saw that no matter what the confusion was, we know who was the author of this confusion. I called her to say happy birthday. The next day, my truck was towed for parking. The police told me where my truck was towed and that there was a warrant out for my arrest. I had to come up with $100 to get the truck back. The Municipal Court in Mansfield Township in Columbus had two offenses on me. The 'Obstruction of Vision' charge from the air fresheners hanging from the rearview mirror was dropped. The second ticket for the 'Unsafe Operation of a Motor Vehicle' still from the air fresheners forced me to pay a fee of $389.

On Friday, I received a letter from McGrady. He was billing me $200 for one letter and three phones calls that totaled one hour.

The balance I owed him was $2,100 to date. Today was my Court hearing at Fort Dix District Court. I fueled up the Chevy and drove the Avalanche down. As I reached the legal office, the receptionist seemed to be familiar with my name as I introduced myself.

"Is there anything on Bryan Porter's court case this Thursday?" She asked. My eyes lit up and focused on 'Thursday' immediately all her other words were foreign to me. In the chaos and confusion of yesterday I must have gotten my days mixed up. I was a day late and a dollar short. Thursday meant my attorney was inaccurate with his phone message. Thursday meant I missed an important Court date. When I called my lawyer, he informed me that the DWI was going to be thrown out but by my failure to appear forced the Judge to place a Federal bench warrant out for my arrest. There was a military arrest warrant out for me and a civilian arrest warrant. I owed hundreds of dollars in car insurance, so I was driving around uninsured. I owed thousands of dollars in legal fees. My wife was warring against me for the rest of my money, my stepson left me, and I missed my daughter terribly. My car was stolen by my brother, two guitars were stolen, a printer, a bag of gold jewelry (including my Mother's birthday gift) and my cell phones. My bank accounts were frozen. Satan was rising against me daily. We were like the sheep headed for the slaughter. Still, nothing could separate me from the love of Christ. I survived comas, jails, repossessions, bankruptcy, rejection, loneliness, etc. I would survive this.

My DUI lawyer didn't know that my cell phones were stolen. He took no responsibility for the confusion with the dates. We scheduled another court date for August 18th. In fact, I didn't have money to buy a new cell phone and I couldn't pay my car insurance, either. Eventually, I learned the attorney that I hired for the City and the ambulance had been disbarred. My strong case had no bearing now. My legal background allowed me to remember that the statute of limitations. It started from the day I filed. They sent me a warning at first and then immediately suspended my insurance on both vehicles. McGrady wrote another letter whining in response of my letter focusing on my defense. Of course, he didn't take it as a client making an intelligent collaborative focus on my defense or a conscious assertion to obtain unsupervised visitation with my daughter. He took offense that I had concerns that we weren't aggressive enough in filing for actions to have supervised visitations removed.

The General brought to my attention the two motions that he filed concerning visitation and child support. He made two motions in four years of representation. He claimed in summarization that he has thoroughly researched my case especially in regards to Sugar's pursuit of a marital share of my personal injury money. In his opinion, he gave candid opinions and for that I may want to replace him for next week's settlement conference.

The nerve of him still mending his ego weeks before the trial. There was no way an ethics committee would allow him to quit this case with a month left. The tension you could cut with a knife. No one is ever going to believe all the drama in my life. On top of that, my family still kept arguing with me on how Sugar could get half of my settlement money. They were not expressing an opinion but drop down, all out, full scale yelling and arguing how much "I know." Everybody knew so much in a family of know-it-alls. Everybody was always focused on my money. How was I spending it? What was I doing with it? It was my money, it wasn't our money.

During the Settlement negotiations, we talked about the visitation schedule and how I would have Charity every other weekend. Finally, supervised visitations were off the table. Sugar had a nervous but amicable look about her while they negotiated the settlement award. Then they determined that I would pay her the amount of $8,000.

Her lawyers were so happy that they secured almost $10,000 dollars for her. The House of Ruth lawyers looked at each other surprised like they couldn't believe it. Sugar, however, looked so distraught and started crying. All this time, she kept focusing on a much higher payday of *my* money. They spoke to her about her obvious look of disappointment, "You should be happy dear. This is a lot of money." They reminded her from their vast amount of experience seeking rewards for their clients, an un-battered woman from a battered woman's agency.

"You're nothing but a sperm donor," Sugar looked at me and screamed sitting in her chair. She was teary eyed, angry, and distraught. Her treatment of me as a father had been emasculating enough, but now she had the nerve to articulate this at me after receiving an $8,000 lump sum award on top of the $12,000 in divorce attorney fees she cost me, not to mention the Child Support I was paying while they still were denying me the right to spend time with my child, alienating Charity against me.

Grounded, I stayed around the church. I often felt it was like the honor bestowed on the tribe of Judah who were instructed to maintain the temple. My television was in the Avalanche and it was parked at Butch's driveway. It was safe there within the tinted glass windows of the truck. Mom wouldn't let me in so I had Deacon For the purpose of me to get more of my things from the house. He went with me on my insistence but made me promise not to say anything to my mother. I took some more clothes including all my suits. There was obvious tension between me and my mother. But she talked sweetly toward Deacon Thomas.

My two weeks of Annual Training was coming up next week on Friday. I had a spare uniform at Sonya's house but I had to get my combat boots from Gary's apartment. I tried to call him but he didn't answer his cell. There was always a lot of confusion. Gary was coming home from New York City and it was close to midnight. It was hard to get a signal in the train tunnels. Finally, Gary called me back and said he was coming soon. As I waited, it was 20 minutes past the time he said. Things around Baldwin and Academy Street got pretty sketchy after midnight. Waiting for over 20 minutes was driving me nuts. I started walking the route I might run into him coming from the train terminal. There was a girl on the corner and so I flirted with her as I walked by to pass the time.

"My boyfriend is right there," she said and pointed at a guy behind me. Immediately, I apologized to her and to him.

"You said something to my girl?" He asked but it was just as much a warning as a question. He was lighting the cigarette hanging from his lips as he stepped close toward me.

"I'm sorry, I didn't...," as I tried to get the words out of my mouth, all I saw was the embers of his cigarette bursting around my face. Everything was in slow motion like when I had that 'matrix moment' before. In my mind, I asked myself, 'Did he just punch me?' I never felt the punch but I thought I saw it coming back as the embers were clear against the darkness of night. Instinctively, I started back peddling, as I looked to the right of me the female was coming at me with a razor blade, in her hand. I kept back peddling and searched my pockets for the pocket-knife I carried. As I looked to the left, the boyfriend was coming at me with a pocket-knife in his hand. They were moving in quick and I was moving back even quicker.

I managed to get my pocket-knife out and yelled for them to back down. Since they mounted an assault from both sides, instinctively I swung hard at the female. I pulled my swing to deliberately miss but I swung so hard her boyfriend stopped charging at me to pull her back to safety. He was more afraid of her getting hurt than coming for me. I kept moving back but I felt a rush of adrenaline. Why were they filled with so much rage and hate? These street people live for a fight, with little else to do with their lives. Feeling so destitute, they had nothing to lose. Did what I say actually call for such violence and possibly my death? We both kept backing up in opposite directions but we were yelling at each other at the top of our lungs.

I should have never let anyone stand that close to me that late at night. I made a new rule from that night on, to never let anyone stand less than an arm's length from me after midnight. I walked down to the Prince-Of-Pizza on Bergen and Montgomery to wait for a bus. I grabbed a napkin and on the napkin I saw traces of blood. My Cousin Ali walked in, his joyful greeting instantly turned to shock and horror.

"What happened to you, Cuz?" Ali asked frowning with his eyes fixated on my face.

"Some guy sucker punched me back there," I said. "They tried to jump me. I think he had a knife," I said still bewildered, trying to process the punch I never saw coming. Did he have the knife when he jabbed me?

"You want to go and get 'em?" He asked. My family was very protective that way.

"Nah, I'll be alright," I said. Ali was a much younger cousin and this guy was definitely a street thug. I didn't want him to get involved with a person who walked around with nothing better to do than carry knives and razor blades looking for fights.

"You better go to the hospital, Cuz. You're bleeding," he said with a look of disgust from my wound.

"I'll be alright. Let me get something cold to keep the swelling down," I told him. I bought a can of soda and pressed it against me cheek. The Bergen Avenue bus came and I caught it going to my Cousin Sonya's house. Mostly everybody was asleep, so I lay down on the couch, keeping the cold can of soda against me cheek until I fell asleep. How strong can a guy be to burst your skin open? But I hardly even felt the punch. Was his pocket-knife already in his hand? Thank God He protected me because they literally tried to kill me just now. If only Gary had been on time. If only I didn't say anything to that girl. The Enemy came to steal, kill, and destroy. I tried to get some sleep. Later, when my Cousin Ace came by to use the bathroom, he had the same look of horror on his face as Ace did.

"What happened to your face?" He asked in shock.

"Some people tried to jump me," I told him. After he came out the bathroom, I went in and looked in the mirror. At last, I saw my skin was cut open above my check. An inch higher and I would have lost an eye. He must have had that pocket-knife in his hand when he punched me. The cut went through the skin to the white meat. I definitely needed stitches for this to heal. I had to go to the Emergency Room of Christ Hospital before any of the women or children saw me. So I left out the house while everyone was still sleeping.

After the hospital and a couple of stitches, I stopped by Gary's later that morning. There I picked up my combat boots. He mentioned how I didn't show up last night. I gave him my latest crazy story. He saw the gauze and bandage on my cheek. I told him how they were coming at me from both sides with a razor blade and pocket-knife. I even apologized and everything. Gary said he did that too and sometimes when you apologize in the hood you come across as weak so they immediately attack. I told him thank God I had that pocket-knife to scare them off. I normally used it on the streets to prepare my meals but it helped scare off my attackers. Thank God if it was an inch higher I would have lost an eye. I needed my eyes with my new corrected vision. I was seeing life more and more clearly every day. I took my combat boots and was ready to get out of this crazy town. Butch loaned me bus fare that he added to the bill I owed him.

On the bus ride down, I kept thinking about all the constant crazy things that kept happening, like getting stabbed in the face, cars stolen, car crashes, trucks being towed, while going through a divorce. My divorce attorney was just as much against me as Sugar was. The love of money was the root of all evil and they all loved my money. My trials didn't come like one after another. It was all at once, like the sky was falling. It was constant devastation shaking up everybody around me. People could not only handle hearing about my trials but they could handle seeing me go through them from a distance. My friends pointed out it was like Job in the Bible. Like Job's friends, some friends came suspicious that I must have done something wrong to make these things happen. I learned how to take one day at a time. I reserved a room at the Lodging Office on McGuire and checked in for a goodnight's sleep. I said my prayers, truly 'Joy cometh in the morning, Lord help me make it through the night.'

Sugar called and arranged to have my first visitation at Uncle Howard's house. I was surprised she changed from the Court papers that all pick-ups would be at her house. I guess she still didn't want me to know where my daughter lived. When I arrived at Uncle Howard's house, we had a great visit. Charity was so excited, she hadn't seen me in a while. I showed her a chocolate cake since I never had been able to celebrate her birthdays with her for the past four years. She had worked on a project at school writing a book. She showed her small book and all the artwork she did. I was so proud of her. As always, I took a lot of pictures of the occasion. We watched a movie on the DVD player. When we were sitting watching the movie, Charity inched over and cuddled with me. Still, I had to let her take the initiative. Finally, it was just like old times. It had been a long hard battle but God was making me victorious once again. Around lunchtime, I asked if she wanted to go to the Roy Rodgers down the street. She said yes. I asked Uncle Howard if he wanted something because I was taking Charity down the street to get some lunch. He said okay but he needed to get ready.

"Take you?" I asked. He said "yes," telling me Sugar had told him that I was still not allowed to be alone with Charity. I asked Uncle Howard why he would agree to that. He should have checked that out with me first and I didn't care what Sugar arranged behind my back. He felt empowered and that he could not break the agreement he made with Sugar. She wasn't his blood relative. I reminded him that he was not an official officer of the Court. He was not authorized to carry out Court functions. Uncle Howard said he watched 'Judge Judy' and a lot of court shows. For argument's sake, I agreed to it for now until I spoke with Sugar later. After all, Uncle Howard was doing me a favor. He let me use his house to have the visit with my daughter, since I was from out-of-state.

After Roy Rogers, we went to my visit his daughter, Yvonne. Later, when Sugar came back, I asked her what is this supervision crap. She tried to act naïve and said it was part of the divorce agreement. McGrady only concentrated on his pay and not what I paid him for. I hadn't received a copy from him since I owed him money still. We were supposed to have a visitation schedule. Unsupervised visitations were approved for every other weekend. Sugar loudly yelled in her anger for Charity to come on they were leaving. I told her in my equally loud voice that I am not coming back to any more supervised visitations. I grabbed Charity by her shoulders as she was trying to go pass me out the door, nervously responding to her mother with all the yelling.

"I'm not coming back here. When you want to visit with Daddy let me know because I'm not doing this supervised visits anymore. There is no reason to be afraid," I said while I looked her into her eyes. I hugged her. Sugar grabbed and ripped her away right out of my arms. She was angry whenever she didn't get her way.

"Come on Charity," she said. Uncle Howard didn't like what was going on and told me to get out of Sugar's face. I was in the doorway with my last chance to hug Charity. He was bothered by all the loud talking in his home.

"I'm not in her face," I said as I stood by the door while Sugar yanked Charity away from my arms. "She has a birthday cake," I told Sugar. Still, she stormed out the door getting in the car. "Come get your cake Baby," I yelled hoping she would be enticed by the chocolate cake I bought for her. Sugar didn't care, anybody else she would have taught Charity to appreciate the sentiment, anybody but me, that is, her father. She sped off in the car. If it wasn't about Sugar, it wasn't important. For memory's sake, I took plenty of pictures that day. Pictures of the chocolate cake with Charity's name written in orange letters. Looks like yet another birthday we wouldn't celebrate together. I thanked Uncle Howard for the use of his home but told him that I was putting an end to any future supervised visitations.

Driving up back home, I stopped at McGuire still on military orders. In the AGE Shop, I wasn't hated but I was tolerated. Everybody else was on a first name basis. There was Steve, Richard, Bob, Chip, and James. Everyone was called by their first names. I was 'Porter,' even by the under ranking people. It was great to get away for the weekend but it wasn't great to go to the AGE Shop. Often, I felt like quitting but God kept encouraging me to go on. I was only four years until my Military Retirement. Butch drove down on Sunday to help me try and get my car back. He heard that the Pontiac Sunbird was at Lil Sis's house so he drove me over there to get it. He was getting intel from Lil Big Sis. Lil Big Sis must have felt it was wrong for them to have stolen my car. She was getting intel from Lil Sis on who was staying at her house in South Jersey. Ultimately, I guess she wanted me to get my car back, too. Funny, all she had to do was call me. When we pulled up to her house we didn't see my car parked anywhere. Butch drove me back to pick up the Avalanche and told me to try it again some other day. It seemed whoever Lil Sis was renting her house to was using my car with her knowledge of it.

Mom saw me when I came by the house to get my mail. She learned how Shakur had stolen the car, whether she knew Lil Sis was involved or not I didn't know. My mother had her head down and said that God would work things out for me. I asked did she know my sister was renting her house to the people that are driving my car around. She kept her head down still, it was more than she wanted to know. They willfully kept themselves ignorant, guilty in what they allowed. No one talked to me any further about it and I was wrong for bringing it up again.

After Guard Drill, I drove to Bryn Mawr, Pennsylvania to the J.G. Wentworth office to finalize the release of my Structured Settlement. Bryn Mawr, a Celtic derivative of my name. Surprisingly, it was Welsh for the 'great hill.' The array and landscaping was beautiful adorned with all types of beautiful flowers and well maintained lawns. Upon return, I was stopped by Pennsylvania police. A computer glitch came up about an outstanding ticket but I was eventually released.

A late July bill came from McGrady for $2,350. Adding to the balance of $4,450. This weekend was July's Drill, at least I had Uncle Sam paying for my room and board for the weekend. Blue Fish and I were grateful to God and to Uncle Sam. After Drill coming back on Sunday, I left my uniform and combat boots at Gary's apartment. On July 27th, McGrady sent me the same bill from June 22nd. Prince George's County Office of Child Support Enforcement sent me a letter showing that their records showed that I was $1,832.16 in arrears. It was only three months for me but I wasn't teaching over the summer. This and my car insurance would have to wait until my Structured Settlement came.

In the midst of all the confusion, I had to report all the arrest on my NYPD Background Investigation. I traveled back to Corona Queens for the final stage of NYPD Recruitment. They wanted us all to fill out every arrest, bench warrant, and summons ever had. They warned everyone that failed to disclose any information was reason for automatic disqualification. I was wondering if I had to include the arrest that was expunged off my record. They should have never arrested me in the first place. I might get a break since it was in New Jersey. How was I going to disclose this DWI? I wrote down the arrest but indicated that it was pending.

The lawyers at M & W sent me a letter informing me our hearing date was rescheduled to August 18th at 8:00 a.m. Desperate for money, I started negotiating for my Structured Settlement to rescue me. Pastor Lanier was not happy that I was cashing in the $30,000 for a mere 60 percent of it. I became strikingly quick in my decision making. There were no other options. I had past due attorney fees, past due car insurance, past due child support, child support incoming, rent, gas and tolls for multiple state transportation. That meant the people around me had nothing to offer up to help me. We prayed but there were few options available.

Most of my nights, I stayed at the Church, Good News Bible Mission. Thursday I grabbed Blue Fish and was driving coming from noon day prayer at the Church. As I was heading toward Journal Square, I started to go straight up the hill as I approached West Side Avenue. As I thought about the traffic that way, I changed my mind and started making a right turn.

The steering seemed sluggish and I didn't hear anything but I stopped the truck. Puzzled, I got out the truck to check on things. I saw a car underneath my high sitting truck. It seemed they T-boned me. They must have tried and gone around me during my moment of hesitation. It astonished me that my SUV was like a tank. Inwardly, I was proud and amused. I didn't even feel or hear this crash and sustained minimal damage.

Two females popped out their car looking at the damage. Their car didn't fare as well against the Avalanche. Their hood and driver's front panel were crushed. They got out the car and were understandably upset when they looked at the damage and began yelling at me.

"Are you all right?" I asked. Feeling it was more important, they were not injured because cars were replaceable. The driver of the car stepped toward me.

"Come on, hit me. Hit me," she challenged me. She shoved her face forward and didn't even seem to want to defend herself. I thought how bizarre, I was more concerned that everybody was alright. Why was she asking me to hit her?

"I don't want to hit you. I just want to make sure everybody's alright," I reiterated. The other female stepped forward. I started getting the impression that they were a couple. She started yelling at me calling me names and moving her hands like a dude.

"Yeah, you need to watch where you are going. We ain't scared of you. Come on, hit me. Hit me," she said dropping her hands and leaning her face at me. What was wrong with these chicks? Why did they want me to hit them? If you wanted someone to hit you in the face, then the police rolled up with their sirens blazing.

"Okay, what happened," the Officer asked as they walked up to us. Now it was starting to make sense why they wanted me to hit them. The cops would of just arrested me on the spot. They would have said I was the belligerent one.

"We were turning and this guy hit us," they both started yelling.

"They hit me," I corrected them. "I was in front of them. They tried to go around me instead of waiting."

"Everybody get their licenses, insurance, and registrations out," the Officer told us. One Officer started taking their statement and the other was taking mine. I handed him mine hoping and praying they wouldn't find out. My insurance card was dated past today's date but when they ran it was reported that my insurance was suspended due to non-payment.

"It says you don't have insurance," the Officer said.

"Yes, I'm late with the payment," I answered. There was no way around it.

"Sorry, we're going to have to impound it," he said as he pulled out his radio requesting a tow truck. Now both vehicles were down. No use crying about it now or why did this happen. I knew exactly why, I didn't pay my car insurance. But the accident was totally an attack from the Enemy that I didn't see coming. They say any accident you can walk away is a good one. It was beyond me what was good about this. As I grabbed Blue Fish, I began on my long walk home praying for wisdom. However, I didn't really have a home now. Most nights, I stayed in the Avalanche. God would see me through this. In two weeks, I would be staying at McGuire for Annual Training. Until then, I truly was homeless. By the time, I got to my mother's I called Butch to tell him what happened, he was shocked that I let the insurance go. I asked him to loan me the money to get my truck out of impound. He wondered where all my money went. I told him how I was getting my Structured Settlement and I would pay him back, even offered to pay him back with interest. Butch was never concerned about interest. He just wanted me to pay back the money I owed him. He never answered but said he would call me back.

My mother went ballistic when she heard. I reminded her that "We are the tested, we are not the Tester." We were not in control when the tests of life come but what we do during the test. She didn't want to hear anything from me. Like Butch, she wondered where was all my money, like the money was going to last forever. I told her most was going toward my divorce. Driving back and forth from Maryland and Pennsylvania, transportation, eating, just like the trip to Maryland I had to finance for Monday. This would be for the final Divorce Hearing. I reminded her it wasn't my fault the other car was stolen. It's not like my mother was supporting me or giving me any money. I lived totally independent.

By Wednesday, Butch left a message that he was going to get my car out of impound. Thank God, we drove down to the impound yard. Butch pulled out a credit card, the daily storage fee was $100 a day. If he was using a credit card he could have done it the same day. Now I had to pay him back $400 because of his delay. Yet no one understood where my money was going. I couldn't get mad because Butch was the only one helping me and I asked other people for help. Butch helped me get the Avalanche out on condition that I kept it parked in his driveway. I couldn't drive it until it was insured again. If Butch didn't help me, I would have lost the Avalanche. I asked Brian's Wife, the Florist, to hold my two ceramic clay flowerpots. She appreciated their magnificence and was glad to hold them for me until I picked out some flowers to plant. I was glad my flowerpots had a home. I had to save Blue Fish, so I decided to give him away to the lady in the CD store next to the, the florist. She was so happy and I was to, finally getting Blue Fish a home. Autumn would be coming soon and Blue Fish needed to be in a warm place to survive. Now all I had to do was find a home for myself.

One evening while getting my mail from the mailbox, Mom was outside. We tried to have a normal conversation. She acted like everything was good. She hadn't a care in the world. I made sure to say things weren't good with my daughter out of my life and that no one was helping get her back in my life. I was upset over the fact they hadn't even seen her in over the past three years. She instantly stormed off into the house and slammed the door on me. I developed a bad habit of shouting what I wanted to say. I stood outside the door shouting still about my hurt missing my Daughter. As usual, mother could care less about my pain. The whole neighborhood could hear me yelling which became a bad habit of mine. From the inside, she stormed at the door and through the window slapped her hand against it in her anger. Again, no empathy about me or her granddaughter. I went and slapped my hand against the window from the outside. Unfortunately, my slap cracked the glass. We were both shocked, our eyes glued to the cracked window. I reverted back to a little kid, I was scared. "I'm sorry," I yelled."I didn't mean it."If I was a child she would have spanked me like no tomorrow.

"You're going to fix that," she yelled behind from the door and she meant what she said. I prayed for God to forgive me. Now another thing I had to pay for.

On Monday, Butch let me borrow his car for my Divorce Hearing down in Maryland. The Judge will reduce my Child Support I'd been still paying for Gabriel who was now 18, expelled from the public school system, and working. Of course, Sugar was called to testify first. Sugar always gets to go first. She kept testifying about the time when I was in a coma. She was crying and sobbing trying to get sympathy for herself. She was taking a moment when I was hanging on for dear life to weep for herself because she didn't know whether I would die. This was so egregious that she wanted sympathy for herself while I was the one facing death. She made the whole time I was in the coma and recovery not able to walk about her. She was so dramatic and manipulated every situation. After a while, I motioned to my lawyer that I needed to take a break from all of this. I couldn't sit in the room any longer while she was crying crocodile tears for herself.

I went for a walk remembering how it was lying in that bed, the pain, and not being able to walk. Why doesn't she talk about when she helped attack me, holding me while I was getting punched in the head? When she laughed with the police while I was about to pass out on the Domestic Escort, throwing all I owned out to the curb and keeping my child away from me for years. I tried to be friendly and she tried to have me arrested for sending her flowers on our anniversary. They seem to take things another way in the Court, if we still had emotions for each other. They obviously had no clue how callously she had treated me in her past 'five year plan.'

At the end of the day, the Judge kept the Child Support for two children the same for just one child. In addition, I was going to have to pay Sugar $8,000. The five hour workday for my Divorce Attorney was going to come out to another $1,000 just for that one day, just another $9,000 day for Bryan not to mention gas, tolls, hotels, food, and travel expenses. Yet everyone asked where all my money was going. In a couple of days, greedy McGrady sent me a letter to remind me to make payment on the outstanding bill for services rendered. The day after his letter, I received a letter from J.G. Wentworth that they were still working on the paperwork. All the traveling was depleting the funds on hand.

I had to report down at Fort Dix tomorrow for Court. With my car stolen and the Avalanche parked at Butch's house, I had to rely on other people. I tried to borrow money but no one had any. Butch was out of town. I had no money but plenty of faith. After exceeding every other option, I put on my Air Force dress blue uniform hoping it would help me get back. My cell phones were still stolen so I couldn't call people and their numbers were stored in my phone anyway. I took the last of my funds to get a bus to the airport and showed up at Curtis's job. I would ask him to drop me off and sleep in the dorms on McGuire Air Force Base. I walked over to the Fort Dix Court House in the morning.

Sargeant Bryan Porter
Air Force Dress Blue Uniform pre - 2001 E-5 Promotion

Curtis worked at UPS at Newark Airport. Sadly, I found out that he wasn't working that night. I was stuck and it was around 11:30 at night, too late to get a bus to Fort Dix. I had no money for the bus anyway and borrowing money already wasn't an option. There was no one to call, especially this late. Who was going to bail me out anyway? Who had my back? I was already out at the airport, and already dressed in my Air Force uniform, so I decided to try to hitchhike down there. With my faith and the uniform, I might find some kindness. Hitchhiking on Route 1 and 9, praying for both success and safety as I walked in the dead of night, reminded me of my long two walks down for those supervised visitations. My life had some challenges but I was a soldier in the Army of the Lord. I wasn't going to cry about it. I kept walking throughout the night under the cover of darkness, with only my old friend the Moon to keep me company. No one wanted to stop for a stranger under the cover of darkness. Despite jerking my thumb like a universal hitchhiker, no one wanted to stop for a Serviceman. How could you blame them? Toward morning, my legs and feet were getting tired. I had been walking all night for hours but I realized that I wasn't going to make it to Fort Dix. I made it as far as the city of Elizabeth and walked into the Trinitas Hospital Emergency Room. Mentally and physically, I was exhausted, dehydrated, and devastated. My faith felt unanswered and I had failed to make a mandatory military appearance. To say that I was devastated would be an understatement of what I was feeling. But like I said, I was on my own. I didn't have a bunch of people watching my back. I had no one to call from the hospital to help me get a ride back to Jersey City. So I called my mother for lack of others to call. My cousin Tim was visiting from out of town. I thought my mother would have come to get me. Instead, Tim had to drive down to Elizabeth alone. He wasn't even from around the area, he was from Pittsburgh. Nevertheless, Tim was a Marine and able to find me. Embarrassingly, I explained to Tim why I was in my Air Force dress blue uniform and stranded cities away. Tim was a Gulf War Veteran and understood the gravity of the situation I was facing missing that appointment. He was worried about me, but I didn't know of the whisperings he was hearing about me behind my back. After I explained how my Avalanche was parked because the insurance was unpaid, Shakur had stolen my other car and had little help from people. I'm sure Mom didn't tell that part with Lil Sis's coming at me with the butcher knife. Tim was worried but his plate was full. I reassured him God would see me through it all. When I called the Fort Dix Courthouse to explain what happened, my failed attempts turned into a medical emergency. How was I going to get this Federal warrant off me? It was explained that the Judge wouldn't be conveying court until September 15th and I couldn't get the warrant removed until then.

Grounded, I stayed around the Church. I often felt it was like the honor bestowed on the tribe of Judah who were commissioned to maintain the temple. My television was in the Avalanche and it was parked in Butch's driveway. It was safe there within the tinted glass windows of the truck. Mom wouldn't let me go in to the house for the purpose of me to get more of my things from the house. Deacon Thomas made me promise not to say anything to my mother. I took some more clothes including all my suits. I gave my mother her space but it hurt as I watched as as she talked sweetly toward Deacon Thomas.

Monday started my orders at McGuire. It gave me both some income, plus most importantly, a free place to sleep for the next two weeks. The Government Credit Card use was authorized again. In the AGE Shop, we had a lot of new people. Meteorologists had been tracking a cyclone that originated over the Bahamas. Two hours before it hit the cost of Florida, on August 23rd it elevated to a hurricane they would name 'Katrina.' In the hurricane of my life, my Divorce Attorney continued to call me threatening to quit and refusing to represent me any further. I was homeless, displaced, and in a constant state of transition. McGrady's newest letter addressed the Court Order he had just received. He advised me that I should comply with all the aspects of it and immediately make payment of the $8,000 monetary award to Sugar. Not surprisingly, he reminded me to make payment on the outstanding balance for services rendered by him. Working on Base put me in a structured some-what peaceful environment. God blessed me with work, food, and shelter. By August 26th, Hurricane Katrina moved out to the Gulf of Mexico and continued to brew. It strengthened to a category five hurricane due to the warm waters of the Gulf of Mexico. Things were also brewing in the AGE Shop. While we were all in the break room talking about politics and the recent base closures, I made some comments but not too many because I was still treated like an outsider. Everyone was in the conversation talking on top of each other. Suddenly, Ronald Reagan became the topic of conversation. So I made some comments about Reagan and they weren't well received. My father lost his job because of Ronald Reagan and the drugs started pouring into the Black Community. The culture in the military was to bow down to Reagan and the Republican viewpoint. He did do well for the military. Tracy Johnson, who was new to our Shop, shot down my comments right away but I ignored him. As we continued talking, he kept talking right over me like I wasn't saying anything. Then he started making his comments directly at me. Again, I was the outsider of the Shop. The Serpent's seed will always have enmity against God's seed, even when I was undercover trying to fit in. It wasn't the first time that Tracy's comments and attitude were disrespectful. Often when I was talking to other Guard members, he would jump himself into the conversation and was always disrespectful and highly insulting.

Often he would waive his hand at me and say, "Porter, you don't know what you're talking about." He wasn't much older than my son. He challenged me on Ronald Reagan, so I reminded him that I served active duty under President Ronald Reagan while he was still in grammar school. Then he said, "We feel . . ."

"We?" I cut him off. So I asked him if he speaks French. Referring to his use of the word 'we.' As he looked at me puzzled and said that he didn't speak French, I told him then he wasn't speaking for everyone else. It did confirm that they were talking behind my back. It was becoming increasingly obvious to me that disrespecting in the AGE Shop had become socially acceptable.

I expressed that he was voicing his opinions and I was free to voice mine. A mutual friend took over the conversation and he was heated about going to college and getting government grants and minorities could get grants and White people couldn't. He kept saying this on multiple occasions. Just how did the conversation go from Reagan to financial aid was beyond me. If anyone had a gripe it was vented at me. I tried to ask how this was possible. When we both applied to colleges, all they gave me was the GI Bill, the same as him regardless of our race. I received no other grants because I didn't economically qualify for them. In the AGE Shop, White men had the opportunity to voice the discrimination that they were feeling, like Affirmative Action wronged them and things of that nature. But every time I said something, Tracy would cut me off. Then I yelled back reminding him that I'm not talking to him anymore. He then told me to shut the bleep up and to get out of his face. He stood up and moved closer to me.

"Mind your business and see if you could make me shut up," I yelled. I was fuming. I didn't like when people cursed at me in disrespect especially when I out ranked them. This was illegal in the military to disrespect a Sergeant like that. It should have ended there and he should have been counseled for disrespecting a Non-Commissioned Officer (NCO), but since he disrespected me, no one saw anything wrong with it. The guys in the AGE Shop never saw me that angry before. I started moving at Tracy to get in his face. One guy tried to hold me back but I was too hyped for one person. It took about two to three of them to hold me back and a couple of guys grabbed Tracy. The guys were freaked to find out I was that strong. I promised myself if there were a room full of people that wouldn't stop me from getting one good punch in and I wanted him to know that. I stopped myself from hitting him, a room full of people couldn't.

It wasn't the first time that guys were pulled apart in the Shop. Tempers flared at times and people lost it. I've played the peacemaker in a couple of shouting matches. The AGE Shop Chief was out at the time and so were most of the other Master Sergeants. Master Sergeant Benedict was left in charge. Despite Tracy cursing at me and disrespecting an NCO, I was the only person escorted to the Orderly Room before the Commander. This should have been handled in house. There was no actual fight between us. The Chain of Command should have been followed. He should have sent me to the Chief of Maintenance first or wait until the Shop Chief returned. Benedict was a weak leader and lacked experienced. He couldn't wait to rush me to the Commander, he always kicked my back in to gain acceptance.

The new Commander of the Maintenance Support Squadron was told that I was sent to him after a physical fight in our Shop. He was told that I had a history of violent behavior. Lieutenant Colonel Smith and Chief Master Sergeant Melvin came into the office. First of all, there were no physical contact between me and Senior Airman Johnson, I told them. Quickly, I pointed out this showing that the situation wasn't as severe as reported. This undermined confidence in what was reported to them and confidence in Master Sergeant Benedict. It didn't warrant immediate discipline and should not have been elevated to their level of attention. Next, pointing out that Tracy Johnson was a Senior Airman and I was obviously a Staff Sergeant didn't put us on equal footing. Once, I was able to explain what happened, how an Airman shouldn't be using the 'F word' at an Non-Commissioned Officer like that. Once the smoke started to clear and it was confirmed that there was no actual fight, but the Commander and the Chief decided to keep me out of the Shop until they investigate things further. I explained that I was being discriminated in the Shop because of my known previous physical accident.

After work, I went home to the hotel on-base. The Governor of Louisiana, Kathleen Blanco, declared a State of Emergency. The National Guard Troops were put on alert and Federal troops were requested to respond. As Katrina kept gaining strength in the Gulf of Mexico, people were finally being warned to evacuate certain areas that were expected to be affected. Many life-long residents lacked the financial means to evacuate and expected to ride out the storm as they did all their lives. While all this was happening, we had our Air National Guard Drill this weekend coming.

Roll call, Saturday at 05:15, I forgot to set the alarm clock. As I walked toward the Chow Hall, the Air Force supplied all the food on Drill weekends. At the Chow Hall, I wasn't sure whether I should get my food to go or secure a ride across base. There was an attractive young woman I noticed sitting alone. For breakfast, I ate scrambled eggs with tomato, ham, green peppers, and onion, grits, a hard-boiled egg, cranberry juice, and some coffee. For later, I grabbed some bowls of Rice Chex, two bananas, half a grapefruit, and a red delicious apple. What I didn't eat, I would eat later in the week. This was Heaven on Earth, y'all.

I started walking and someone offered me a ride. I was ordered to report to the Orderly Room until I was cleared to go back. The AGE Shop Chief wasn't happy to find out that I was set over to the Commander while he was out. He felt Master Sergeant Benedict over reacted, as well, but he believed their reports that I was to blame. My light was not shining. The Commander told me to report to the Medical Clinic later and talk to someone there. Until then, I would continue to report to the Orderly Room. The Orderly Room is the Squadron Commander's Administrative Staff that operates the Squadron.

I didn't mind not being in the AGE Shop. I saw a lot of old faces, some even from active duty from the 1980s. People treated me much nicer than they did in the AGE Shop with their clicks. The discrimination that I received from my traumatic brain injury placed me at fault with every disagreement.

After the Medical Squadron, I walked back to the O Room. There was a hawk soaring high in the sky, flying free without a care in the world, flying majestically. I came across Tom Brooks from active duty. Many members of the National Guard and Air National Guard worked on a daily basis besides the traditional monthly commitment. We started out on the Flight line working the planes. He remembered my name. Wearing names on our uniforms didn't hurt. He said we lived in the same building in the barracks. I vaguely remembered him but my memories were challenged since the brain injury. He remembered the Bible Study I ran on Fridays in the Recreation room. Tom offered me a ride to the Chow Hall at lunch time on the other side of the base. As we left the Squadron office, we talked about our families. Tom said that he and his second wife were into camping. 'Family Life Today' ministries pointed out that family camping trips were a common and important factor in well-functioning families. It reminded me about our trip to Portugal, or camping out in the backyard in Maryland. I thanked Tom and mentioned how it was hard for me to get rides in the AGE Shop, which I had been in for three years now. They thought of Crew Chiefs as the enemy because we broke their equipment.

While we drove to the Chow Hall, I observed another hawk in flight. It was soaring through the sky, high above the heavens. For lunch, we all ate for free. I had a slice of pizza, a tomato wrap consisting of roast beef, and a salad. We ate like kings on Drill weekends.

It was still Saturday, the Governor of Mississippi declared a State of Emergency, alerting the National Guard. Governor Blanco of Louisiana sent a letter to President Bush asking him to declare a Federal State of Emergency. President Bush declared a Federal Emergency and FEMA was authorized to respond with recovery efforts.

I wrote Lieutenant Colonel Smith a letter documenting a list of recent personal crises in my life that may have led to my reaction of Senior Airman Tracy's disrespect. I apologized first for my behavior and was glad that the members of the AGE Shop were there to prevent us from further regrettable action. I spoke of my record indicating from my lengthy career that I was capable of better behavior. Some discrimination I felt was from my own shortcomings. I was a poor witness for Christ in my Shop. It didn't reflect my personal life. I did everything I could to just get along, unlike I did during active duty. Despite my efforts, they still disliked me enough to form no close bonds.

I focused on my previous 16 years of Good Conduct. Addressing the recent stress I was under was unrelenting, including four physical attacks with family members, one car stolen, one truck impounded, two guitars stolen, two cell phones stolen, one printer stolen, detained by the police four times, arrested twice with no crime committed, placed in Psych Ward and released, blocked from seeing my daughter, mounting legal bills over $4,000 from divorce attorney, and two pending arrest warrants. Now on top of these things, this under ranking Airman disrespects me and curses at me. As my Commander, he couldn't condone it. I have a course of action that will allow me to clear myself of any legal recourse. Unfortunately, I must ask for your continued patience to process the court systems. I have documentation to support my request for a little more time. While I am waiting for the proper court dates, I am fulfilling my annual training requirements and attempting to satisfy all my drilling requirements to qualify for a good year before the end of the fiscal year.

By Sunday, Katrina upgraded to a category 5 hurricane. New Orleans Mayor Nagin issued the first ever mandatory evacuation in the 287 year history of New Orleans. For some, this warning came way too late. For most were unable to evacuate anyway. On Monday,

August 29th, the flooding broke the levees and eighty per cent of the city of New Orleans was underwater. This was detrimental, all their food, water, and other essential supplies were now cut off to them. Coastal areas and beachfront towns of Mississippi received ninety per cent flooding. An estimated 1,245 people were later estimated to have died during hurricane Katrina. Property damage was estimated over $108 billion. People began debating whether the people were at fault for not evacuating. They debated whether the local, state, or federal government was more responsible for the recovery efforts.

While I waited for the Commander to evaluate me, I continued to report to the Orderly Room. I met my friend Charlie Brown from Active Duty. He gave his life to Christ Jesus through our Bible Study. Even then, Charlie became a devout believer fervent in study of the word. As we were catching up, I shared with him some of the struggles I was going through. He was first sorry and a little mystified to hear about my divorce. I was as shocked as he was because Sugar and I seemed to be so rooted in Christ. Then I shared the coma incident and the years of supervised visitation. He shook his head and informed me of another mentor of ours, whose wife divorced him. This was a strong brother in Christ and a renowned family man. Then he said another Christian mentor's wife divorced him as well. It made me sad to hear of such righteous and holy men of God, good husbands, and good fathers go through these painful divorces. The Devil was attacking more marriages than just mine. Truly, the Enemy comes to steal, kill, and destroy our families but great is our God.

By Wednesday, the Commander released me back to the AGE Shop. It was fair because nothing was ever done to Senior Airman Johnson. I didn't want to go back but it was my only source of revenue at the moment and I had four years until I could get retirement benefits. They assigned me to refuel all the power units, electrical, and floodlights in use on the Flight line. It got me out of the Shop and allowed me income, child support, and a temporary home.

People all over our Refueling Wing were being asked to donate cases of water for the victims of Hurricane Katrina. As I drove back and forth refueling equipment, I saw pallets of water parked all over the Flight line. These pallets were stacked over six feet high with cases and cases of spring water. People were eager to send these supplies to the needy victims. Why were they just sitting here on the ramp and not being sent down there where it was needed? We had tons of water for the people of Mississippi and Louisiana.

Friday after Drill, one of the new guys in our Shop dropped me off at Curtis house in Willingboro. I couldn't get the older Shop members to drive me around the Corner. What a blessing! Curtis was home and drove me to Lil Sis's house and we saw my Blue Pontiac Sunbird parked in the driveway. Thank God, I kept a spare key. Lil Sis was living back in Jersey City but whoever she was renting to was driving my car around like it was part of the package deal. Still, I was wearing the uniform of the day. I thanked Curtis and warned him that he didn't want to see what was about to happen next.

Curtis was a very calm natured man. I used to be that way. But as the lion and the bear transformed David, I was built for confrontation now. "Just grab your car and go home," Curtis yelled from his car. I marched to the front door and banged hard on it. It was good that I was wearing my battle dress uniform because I was ready for battle.

"Come out," I roared. Whoever knew Lil Sis was about to know me even better. "Come on out! You want to steal from me," I was seeing red banging on the door of the house. So angry and adrenaline pumping, I started pacing back and forth up the driveway. All the court dates I missed, all the times I was stranded, my life became so complicated because of these thieves. They had to be in the house in these suburbs if the car was in the driveway. "You let me catch you," I yelled, walking to the car and starting the engine. I'm sure the whole neighborhood heard me. It was good they never came out. I had no compassion for thieves and I would have stomped them good, especially with all the added drama that was coming at me lately. Jesus taught 'It's not what goes into a man that defiles him but what comes out.' On my journey as a warrior, my anger had been magnified and it bursting out now. Out of the abundance of the heart, the mouth speaks. My hurt and pain were louder than my witness for Christ. It was only natural how I felt but God was calling me into the supernatural. I had to deal with the anger that was coming out and defiling me. It says to anger but sin not. I was going to stomp this person into serious physical harm. And this journey would truly be a hard one.

As I drove away, I appreciated being back in my car again. My anger was started to dissipate. Seeing things more clearly, it wasn't just my car. It was my car, my guitars, my rights, my daughter, my dreams, my dignity, etc. I was feeling the blessings of God at one moment and violated the next. My life felt like a hurricane ripped right through it. People were arguing and physically attacking just about everywhere I went. It wasn't a pity party but I knew it was a test. My mother didn't normally act like this. She didn't act like this to anyone else. Even my brother was still living there unchallenged. Paul spoke how to keep him from becoming conceited God sent a thorn in the flesh, a messenger of Satan to torment him (2 Corinthians 12:7). It was like it followed me around effecting people but it could only do this if God allowed. My daily prayer for a hedge of thorns around me like Satan said that Job had he couldn't penetrate. What doesn't kill us only makes us stronger and I was feeling the growing pains. As I drove back to Jersey City, I gave God thanks. He had given me the victory and I had my car back again. I had not only my car back but also a place to sleep again.

A letter came from J.G. Wentworth. A Court appearance was scheduled for September 23rd to show cause why there should be a transfer of my structured settlement. After Labor Day, the School year started and I was going back to substitute teach again. This and Guard Drill were at least paying the Child Support. My daughter was being provided for and this was good. There wasn't much left to live off of. Blue Fish had a home and my ceramic pots had a home. I kept praying and God would supply. For the meanwhile, I had my car back and I crashed at the church some nights.

Since I was gone for most of August, I noticed Will's cousin had been hanging around a lot. He didn't attend our church services and lived right across the street. He was unemployed and needing some guidance in his life. I discerned something wrong so I asked Will about him. Will became defensive and told me that Pastor had asked him if I was bothering him there because the Annex was there for him. I was surprised that Rev would say that behind my back. He must have felt Will needed more encouragement than I did so I just left. This gave me one less place to sleep. I still had two vehicles and money was coming from my time spent on Annual Training. It allowed me to get basic insurance on the vehicles again.

I started sleeping under the Pulaski Skyway right where Route 1 and 9 curves into Broadway Avenue. One night while it rained, some lightening hit a transformer on a pole. The lightening cracked through the night sky like a whip and I was startled from out my sleep again. Faint sirens were heard in the distant night. I just kept moving locations, so the cops didn't get wise to me. I trusted the Lord to protect me.

I received another letter from McGrady complaining that he had not heard from me in the past few months despite his letters asking me to contact him regarding the outstanding legal bill. He claimed the bill was sent over six months ago and no payment made yet. Now that the case was concluded successfully, the bill must be paid now. If payment was not received by September 21st, two weeks, he would initiate a lawsuit in the District Court of Prince George's County to collect. My estimates of payment to him were well over $12,000 but he still was seeking more.

I talked with Errold, Allan Berry, and Aunt Cindy to arrange a concert at St. Michael's church on Virginia Avenue down the street. This time, it would be clear that Aunt Cindy would headline and Michele Wright sing. I would only give a couple of selections and play bass with Allan for them. Since Errold and I worked so hard for the other concert, this was easy to promote. Unfortunately, it was last minute and to advertise I had to start because we were already behind. Aunt Cindy and Michele were two of the most popular Gospel singers in Jersey City. Another misfortune was we lacked the finance to properly design and print the flyers.

They were offering more days at the AGE Shop. My pay was substantially more with my rank and years of service. In addition, I would have a place to sleep again. God provided and now I had not only a bed to sleep in but also a private bath, my own refrigerator, and cable. Hallelujah!

The Lord blessed me with more days at McGuire Air Force Base in September. On the Air Force Base, the All American Inn was only $25 a night. Plus, I could use the room phone to save minutes on my calling plan on my cell phone. Returning to duty, cases of water were still stacked on the Flight line since late August. It was major news how the Mayor Nagin and Katrina victims were suffering in the Super Dome with limited supplies and little security. There were tons of water and food just sitting here. Some people said that they couldn't coordinate because the runways were so damaged. We had C-141s that airdropped its cargo and didn't need to land. We had KC-135s and KC-10s to refuel these aircraft to accomplish the mission. We were the Air Force with the capability to respond globally to any threat or condition. Then someone told me that since the water had been exposed to sunlight and the elements for so long, it became a biological hazard.

People said it was no longer drinkable so we couldn't send it. The cases of water were sitting on the Flight line Ramp uncovered under the direct sunlight of August under temperatures that exceeded 100 degrees. What a waste of tons of life giving water to someone's mismanagement. In other news, I met my friend Charlie Brown again from Active Duty. He had some horror stories of some past roommates but offered I might want to stay with him until my check clears. This was an unexpected blessing. Truly, Jehovah provides.

Within the AGE Shop, we started to debate whether the African-American Mayor, Ray Nagin, was at fault or President Bush. By a debate in the AGE Shop, I mean the entire Shop against me. Still, I wasn't backing down from having intelligence and independent thought while either these guys were blind to every Republican notion or lacked any independent thought. I defended the people who they criticized. They should have evacuated the region. It didn't matter to them that these life-long residents never experienced a flood of such devastation. Further, I pointed out that, 'those people,' as they put it, lacked the resources to evacuate. They didn't account the patients trapped in hospitals, families with pets, the poor, or the elderly that were unable to evacuate. Still, they blamed the Mayor who admittedly said that the City of New Orleans was unprepared for a natural disaster of such magnitude. The State government and Federal government officials also said they were overwhelmed to respond to the devastation that Hurricane Katrina called for.

To add, I presented that the Mayor of a city did not have the resources the Federal government had. A wiser man would have kept his mouth shut and agree with the group. It didn't matter that many of the local New Orleans Police abandoned their post and Emergency Workers. The Democratic Mayor was understaffed, under equipped, and overwhelmed with 80 percent of the city submerged with its food, drinking water, and supplies lost. These guys still would never blame a Republican president for anything, especially in front of the others.

Thanks to God and His perfect planning, September 15th came and I could finally get this arrest warrant removed. I was in the vicinity and excused from work to take care of this Court appointment on Fort Dix. At Court, the charges were downgraded to Reckless Driving. Thank God, I really dodged a bullet but the Reckless Driving still carried five points on my driver's license. It came with a $700 fine, as well, that I had to pay immediately. That Thursday evening, President Bush addressed the nation from the city of New Orleans. He acknowledged the victims stemming from the Mississippi Coast to Alabama, and to parts of Florida. He spoke about the kind of devastation no citizen of this great and generous nation should ever have to experience, about fellow Americans calling out for food and water, about vulnerable people left at the mercy of criminals who had no mercy, and about the bodies of the dead lying uncovered and untended in the streets. President Bush was responding to the looters taking advantage of such perilous times.

Although I was never a fan of President Bush, his message was very inspiring at a time when it was needed. It birthed hope and comfort for all Americans, as Bush said, still searching for food and lost loved ones. He announced the previous day that he took full responsibility for the confusion in the delayed response in the recovery efforts. No way all the blame could fall on one man but a sign of a good leader was to take blame. He echoed the cry, "The buck stops here."

Later that month, a letter came from J.G. Wentworth about the money I had waiting for from the Structured Settlement. My attempts to try and raise my Settlement amount by threatening to use their competitors were no longer an option. The letter gave the dollar amount of $17,200. To most, it seemed like a large sum of money, despite the fact that it was subtracted from $30,000 was signing away $12,800 with a pen. No other options presented themselves. I owed too much money. A Court date of October 21st was set and pending that date, funds would be available within 72 hours. Not the best of news but a victory for me and better days ahead. When I spoke with Reverend Lanier about it, he shook his head not liking the fact that I was losing nearly half but he knew I was in a peculiar situation with everything going on in my life. And no one else was helping me with any of my mounting bills.

By the time October rolled around, my second concert at St. Michael's was supposed to start at six o'clock Sunday. The headliners were Cynthia Hines and Michele White. I was hoping their names would draw a crowd. My name couldn't draw flies. Lack of finances didn't allow me to properly produce professionally made flyers. The amateur copies had a ripple effect. First, Aunt Cindy bailed out from the concert. There went Alan's guarantee. Then Alan and Michele pulled because their Pastor had an impromptu evening service. I always prayed about these events and felt led of God's spirit. Nevertheless, no one showed up. Minister Roddey gave the opening prayer, and Errold had to fill in on the organ. We never practiced together so he didn't know the arrangements on the songs I selected. Gary was there with the video camera he borrowed and made a video. The concert was not the financial or musical success I wanted.

October 5th rolled around, and some confusion came about with my Public Defender in connection with the above matter was not completed. Now I was obligated to pay $200. In better news, Lil Big Sis's birthday was today. My friend from Active Duty, Charlie Brown, lived in South Jersey and offered me to come stay in his house. He warned me that to keep cost down he kept the heating bill low. Well, Blue Fish and the plants couldn't survive in that cold but Bryan could. Jehovah Jireh, the Lord Provides, I had a home. October 21st finally came, which was the court date for my Structured Settlement. Three business days later the funds were finally available. Immediately, I wrote McGrady his check for $5,500 to get him off my back. Despite still making recent Child Support payments, I was in arrears for $2,700. So, I wrote a check now that I had the Structured Settlement money. Next, I paid the speeding tickets for the Avalanche. All the points I acquired triggered me to take the Driving Course to lower points. So, a check was written for that as well. For the next three years, I would be paying a surcharge to the Division of Motor Vehicles. Thank God for providing. But every time I turn around, someone else was getting a piece of me.

The 2006 School year was ending. If I went back to substituting at the end of May, I wouldn't have to indicate the leave of absence pursing the divorce on my resume. Then there wouldn't be any gaps. The economy and gas were crazy. Fueling the Avalanche was expensive and I had to come up with $8,000 in cash to pay Sugar for our divorce settlement. The Blue Sunbird was reliable to get me back and forth to work. A temp agency got me a forklift job with Grainger in Robbinsville, which meant no more one hour commutes to Jersey City.

Andrea Yates murdered her five children so their souls would go straight to Heaven. She was found not guilty by reason of insanity in her retrial. Later, she was moved to a low security state mental hospital.

Charity told me that she would be starting school in September and going to Baltimore School of the Performing Arts High School. I wondered how, since she lived in Prince George's County and was going to a perfectly fine Performing Arts School. She said that Sugar felt that the school wasn't good enough. Sounds just like Sugar, all those other children were going to graduate from that school but it wasn't good enough for her.

"Are you moving to Baltimore?"I asked.

"No I'll be getting on the MARC train," Charity told me. The MARC train stands for Maryland Area Rail Commuter system. It's an express train capable of reaching speeds up to 125 miles per hour. Commuting time would be short when traveling at speeds over 100 miles an hour. It was going to be expensive commuting there five days a week, I thought to myself.

On December 30th, Saddam Hussein was executed by hanging. He was sentenced by his own countrymen for the murder of 148 Shi'ite Muslims. On January 10, 2007, President Bush ordered the buildup of 21,500 troops in Iraq. The war was growing unpopular. American casualties were over 3,000, thousands of Iraqi casualties and the war was costing approximately 400 billion dollars. Three days later, I celebrated another birthday. Praise God!

Times we're getting tough during the Bush years. My hard work paid off Grainger when hired me full-time. My hourly wage went up substantially. Another plus was receiving these $50 gift cards and stock options at work. Despite making some of the most money in my life, I often had to choose between buying food or gas with my weekly paycheck. So, I decided to start sending my daughter the gift cards written in her name. The extra money would have been nice but I was happy to send the $50 gift cards to my daughter down in Maryland. I was so happy to send it in addition to the child support and place it directly in my daughter's hand. These cards were made out in her name so Sugar couldn't use them, unlike the child support. When I spoke with Charity on the telephone, I told her how I wanted her to relax and get something to eat or enjoy a nice drink. She thanked me when she received it and told me how she liked to get a coffee at Starbucks.

Has my baby girl grown up that much? She was just eight years old when they took her from me. Now she's in high school at the School of the Arts in Baltimore sipping coffee. Some of the gift cards I had made out to my mother. She thanked me when she received it. Her voice was sincere unlike I heard from her in years. Before I gave her thousands and now she was thankful for $25 dollar gift cards. God was so amazing.

Leaving Praise and Worship practice one Saturday, the police pulled me over because of my red rejected Inspection sticker on the my car. The cop asked for my license, registration, and insurance. He searched and said that there is a warrant out for my arrest in Jersey City. I said to him, "Man, I haven't lived in Jersey City for over 2 years now." He acknowledged it was from two years ago. Thank God, I could call on my cell phone my friend Curtis. The Township of Riverdale wanted to make money more than arrest people. My bail was $2,500, so I borrowed $250 from Curtis and had to report to the Jersey City Municipal Court on Monday to straighten it out.

For Annual Training this year, the Maintenance Wing deployed to Gulf Port, Louisiana. We reported to and worked side-by-side with Louisiana's Air National Guard Unit. When we went into town by the beach, you could still see the devastation that Hurricane Katrina had done to the region from two years previous. Remnants from the powerful force of the wind were even now apparent. Some buildings were still abandoned or demolished. Areas were fenced in. Trees and limbs were still leaning or uprooted from the ground.

It seemed that the locals weren't too used to African-Americans in there Shop. They told my management how they didn't like me being there. The Sergeants above me became protective, look at God. They seemed always against me and here the Lord was making all my enemies a footstool. They gave me time off with no arguments from me. I had a good time in Gulf Port, Louisiana.

I had to make the choice no parent wished to make. Should I spend hundreds of dollars in gas and tolls to physically see my daughter or just send her the money, in addition to my Child Support. It was going on a year without me seeing Charity's face. Sugar wasn't going to let her come up and visit me or her grandparents. Even when I called Charity on the phone, sometimes Sugar would answer and tell me that Charity was on punishment and that she wasn't letting her talk on the telephone to anyone. I responded that I wasn't just anyone, I was her father and I should be excluded from that list. Sugar never saw that as reasonable and just hung up on me not letting me speak to my own daughter.

O.J. Simpson was arrested on September 16th, for breaking into a hotel with a group of men and stealing various sports memorabilia at gunpoint. At later times, I sent more gift cards to Charity. I asked her to call me when she received them. I wasn't sure if Sugar was using them herself. Charity never seemed to call when I sent them. When I finally would call her, she told me that she did get them and thanked me. She was wondering how would she be able to pay for the MARC train to Baltimore.

"You paid for the train to go to school," I yelled out. "That's not what that's for, you were supposed to relax and enjoy some down time with that money. That transportation to school needed to be figured out when you make decisions like that," I yelled in protest. Charity remained silent, she had been programmed that the school they chose was the best and all other dance schools were inferior regardless of the economic means.

On December 10th, 2007, Senator Barak Obama from Illinois announced running for President. As if a Black man was ever going to be president. How could anybody win against Hillary Clinton? She had a multi-million dollar war chest for campaigning. Even the Republicans had the utmost respect for her.

E-Harmony was great for meeting Christian women. I met a girl from Maryland, so I set up a date while I was driving down to visit my daughter. After yet another Supervised Visitation, I had a date with Victoria. She had a wicked cough. She was obviously catching a cold. Since the date was going well, I didn't care that she was coughing. She was a good kisser and I hadn't kissed anyone in a long time.

Coming back from Maryland, I started coughing real bad. I must have contracted the cold from Victoria. My cough was deep and scratchy. It seemed I caught the cuddies down there. No one wanted to be on the receiving end of my dry scratchy cough. I saw a doctor and he prescribed some medication for my cold. When I went to the Pharmacy to get it, the cost was overwhelming. There was no way I could pay it on a weekly salary. Going home I went continuing my dry scratchy cough. My roommate became so concerned hearing me coughing my lungs out, he loaned me the money to buy the medication. He told me to ask for the generic equivalent at Walmart Pharmacy. Despite getting paid weekly, I was choosing between gas for work or food to eat. Inflation was rising and economy was expensive.

At Grainger, we all gathered for our morning briefing. I had just returned from my Air National Guard Drill. My Section Supervisor wasn't happy with me leaving on Military duty. He insisted that I only had to be released for Active Duty Training. Master Sergeant Jimmy told me that all our orders read 'Active Duty training.' The conversation escapes me but me and the guys were talking and the tough Ex-Philly Cop Twin told me to get the 'Get the F out of here before I punch you right in the face.'

For the moment, I was shocked and insulted. It felt highly uncalled for, so my reaction was to just walk away. We were in a circle and the supervisor Jackie saw me walk off. He immediately dismissed the Pickers and motioned for me to follow him off the floor of the warehouse. He spoke no words to me but by his body language and the fact that we were leaving the floor meant that this wasn't good and I was in trouble. As I tried to speak to Jackie, he told me that he didn't want to hear it and pointed me to wait in this room as we left the warehouse floor. He went and got Woody as if I did some egregious act when all I did was walk away from someone who curse me.

It wasn't surprising that Jackie didn't even ask me what happened or why I walked off. I had been praying for weeks while I was feeling slightly persecuted at work. I was leaving it in God's hands and trying not to offend anyone. Woody came in the room, no nonsense but more experienced, and asked me, 'What happened?'

Wow! Jackie couldn't have simply asked me that, to see if I actually had a good reason for walking away for those brief ten seconds. Was it such a crime to walk away for 10 seconds rather than what was said to me? Now I had to tell the story and not get my Philly friend fired for threatening me. As I thought about it, it was the normal way he spoke to people and not a true physical threat. I just didn't appreciate the language.

Someone told me to 'Get the F-out of here before I punch you right in the face.' Woody was quick in his evaluation. He knew the company policy and any fight or threats would result in immediate termination. Jackie looked away as he now understood that why I walked away and would not be subject to any disciplinary action.

"Give me the name of the person who said it," Woody said. Woody asked and now realized I had justification for walking away. But if I gave him the name of my foul mouth friend he would be fired.

"Well we resolved it," I answered, covering for my friend, and withholding from revealing his name.

"Give me their name," Woody demanded again. He was a man of few words and I was not going to give him the ammunition he needed for firing my Philly friend.

"I will not," I remained silent. This guy was divorced like me and had a daughter. I was not going to be the reason he couldn't support his daughter, especially when I couldn't even see my own daughter.

"Then you are suspended for two weeks," Woody said without hesitation. It was not what I expected or what I prayed for with the persecution but I was firm not to furnish the name of my friend. Woody had an idea who said it but I wasn't going to be his puppet for firing this ex-cop. If he wanted to fire him, he would have to find another way without me. My orders were coming up next week anyway and I would be working for the Military making much more money.

Being laid-off gave me time to visit some of my old stomping grounds. So, I visited this place that had a tasty turtle stew. A craving for some Crown fried chicken came on me and I had to satisfy. The chicken was greasy and delicious.

Now that I was laid-off, it gave me the opportunity to visit my little princess at school. Catherine, the daughter of Curtis, was a sweet little angel. She was always being sweet and I encouraged her in the pursuit of violin. She had a recital at school and so with me now laid-off, I decided to go before I left for Active Duty Training. While there, I had a medical emergency and my heart started racing.

They got the School Nurse and she told me my blood pressure was through the roof. I was paying for all that turtle stew, fried chicken, and greasy burgers I had to eat to get back and forth to work. Thanks Murray's Meat Market. I think it was a reaction to the generic cold medicine I was taking. Anyway, I hopped a flight and flew done to Wichita Falls, Texas.

While at Sheppard Air Force Base, Human Resources from my civilian job emailed me information about a telephone conference. I responded to their email that I was busy on military orders and unable to stop training to meet them at their specified time. While at Sheppard, I didn't receive my direct deposit from my civilian job. I called Human Resources and they told me my pay was being delayed. The supervisors at my civilian job were very upset I didn't conference them but the Military had a rigid training environment. Broke, I was stuck down in Texas, so I started using my Government Credit Card to eat. My intentions were to pay it back when my civilian pay came in. A week's pay and vacation days were available to me.

After 2 weeks, I finished my 5-Skill Level upgrade training. When I flew back to New Jersey, I called into my job letting them know I was back to conduct the conference. They informed me that my employment with them was terminated. While on the call, I was still in my uniform. My military orders didn't officially end until midnight. I let them know that I was still on military orders. They seemed prepared and unfazed by the legal ramifications. I knew my rights and they couldn't do that. Immediately, I called the AGE Shop and reported to my superiors how my job fired me and I was still on orders. Their immediate response was 'they can't do that.' Those were my sentiments exactly. As I kept driving and talking on my cell phone, the police eventually pulled me over. In addition to losing my job I now had a traffic ticket for driving while on a cell phone. When it rained, it poured.

To make matters worse, my roommate had come to the conclusion that he needed to be in the house alone. This couldn't have come at a more awkward time. Vacation was over, I was now back in the hot seat. I had no ill feelings, knowing this day would eventually come. I fled to Jersey City, reporting to the Unemployment Office to start my claim to get some income.

Charlie wanted me out as soon as possible. With no job, no Unemployment, and no prospects, it was challenging to say the least. Having a severe lack of funds forced me to look in places beyond my normal perspective. Necessity truly was the mother of all invention. There were funds in my Military Retirement funds, the Thrift Savings Plan. After I requested my money for cash at hand, I opened a Storage to put all of my things. Charlie rented a truck, packed all my stuff, and brought it up to Jersey City for me.

Back in Jersey City, I would hang at my Mom's house or Extra Supermarket. I came in and saw Mom eating breakfast in the kitchen. I asked her about Shakur. She told me I should know where he is since I told the police where to pick him up. I went from insult to rage in two seconds. Shakur was getting arrested since he was a teenager. It was not my fault.

"You said what?" I yelled in reaction to her sarcastic tone. I was in total disgust and pushed to a point for the first time in my life where I resented her. "Since when did I ever know where he hangs out to tell the police where he is?"

"Well, that's what he told them," she snapped back, shaking her head. She always latched onto something someone else said about me and argued it to death.

"Well, what did I just tell you?" I lashed back in a rhetorical tone.

"Well, that's not what your Brother told me," she said, telling me that I was lying about the situation. I was not only a snitch now but also a liar.

"But what *did* I tell you?" I fired back again. This was also for the constant arguments we were getting into about Sugar having me arrested or keeping me from my daughter. My mother would always take her side and argue with me 'Sugar said.' I would argue back 'what did I say?' As always with all the hurt and anger, my voice was thundering.

"Get out! Get out of my house!" She yelled. It seemed like she always yelled for me to get out. I stormed out and left some more choice words. Across the street, I walked to Extra Shopping Complex and saw my friend Brian. We were catching up and talking about things, I noticed there was a police car in front of my mother's house. I excused myself and walked over to check that everything was okay.

The Officers were out of the car. One cop was an older Black Sergeant, obviously the senior of the two. The second cop was White and younger. I explained that my mother lived here and my niece walked out of the house and said "There he is," pointing at me. The senior Black Police Officer asked, "Is that him?" "Yeah," I heard my Niece say. "Were you screaming at your mother?" He asked me.

"I don't like the way you were talking to here," my Niece told me.

"I could care less. I'm talking to my mother and you need to mind your business," her Uncle told her in his loud authoritative voice in front of the cops.

"Now wait a minute!" The Black Cop said trying to get control of the situation. "You be quiet," he told me.

"No, you wait a minute," I thundered at the cop. "That's my Niece and you gonna to come here, seeing an older Black man, and you want to hear a young girl? She doesn't even live here. She doesn't have any identification proving she lives here." The cops would have jumped on me but I was making perfect legal sense and my paralegal side was kicking in strong. "Now I'm a licensed ordained minister and a member of the Minister's Alliance. I'm a Sergeant in the Military and I want to be treated with some respect in my community."

"I don't like how you talked to her," my Niece said again.

"And I don't care." This was the pot calling the kettle black. Here is my free-loading Niece taking advantage of my mother showing her little appreciation or gratitude giving a place to stay and food to eat and judging me on how I'm treating her. "What are they gonna do? Arrest me because you don't like what I said? That's not a crime." They cops looked at each other. They had little power to exercise over me when there was no crime committed. My mother came out the door and told the police that everything was alright. I stormed away rolling my eyes, returning to my conversation with Brian.

Letting Brian hear all that had happened, the accusation of me telling the cops where to arrest my brother, my Niece calling the Cops on me, Brian's family didn't have such dysfunctional dynamics.

Months went by but the unemployment never came. My cousin Julius invited me to stay with him while I was waiting for my money to work out. He bragged how he had a parking lot I could park in. This was a huge bonus, parking in the Journal Square Area. I was living off selling my drinks at the Train Stop and odd jobs. Mom's anger kindled against me and I wasn't allowed in her house. Still, I stayed around the Extra Parking Lot, ministering Jesus and selling juices. As much as I made, I spent in ice keeping my beverages cold in the summer heat. I was waiting to hear from the Department of Labor while I was on Active Duty. My faith said my pay day was coming.

God protected me through all the family confusion. For whatever reason, Mom wanted to keep me from the house. The police came looking for Shakur. I wasn't allowed in, so I couldn't get blamed for anything. Yet somehow my name was still being thrown around even though I hadn't been allowed in the home. I stayed with Julius. I brought plenty of food I received from the church. This helped feed Julius and his Son very well while waiting for my funds in my Military Retirement Savings or unemployment to arrive.

Senator John McCain won the Republican nomination for the Presidential Election. He chose Governor Sarah Palin from Alaska as his running mate. I couldn't see America ready for a woman Vice-President and certainly couldn't see America allowing a Black President. Barak Obama received the Democratic nomination over Hilary Clinton. They might as well have handed it to McCain. If he chooses Hilary as a running mate, it could make an even playing field. However, he chose Senator Joe Biden, a seasoned Washington insider.

Just as I couldn't see Obama winning the Presidency, I couldn't see my car in Julius' parking lot he bragged about. Later we found that my car had been towed. Only residents were permitted to park at this Journal Square location. All Julius, who bragged about his parking lot, had to do was sign me in as a guest and I would have had parking privileges. His mistake was costing me money daily on the impound lot. My Military Retirement funds check hadn't arrived yet, so I had to go borrow the money from loved ones. I prayed the prayer of faith in Jesus name. Whatever I asked shall be given to me. No one was giving me anything, they just were loaning me money or using a credit card and it would be like pulling teeth.

After the prayer, I provided the action of faith. So, I asked Lil Big Sis and she said no. Then I asked Butch and he said that he couldn't right now. My last hope was for Mom to help. She talked to me through the doorway, not allowing me in the house. She was so upset to find out I had my car towed. I explained Julius had told me it was alright to park there while I stayed with him. She was disgusted and told me to wait at the door while she got her credit card. As she handed me her credit card, she started fussing at me.

All the things I did for her or for family, I never talked down to them. She fussed at me like a child, I never heard her talk to anyone like that. The money she was getting back as soon as my unemployment or Thrift Savings Plan check come.

"If you feel that way then don't do it," I said in my pride. This was not God. A gift from God doesn't come that way. It doesn't demean you, insult you, or strip you of you dignity. This wasn't even an act of faith. They knew that I'd pay them back. I always pay them back. Butch and Lil Big Sis had some major legal battles coming up. Normally, they were always there for me. Me running my big mouth wasn't God, either.

"Well, then I won't," she shrieked. She shut the door and the matter was closed to her. Of all the people I asked to help, none of them were too concerned with my situation. Days went by as I checked the mail daily. Every day was $100 plus dollars in storage fees.

I received a letter from the Assistant Director of the Department of Labor Veterans' Employment and Training Service. Enclosed was a federal privacy act release form to file my USERRA claim, an important first step in the process. Hallelujah! Another envelope appeared as a check. God answered my prayers. As I ripped it open, I saw the check and God answered prayer. Immediately, I cashed it and went to the impound lot. I wasn't quite sure of the amount. When they told me $800, I was speechless. Anyone I asked could just use their credit card and I would have paid them back that same week. As I rolled away, I decided to treat myself to a hotel. I played some Marvin Gaye and should just be grateful for God's mercies. I received my check. I was back in my car, and I had a hotel room tonight. However, despite my mind telling me to be thankful, the tears streamed down my face. I was waiting for these funds from my Military Retirement Plan and the Devourer has taken most of them in this single action because I trusted Julius and listened to him. No matter how I felt, God provided and He would continue to provide.

I went for my routine checkup with Dr. Kim at the VA Clinic downtown. I mentioned how I was living out of my car now and waiting for my USERRA Claim to get my job back. A Psychiatrist was visiting and Dr. Kim was anxious for me to see him. The Psychiatrist recommended that I stay at the VA Hospital in the Domiciliary. There was temporary lodging there to solve my homeless problem. When he heard about my Traumatic Brain Injury and swelling of the brain in three areas, he immediately determined that I should no longer serve in the military.

"How could you determine that?" I asked. "I was evaluated and approved for duty eight years ago by Military and VA Doctors," I fired back at him. He just smiled with his superior smug smile.

"I still don't think you should be deploying with the military," he said with such arrogance without any evaluations or hints of negative performance for eight years.

"Well, my Psychologist has been approving me for duty since 2001," I let him know.

"You do know the difference between a Psychiatrist and a Psychologist? Don't you?" He asked as his arrogance continued. I shook my head indicating 'no' to him.

"Well, I can prescribe medications and they can't," he said with this look like the world revolved around him.

"Well, my Psychologist has a PhD," I quickly responded. This cocky Psychiatrist was very young and not as far accomplished in his field.

The cocky Psychiatrist gave me an address to the VA Hospital in Lyons, New Jersey. There was a Domiciliary I could enroll into. When I drove out there and tried to enroll, they told me the rules of the Program. One rule in particular was I couldn't leave the property for the first 30 days. My mind flashed to my Weekend Guard Drill but first I was get into this Program and worry about that later.

When filling out the application, they wanted to know the reason why I was homeless. My reasoning for losing my civilian job while on military orders was responded to that "they can't do that." My response to that now was "they did." Then they asked if I have a drug or drinking problem. To not condemn drinking as a Christian opened a big denominational can of worms. As I found seeking refuge, the Domiciliary took a superior approach and told me the only reason I had to be homeless must be from a drug or alcohol dependency.

Admission to consuming alcohol occasionally to them was as an admission of guilt. Any Veteran admitting they drink is an admission of an alcoholic problem. I found that while I received the sanctity of a place to sleep and food to eat. My time would now be regulated by daily multiple mandatory Alcoholics Anonymous meetings and Narcotics Anonymous meetings. This is not what I signed up for, but having a bed, food, and daily showers was nice. I reconciled with my old family the Military. It was good being around all these Vets. When we get together hard times bond us regardless of race, social, and state affiliation.

Despite my newfound comforts, the monthly Weekend Drill was coming up with the Air National Guard. Despite being in a VA Hospital, they had no accommodations for active Military commitments. If I left to fulfill my Drill Weekend, I would be expelled from the Program and not allowed back. After days of thinking about it, I decided to trust God and leave. He would guide my footsteps through this process. After Drill, I spent time at my Cousin's house or in my car. Sleeping in my car bothered my mother a lot. She invited me to come stay with her for a while.

A mother's love has a universal strength. Today I borrowed "Alexander" the movie by Oliver Stone from the library. Stone said in an interview that a mother will be the greatest teacher in a person's life. From Alexander's mother and father, I learned some timeless age old truths. The movie opened with Anthony Hopkins reminiscing at Alexandria, Egypt about many accomplishments of 'Alexander the Great.' Some called him a tyrant, but never has a tyrant given back so much. There were 18 Alexandrias built that showed an empire more than just of gold but of the mind and intellect that all men reach and fall.'

For 100 years, the Persian kings bribed the Greeks to fight for them as mercenaries. It wasn't until Philip the One-Eyed, Alexander's father, who united them and built a professional Army. Alexander's mother, Queen Olympia, was considered by her non-conventional ways a sorceress. Queen Olympia told Alexander to grab one of her pet snakes, when he was just a child. She warned him not to let the snake see him hesitate or show fear. That moment of weakness could cause the snake to strike. As she taught this, it went straight into my spirit. She told him that people are like snakes. You can nurture them, care for them, and feed them but one day that may turn on you.

Philip saw that Alexander gloried in battle and cautioned him that his mother encouraged him too much looking for glory. Philip told him that there is no glory without suffering. A king isn't born, he is made by steel and by suffering. Fate is cruel. The glory that one gets in the end gets taken away.

My prayers were not being answered in getting a legal Settlement and financial compensation from being fired from a job. Unemployment was a blessing and money was steadily coming in. Other Americans couldn't quite say the same in these last days of the Bush Administration.

Financial wows weren't only being felt by me but by the nation as whole. Stores started closing and thousands of employees were being laid off. A decrease in automobile sales caught the attention of Wall Street. Fannie Mae and Freddie Mac guaranteed mortgages and lowered borrowing cost, crippling the housing market. Over $100 billion bailout money was approved by Congress to maintain its functioning to homeowners for this crisis.

On a triumphant day on November 4, 2008, Barak Obama defeated Senator John McCain to become the 44th President and the first African-American to serve in that office. *Never* in my wildest dreams did I believe, with the racial climate in America, we were ready for anyone with a dream to become President. Had the dream of Martin Luther King finally come to be realized? The Black Community was shocked and overjoyed. Millions of Americans who voted made history. There were celebrations all around the country. Yet there were some who agonized over this, as well.

The road ahead would not be a smooth one. Senator McCain congratulated President-elect Barak Obama and said during his concession speech that difficult days were coming for our nation. A recession hit the economy only to rival the Great Depression. The cooperation of every American would be needed to get through the difficult days ahead. My unemployment check supplied me with a steady income. Mom was grateful for the rent. Another car was repossessed but I thanked God everyday for a warm home. Reverend Lanier came to pick me up on Tuesdays and Friday nights.

As the year was ending General Motors, Chrysler, and Ford were all on the verge of bankruptcy. Besides gasoline sales, this included car dealers, mechanics, auto detailers, etc. Millions of jobs were in jeopardy. An 80 billion dollars bailout was proposed to save the auto industry. Ford opted out, deciding to take its chances and not participate by receiving government loans. People were reevaluating the true meaning of Christmas. Family was more important than meaningless presents. Count your many blessings.

President Barak Obama ordered U.S. military troop buildup in Afghanistan to 36,000 to accompany the 32,000 NATO forces on January 30th. I was blessed to see another birthday. I thanked God. I had no job, no car, and little communication with my daughter. I just had my Air National Guard job and unemployment. People were losing their jobs and homes every day. Best be thankful for what you have. A home, a job, and a meal. So, I checked into transferring over to the 113th Infantry Regiment, in the Jersey City Army National Guard.

There, I was scheduled to deploy to Iraq as a Medic. By February, President Obama approved an additional 17,000 more troops.

Rarely in my life was I unemployed. Since high school, I worked a full-time job. Maybe I could transfer over to the Army and get deployed to Iraq. I would make money as a Staff Sergeant. Sugar would only let me see Charity through supervised visitations anyway. Rarely did I get the opportunity to see my daughter Charity. There were little to no funds to travel. Deployment to Iraq meant I didn't have to pay any taxes in a Combat Zone. I would come back with so much money. I wonder if they would let me transfer.

One night, I woke up from a horrible dream. The emotions and memories of the dream were so real and vivid even after I was awake. I was still convinced my Nephew Trè was dead. Still in the darkness of the morning, I walked down the steps and asked me mother for clarity. My short term memory still troubled me but I trust no one to share the severity of it.

"Ma, is Trè dead?" I asked still experiencing the pain and confusion. My mind was telling me my dream was real. She stared at me with a look of attitude, disgust, and anger.

"You know Trè is not dead," she rebuked me sharply. When she answered me like that, it always triggered a response of attitude back. Looks like they would have been sympathetic about my short-term memory problems but my family was always the least helpful in that area.

"If I knew Trè was alive, why would I be asking?" I answered back still devastated by my nightmare. She continued to stare at me still in disgust, still in disbelief.

"Trè is not dead," she answered with total distain. Her response still did not relieve the sense of mourning I felt over my nephew. I felt in my mind and heart a sensation of lost and emptiness. To keep the peace, I began to explain to her the dream I had and how real it felt. I didn't see how it happened or what had happened but it happened. In my mind, Trè was gone and trying to explain that to my mother was a challenge. She was unable to relate to the effects of short-term memory loss from brain injury or hide her emotions on her face. She stared while listening to my story. All I could hear echoing in my mind was her saying "the Doctors said you'd never be the same." After I finished, she didn't seem to be any more understanding about my feelings. "So just pray," she said.

For the next couple weeks, my main prayer was for Trè's safety and his life be spared. I wanted for my new National Guard Unit to contact me, so I could start Drilling and training. I wanted to be in the number of all those troop deployments. The Jersey City National Guard Unit was activated. But I wasn't called, then I received a call I've been regretting.

"Bryan," my cell phone rang and it was Lil Big Sis calling. "We need you to pray," she said crying.

"What's the matter?" I asked attentively.

"It's Trè," she said crying. My heart sank. I was hanging on the edge of my seat. "He ran into the street and got hit by a car. Our Cousin Mike said they hit him up so bad it knocked him under his car. They had to jack the car up just to get Trè out from under it. He's unconscious and the Doctors don't think he's going to make it. They took him to the Medical Center but now they're going to transport him to the Children's Hospital." I wish my response could have boosted her faith but all I could think about was the dream I had the month previous. My words were uninspiring and my faith was weak. "This is just like when you were in your coma," Lil Big Sis said. "We told that Devil that you can't have Bryan. And we have to believe that Trè is going to make it through this," she said.

My response to her was 'yes' but my dream crept back in my mind. I thought that truly this is why I had that crazy dream. But I had been praying for Trè's life all this time, and prayer changes things. Lil Big Sis prayed with me. We called Shakur and told him the bad news. He wasn't taking it so well. He and Trè were inseparable.

We rode down to Children's Hospital in New Brunswick. The sight of my little nephew with all the heart monitors hooked up to him, IVs, respirators, and feeding tubes. Trè lived but he lived the rest of his life as a paraplegic. He would never walk, talk, drink, or eat solid food again. He lay in a bed and needed around the clock medical care.

By June, 10,000 more Marines were deployed to fight against the Taliban in Afghanistan. Still, October proved to be the deadliest month for U.S. Troops in Afghanistan with a total of 58 troops being killed. President Obama was expected to still send additional troops to help in the crisis. The real question would be how many to deploy. Some strategist suggested up to 35,000 should be necessary. Good news on the 9th of October, President Barack Obama won the 2009 Nobel Peace Prize for "Strengthening international diplomacy and cooperation between people."

October started the fiscal year for the Government. Military strategist planned to reduce Air National Guard slots in Atlantic City and merge them here with the 108th at McGuire. This was the perfect opportunity for me to move over into the Army. Easily, I could get deployed to Iraq or Afghanistan. Unemployment was so high, there weren't any job prospects to be seen anywhere stateside in this slow economy.

On this day, November 10, 2009, John Allen Muhammad (aka the DC Sniper) was executed by lethal injection in Virginia for the killing seventeen people and injuring ten others. During December, President Obama gave a speech at West Point announcing to expand the role of the U.S. Military in the war in Afghanistan by sending 30,000 additional troops. The U.S. military forces in Afghanistan would now be 71,000 strong. Christmas was dismal but my sisters still worked their magic with handsome sweaters and shirts for me.

All this time, I gave no thought walking past the Jersey City Armory. It was the home to the Army's 113th Infantry Regiment, one of the few National Guard units with roots dating back to the Colonial days. Now with the green light, I stopped by and talked with the recruiters seeking a transfer. I requested to branch into the medical field, so that I could transition back to civilian life with a marketable trade.

Everybody seemed to be on board. My 108th Maintenance Commander had no problem signing my transfer paperwork, since they were reducing forces. The National Guard Recruiters were anxious and stated the 113th was about to deploy over to Iraq. I was a mercenary for hire. I would have volunteered to go anywhere for steady employment. Truth be told, I preferred Iraq over Afghanistan. God will give you the desires of your heart. My chances of coming back alive were greater in Iraq anyway. Afghanistan was a blood bath. Anyhow, after 20 years of the Air Force, "You in the Army now, Son!"

Chapter 5

You in the Army Now

M - 4 Assault Rifle

R inging in a Happy New Year 2010! As this year starts out, I've successfully graduated my Medical Assistant program. Now I was certified in Phlebotomy, Medical Assisting, and EKG. Finally, I couldn't wait to start working in the medical field. My ambitions were to apply for Nursing School and seek a Commission as an Officer in the National Guard. 'Captain Porter' had such a nice ring to it. Deployment would have to wait for now. They were viewing my vast medical history. The Army wasn't viewing my traumatic brain injury and the coma quite like the Air Force did. My desires to join the Army and deploy to Iraq were now on hold and hanging on a wing and a prayer. My desires to escape my poverty, unemployment, failures, and not seeing my daughter would have to wait. The island nation of Haiti was devastated by a 7.0 earthquake that devastated property killing thousands. In moments like these I would be activated to provide medical support. The next day was my birthday. President Obama started an 'Open Doors' program to assist in the housing of homeless veterans. Thank God, I wasn't homeless right now. However, I can't say the same about all the earthquake victims in Haiti. In an instant, thousands of people lost their homes, property, lives, and loved ones. Argentina's military set up a field hospital to help the huge number of injured in Haiti. Bodies of victims were being piled up on the streets. International rescue teams started arriving in Haiti within 24 hours. First Iceland, then Cuba, and Peru set search dogs and 50 tons of food. By Wednesday, the United States Coast Guard was arriving with helicopters, aircraft, and cutter ships to aid in rescue efforts. Still, their response time was faster than federal relief was sent under the Bush Administration to American citizens during hurricane Katrina. The U.S. Air Force Combat Controllers landed and took control directing over 2,500 flights without incident delivering over four million pounds of much needed emergency supplies.

By Thursday, twenty countries were helping provide supplies, manpower, and financial aid to Haiti but my Med Com Commander threatened to get rid of anyone who volunteered for Haitian Relief. As a Medic, this was one of the reasons that I joined the Army National Guard. To be denied because of the selfish ambitions of our New Jersey National Guard's Surgeon General was counter-productive to Big Army's objectives. With all the injured, medical support was in great demand. Death tolls were estimated to reach 200,000 souls.

Another birthday rolled around and God never spoke to us about a fast. There would be plenty of cake in this house thanks to Lil Big Sis, the party planner of our family. She bought me a cake from our favorite Italian bakery, Monteleone's. The Porter family had been buying cakes there for over forty years. Mom, Lil Big Sis, and Double K gathered round and we had a good time with each other. My daughter sent a birthday text which was progress. Sometimes that's all we could ask for. She wasn't trained to do anything more than that for my birthdays. Lil Sis always sent me a nice birthday present. All my money went to child support and it wasn't much. I didn't earn much and couldn't afford an apartment. If it wasn't for my mother's generosity, I would be homeless on the streets without a pot to piss in or a window to throw it out. Even my wardrobe I owed to my sisters.

The New Orleans Saints defeated the Indianapolis Colts in Super Bowl 44. This victory was a triumph for the Saints franchise with their first NFL Championship. It was also a boost in morale for the entire city of New Orleans, still recovering from the deadly aftermath of Hurricane Katrina five years ago. My prayer of faith was that an overdue victory was looming. Faith never gives up and God never fails. Unemployment was coming to an end for me but the economy was still very slowly recovering. Surprisingly, I was on it for two years. What a blessing! It seemed it was as much a plot as the political strategy of obstruction to not support President Obama. The product of not supporting any program to recover the economy was hurting every unemployed American. Businesses had money but jobs were not being created. Medical Assisting was not opening any doors, either. Not even my bilingual classmates were getting hired. As a backup plan, I chose the Security Guard field as an option. Certification was necessary in both New Jersey and New York. New York was my selection where the opportunities for employment seemed far greater. My Security preparation took sixteen hours of job training, eight hours of Pre-Assignment training, as well as Fire Safety Officer Exam Preparation. Working in New York City as a Security Guard also warranted a Fire Guard certification.

June rolled around and news from my transfer to the Army National Guard finally came through. The Army's Surgeon General approved my Transfer Request. The traumatic brain injury, the swelling of the brain in three areas, and being in a coma were all being waived. The Supply Sergeant met us at Fort Dix to issue us our uniforms to start training in August at Sea Girt. My becoming an Army Medic seemed a long road but God was true to His promises. I could start working in the healthcare field and possibly become an Officer as a Nurse. In that profession, they would waive the age limit that I passed. We went into a Military Clothing Store and were issued our duffle bags. In them, we stuffed our battle dress uniforms, field jackets, and boots.

When I got back home, I started looking for Security Guard jobs. Macy's in New York City had job openings. I imagined all the overtime I could get working there with all the parades. Most of my money was spent going over New York for job interviews. Coming back from Macy's, I took the PATH to Journal Square. Humped down to Storms Avenue and decided to drop by to see Joel at his Christian Bookstore. The strain from the luggage bag forced me to rest by the Coptic Orthodox Church, catching some shade. Then I humped it to the Old Bergen Church between Highland Avenue and Mercer. This was a historic church with the congregation was founded in 1660. In 1680, the first building was erected, while the present building was erected in 1841. In 1967 Trinity United Presbyterian Church was formed with a merger of three Presbyterian Churches. Also it was the year I was born. Lastly, in 1970, Bergen Reformed Church joined in union with Trinity United Presbyterian Church. History always fascinated me, especially about Churches. Churches were not only about the buildings but also about the work and offerings raised to pay for the buildings. It was about the people, the families, and the sacrifices made.

No Shame In My Game

After 20 years of the Air Force, I was in the Army now. Starting my Army National Guard Drilling once a month at Sea Girt with the Medical Command (Med Com). The members in the Army embraced me and to say the least, it was comforting. When I went away to my Army National Guard Drills, I wasn't treated as an outcast. I wasn't treated like a guy no one wanted to hang out with. I didn't have any incidents where I had to be rushed to the Commander. At last, I was part of a Unit in which people had my back. There was this particular couple in my Unit, Ivan and Brenda. They always made sure there was room in their car for me. They took me everywhere with them after Drill. Anywhere they hung out, I had an invitation and a ride.

Sea Girt had large grass fields for marching and formation. The Marching Bands trained there and the State Police. Even an army of Canadian Wild Geese took residence there. At Sea Girt, we took and recorded soldier's height and weight. Then I learned how to take blood pressure with a stethoscope. Clumsily, I deflated the blood pressure cuff and squeezed the ball pump. After several readings, I finally streamlined the process. Our Commander was Colonel Bird. She wasn't just a lieutenant colonel. She was a full bird colonel. She was a tough old bird who was the Surgeon General for the state of New Jersey National Guard. She said something that inspired us, that if soldiers didn't have their medical procedures documented properly, then it didn't happen. This is why I joined the Army, to support our American troops and to save lives. I wondered why I didn't receive my '20 Year Letter' from the Air National Guard. It was quite an accomplishment and I wanted all my accolades. Macy's hired me, thank God. After two years of unemployment, the economy was still slowly recovering. Some blamed it all on President Obama. How could they dismiss Senator Mitch O'Connell and the obstructionists that controlled the Congress? At Macy's, I was assigned to Loss Prevention. They issued me a black suit, tie, and an earpiece. We looked like Secret Service agents. We were Visual Security assigned to the doors. Our presence there deterred a lot of theft. We wore earpieces to one of the most advanced surveillance Control Centers in the world. Their cameras even helped during the 9/11 bombings. I enjoyed working there and having a daily inspection before each shift. It was run like a military operation using the police's 10-40 Codes. It felt so good working again. But as soon as I started working again, I had to take a Military leave for Medic training. Did they have to let me go? What could they do? Fire me yet again?

I started training for the Combat Medic Course at Fort Dix with the 2nd Battalion 254th Regiment. Most of the fellow Soldiers in my Class were from various New Jersey National Guard Units throughout the State. My friends, Ivan and Brenda, were from Medical Command Unit at Sea Girt. My new Army unit was much closer than my Air National Guard AGE Shop in the 108th. The guys there wouldn't even drop me off at the back gate or ride with me to lunch. My fellow Soldiers, my new Battle Buddies, took me everywhere during Drill, and always had my back. They always took care of me, especially Ivan and Brenda, my Battle Buddies. After Drills, we would go to a Mexican restaurant called Jose's. My favorite entrée was the steak ranchero. It was so rich in flavor with peppers, chilies, and spices.

In the Army, a battalion is basically 1,000 soldiers made up of 'companies' commanded by a lieutenant colonel. The companies consist of 80 to 250 soldiers. The company commanders are majors or captains. Companies are made up of platoons. Platoons are commanded by platoon leaders, lieutenants, who are assisted by platoon sergeants. Platoons were made up of squad leaders who were led by sergeants called platoon leaders. There weren't even 50 people in our entire Medical Command. We basically were split into two companies of four squads.

Med Com was so small they didn't even an Armeror qualified enough to keep the armory. They provided little to none on weapons training, which was something I craved for in my Army training. Mostly all we did at Sea Girt were height and weight checks for soldiers needing one for deployment. The Top ranking NCO, Top, was trying to bring our tiny unit run more like a full battalion. We started meeting outside for Formations for drill. We had to share the field with a large flock of Canadian geese. We would conduct formation in those grassy fields and Top wanted us to start having more PT (physical training). I must say we shared no joy doing push-ups in a Goose poop ladened minefields. But we were grunts and a grunt can take it.

In the Army, the distance for running was different as well. The Air Force only required one mile and a half while the Army's standard was two miles. Back in the Air Force, I was one of the fastest people in the Squadron. Never did I need to train for it, being the former Captain of my high school track team. But I was in the Army now and things were different.

Normally, the Combat Medic Course takes place at Fort Sam Houston in Texas. However, it was cheaper for our units to keep us in State. God had truly blessed me. Uncle Sam provided us Barracks to live in during training. No rent to pay for me, just three hot meals and a cot. The hot meals consisted of breakfast, lunch, and dinner. The

Air Force took over management over all the Army Chow Halls on Fort Dix, so the food was nutritious, delicious, and free. Uncle Sam was always my favorite Uncle. To avoid Base closures, the branches were merging for survival. Fort Dix was for Army, McGuire Air Force, Lakehurst a Naval base, and a Marine Detachment. The Medic Course would be divided into three Phases. Phase 1 began teaching an overview of Basic Life Saving, an introduction of Emergency Medical Care, basic anatomy, and Cardiopulmonary Resuscitation (CPR). Upon completion of all three courses, we would be certified in CPR and as EMTs. One of the first things they instructed us about was the scope of our authority. We had as EMTs to learn legal terminology, such as negligence, advanced directives, abandonment, living wills, do not resuscitate (DNR), duty to act, etc. There were certain rights people possessed that EMTs couldn't have the authority to violate. People had the right to refuse medical attention. This right is called 'consent.'

The legal definition of 'consent' is when a person possesses the sufficient mental capacity to make intelligent decisions. If consent isn't given by the person, they had the right to refuse any medical attention. This right could only be overridden if that person was a danger to themselves, or a danger to others, or to property. The person must suffer some underlying mental disorder. There are presently people walking the streets with obvious mental disorders and it is still hard to commit them because they haven't given consent.

My Training Instructors served as Sergeants from various local New Jersey National Guard Units. They came from all walks of life as First Responders: a Paramedic, a Firemen, and a State Police. After a month, we finished Phase 1 of the Army Medic course. We were all now CPR certified and I had an 87 grade point average for the course so far. There is no shame in my game.

Leave No Man Behind

As Phase 2 began, Master Sergeant Cosmo told a joke, "Sergeant Porter is so old, he fought in the battle of Jericho." Everyone seemed to have jokes. They took us to a building and prepared us that inside we would find rooms set up for scenarios we might encounter in the field. Since I was a Sergeant, they sent me in leading the team first. We were all armed with our M-4 rifles and the mission was to go in and find the American soldiers and give them medical attention. We entered into these dark rooms. I was amazed how they transformed these rooms to appear like a Middle Eastern village. Women were walking around in their hijabs and wailing. The rooms were filled with smoke and resembled a war zone. We were told to go into all the rooms to look for the wounded. Mannequins in camouflage uniforms were lying on the floor. When we found one, we called out to our Training Sergeants. They would ask us what their vital signs were. We dropped to our knees, checking to feel breathing and establishing if they had an airway. The first thing we assessed was if there were signs of breathing. The Instructor would tell us whether they were breathing and whether we would have to use an artificial airway device. Then we would use the Head/Chin Lift to establish an airway. We would say there was equal rise and fall of the chest. Simultaneously, we had to check for a pulse. Since we were checking mannequins, we would always smile and say they had no pulse while checking the carotid artery. Our Instructors didn't smile, feeling we weren't taking the training seriously.

My Team went to several rooms, looking for the wounded. There was a wounded soldier I found on the ground, so I knelt beside it and called out for a Training Instructor. Staff Sergeant Pathfinder came and after a routine assessment of the airway and circulation, I placed the mannequin in the Head/Chin Lift and they told us to move out. After I gave the Team the order to move out, the Instructors called the scenario over and we came in for an evaluation of our performance.

"Okay, how do you think you did?" Staff Sergeant Pathfinder asked. We shook our heads as we were pleased with ourselves.

"Where's your weapon, Sergeant Porter?" she asked me. In all the excitement, I hadn't noticed one of the wailing women in her hijab snuck off with my assault fire while I was tending to the wounded. How was I supposed to administer medical attention and hold on to my firing arm at the same time? "A lot of you were focused on your patient not aware to everyone around you might become hostile. You have to secure your weapon at all times. You might want to sit on your weapon while giving medical attention."

"How many Medics did you start out with, Sergeant Porter?" Sergeant Choc asked.

"Six, I believe," I answered.

"And how many do you have now?" He asked as the inquisition went on. As I looked around, one member of my Team was missing. Sergeant Choc took out his wallet and handed me a VFW business card with the slogan, 'We will leave no soldier behind.' All the Training Instructors were cracking up. Everybody had jokes. They didn't seem to appreciate our mannequin joke.

Later, we practiced our patient lift techniques. After the Phase was completed, they administered the test. When the results came in, they called me out of class and told me that I failed the course with a 69. It was only one point away from continuing on with my Class. Never before in my life did I fail any test. Information was becoming much harder to retain after the brain injury. All my Training Instructors were apparently sad for me. They all looked so sorry to see me leave. Surprisingly, they documented everything quickly and I had a whole package of forms for me to sign, documenting my failure. Immediately, I called my Squad Leader and my Platoon Sergeant to tell them the bad news. They weren't too disappointed, encouraging me that they would give me some studying materials and I would pass the next time.

Meanwhile, when I reported back to work at Macy's, my friends were wondering where I had been. The girls working at the make-up counters had noticed I was away and totally ate up my war stories. My modest attempts explaining I was merely away with the National Guard gave me cool points throughout Macy's. They were impressed to hear that I served in both the Air Force and the Army. Whenever I was asked about serving, I boasted about my twenty years in the Air Force every time. Uncle Howard and Mom joked that they didn't think the Army would take them so old, every time. With an inflated ego, I was wondering why I hadn't received my milestone '20 Year Letter' from the Air National Guard yet. So, I made some inquiries and sent some emails to the 108th National Guard Headquarters.

August rolled around and at National Guard Drill, I received a Training Seat Reservation Reminder congratulating my selection to attend the Army Medic School at Fort Dix from October 3rd, Phase 1. You could not imagine how awesome I felt. God was blessing me with yet another opportunity to receive my training to be qualified to deploy to Iraq. He keeps on blessing me, over and over again. There I would be able to escape the lack of employment the entire Nation was experiencing. Financially, I would be in a tax-free Combat zone, stacking up cash, with nowhere to spend it. Being in a line Unit were everybody had my back, working on skills to bring back to civilian life. My life was finally turning around for the better again. Thank the Lord!

Macy's had no choice but to let me go on my new Activate Duty Orders. The same training arrangement was made at Fort Dix with 2nd Battalion 254th Regiment once again. This time, my fellow Soldiers taking the Course came from all parts of the Country. There were very few jobs in this economy Bush had brought upon us. Soldiers came from Washington State, New Hampshire, Oregon, Connecticut, Kentucky, and I represented New Jersey. Now more funding would come to Fort Dix for their earlier success. Master Sergeant smiled and greeted the new class.

"Sergeant Porter, it's good to see you back. What are you planning to do?" He asked.

"I'm just going to try to lay low and stay out of trouble," I replied. Master Sergeant Cosmo paused shaking his head.

"Sergeant Porter, you're the type of guy no matter how hard you try, you can never lay low," he said smiling. I smiled back, 'there's no shame in my game.' Fort Indiantown Gap (FIG) of Pennsylvania was now cashing in because they held rank over the jurisdiction Course and added some of their Training Instructors. My old Training Instructors were there as well. Repeating Phase I again, we covered a general overview of Basic Life Saving skills, an introduction of Emergency Medical Care, CPR certification, basic anatomy, negligence, advanced directives, abandonment, duty to act, and consent, both implied and expressed.

Master Sergeant introduced this Corporal to our entire class. Corporal was a rank rarely used in the Army today. It is between the Sergeant's and Privates. Routinely, Corporals were skipped straight to the ranks of Sergeants. Corporals still possessed the authority of an NCO. He was in charge of all the activities to support our training. There were some Privates activated as well. No more mannequins during training. We would have breathing living bodies to work with.

Our entire class passed Phase 1, so we all moved on to Phase 2. Master Sergeant Cosmo took us running the next morning for PT. Instead of a mile and a half, he said, we would now run two miles. He waited until we were winded, explaining how oxygen was being deprived from our brains. He was quizzing us under duress about assessing the patient, normal heart rates, where were the major arteries, bleeding control, different types of shock, establishing airways, respiratory emergencies, lifting, and moving patients.

Shots Fired

The Fireman's Carry was one of my favorite ways of transporting the wounded. You just simply bend down to your knees, place the wounded soldier's arm over your shoulder, and stand up straight. Surprisingly, it was so easy to lift someone's body weight if you just lift with your knees. Using the Firemen's Carry, a Medic or First Responder could transport a body alone. Next, there is the Two-Man Carry. As the name suggests, it takes two men. One would be at the head grabbing the upper torso and the other at the feet. These carries didn't require a backboard, stair chair, or a stretcher. Training on the aforementioned equipment came later. They made a scenario where we came to a field where soldiers were wounded lying on the ground. Some were bandaged, some had legs in cast, or arms in slings. We were ordered to run to and grab every wounded warrior, taking them out from harm, and then go in and grab as many as you can. Being the Captain of my high school track team had its advantages, although I was significantly order than my fellow classmates, in some cases by 10 years. Still, I was faster than them all. Known for snatching soldiers in the Firemen's Carry and then speeding them off to cover. There was certainly 'no shame in my game.'

Later, the Master Sergeant introduced my entire Class to the Corporal. The rank of Corporal was a ceremony rank used more in the Old West times. Still, Corporals out ranked privates and had the authority of an NCO. He was in charge of all the activities to support our training and a sinister grin to match. They finally issued us our M-16s. In the Air Force, we only fired the M-16s annually but they were never issued to us. Here in the Army, weapons were handed out as part of our daily drill. We started Phase 3, Master Sergeant Cosmo introduced Private Lauder from my Medical Command Unit at Sea Girt. Private Lauder shared his experience when a roadside bomb exploded. He shared after the explosion a bus load of soldiers were lying everywhere. Some were bleeding, some dismembered, and desperately in need of medical attention. Immediately, he sprang into action and started bleeding control. He asked for everybody's belts to use for improvised tourniquets. The Class was impressed by his quick wit and calmness under pressure. Later that day we started marching up to the Forward Operating Base (FOB) to train in a tent city. One of our many tasks was to perform Guard Duty at the front gate of the FOB. Within the FOB my rotation came to guard the front gate. I was paired up with a Private. Staff Sergeant Cannula came down and instructed us.

"Don't let anybody pass the gate that doesn't have the right credentials," he ordered. We propped up our weapons in the Guard Shack and made ourselves comfortable. We were issued M-4 carbine assault rifles, a blank magazine, and little to no instructions. We never pulled Guard Duty and didn't know what they had in store for us. The Corporal was in charge of the mischief. He had a pickup truck and a boat load of privates to ensure chaos. My Battle Buddy at the gate was a Sister Soldier from Connecticut. She was a Private 2nd Class, which meant I was in charge. I felt trouble stirring.

"Look alive," I told her. "Here they come. Lock and load!" What was I saying? We were only shooting blanks.

The Corporal started approaching us in the pickup truck with Privates mounted on the side rails. They rode in armed heavily with their weapons and with serious faces. The truck stopped at the gate.

"May I help you?" I said, armed and strapped with my M-4. The adrenaline rush I was feeling was exactly what I joined the Army for. At heart, I was always a warrior.

"We're from Blackwater," the Corporal said. Blackwater was the largest mercenary army in the world. They presently were performing security duty in Iraq. Blackwater Agents guarded military convoys, military installations, U.S. Embassies, U.S. Officials, and provided support for armed forces and the CIA. They provided training for the Iraqi Police and Iraqi Military. "We wanted to go on Base to check a couple of things," the Corporal said not cracking a smile never breaking character.

"Show me your IDs and you can proceed," I replied as if we never met him before. The Corporal looked down and fumbled in his pockets.

"Seems like we can't find them," he replied.

"Then, I'm sorry. You can't enter," I snapped back. The Corporal turned his truck around and sped off. They waited 15 minutes to return, this time with Soldiers sitting in the truck bed armed to the teeth.

"Good afternoon," he said as he pulled up, acting as if we never met before. "We would like to access the base."

"Let me see some ID." They pulled out some ID and I gave them the green light. They speed off on Base, turned around, and sped back outside the gate. After a few minutes, they returned.

"Here they come again," I replied with my eyes gleaming. The Access Gate we guarded was simply comprised of a one man guard booth. There was no actual gate to protect. No obstacle to prevent someone from traveling through but you.

"Why do they keep coming back?" the young Private whined. "I wish they'd stop." Quickly, I turned my head in astonishment. As a Sergeant, I didn't have to be politically correct. I had the rank and the authority.

"They're doing what they are supposed to do. We are doing what we are supposed to do." She was fresh out of Basic Training with the immaturity to match. "This is fun," I told her with enthusiasm.

The Corporal with his band of merry men approached us yet again weapons down.

"Need to get on," he asked innocently, looking me straight in my eyes. He then held his head down. His troops were sitting secure in the truck bed.

"Let me see some identification," I said but I wasn't asking. The Private soldiered up and stepped by my side. Her weapon pointed down this time. We were locked and loaded.

"Let me see," he said, fumbling again through the many pockets of his battle dress uniform."Seems like I don't have it on me," he frowned.

"Well, you can't get on without proper ID," I reinforced the point. The Private had my back, looking stern with her warface on. The Corporal looked me into my eye and within a split second slammed his foot on the gas pedal. They sped off in the truck, leaving a trail of dust behind them.

Instinctively, I raised my M-4 rifle, took the safety off, and fired into the direction of the dust cloud. Eagerly, the Private followed behind me, letting off a shot. The blank rounds we were shooting let off more of a loud noise rather than causing any bodily harm. Not to be outdone, I double tapped ringing more gun fire to cover the cloud of dust with our outrage.

A sense of satisfaction came over me. The Private herself was finally smiling. "See? I told you this was fun," I reassured her.

My words were short lived, as the telephone rang in the guard shack, silencing the resounding ringing of shots fired.

"Sergeant Porter," I heard as I picked up the telephone. Right away, I could tell it was one of my Training Instructors, Staff Sergeant Cannula, on the other end.

"Yes, Staff Sergeant?" My response let him know I understood who I was talking to and who out ranked who.

"Did you fire your weapon at the Corporal?" He asked, unable to process what he just heard. I was not authorized to fire.

"Sir, no Sir!" My response gave little room for further discussion on my part. Staff Sergeant Cannula paused in unbelief at my response. Truly, we were both aware that I fired the shots. The good thing was that I still had the casings to put back in the magazine. There was no way to prove I fired with blanks.

"Okay Sergeant Porter. Okay." I could hear him smiling over the telephone as we came to an understanding. There'd be no admission of guilt by me. There'd be no proving I fired anything. There was 'no shame in my game.'

Just like the beginning of Phase 2, they had some scenarios where we would go in and provide medical support for the wounded. At this stage, we were far beyond just reading blood pressure. The Fort Indiantown Gap Training Instructors turned into Drill Instructors. They were old school and liked to get in the face of Medics while they performed the full scope of medical care on our soldiers. They screamed at the top of their lungs creating stress and anxiety to see how Medics respond under pressure. We took turns going into the scenarios, being the NCOIC of the mission, assigning where our Medics would go for triage and wound care.

Black Hawk Down

We started marching on the back roads of the Post while conducting armed patrols. We would encounter Privates lying on the road, so we treated them as wounded. After checking their ABCs (airway, breathing, circulation), the Training Instructors told us their vitals. We verbally told them how we would treat them to prevent shock. After a round, pickup trucks would come by and we performed mounted armed patrols. We stopped once new wounded were found. Without hesitation, I had sprung over to the Soldier lying on the side of the road. The Training Sergeants told me his vitals after the ABCs. I told them the treatment I would administer an IV to prevent him going into shock. They said to give him an IV. I began to move along as if the scenario was over. My Instructors were clear that I was to give him a real IV. All of a sudden, the training turned for real. Taking his arm, I inserted a real IV line into his median brachial vein. Being a Private in the Army was like being a human guinea pig but this was quite literal. Inserting a real IV line was more gratifying than working on mannequins. Still, I wondered whether we would be treating a collapsed lung or tracheotomies on anyone. I'm sure they would. A unique prospective Training at MDL Joint Base was the opportunity for Blackhawk training at Lakehurst Naval Air Station.

Our Class had a unique opportunity to train at MDL Joint Base next to the Naval Air Station in Lakehurst, New Jersey, a place known for the infamous Hindenburg Disaster in 1937. That day, a German zeppelin aircraft (blimp) filled with hydrogen gas exploded while attempting to land. Over 30 people lost their lives engulfed in the fiery inferno. We were here at Lakehurst to train how to save lives. We airlifted wounded soldiers with a gurney and hoisted them up to a hovering Black Hawk helicopter.

We trained in securing the wounded to a carrier crib and hoisting them up to safety into the Black Hawk helicopter. First, we had to stabilize the patient wounds. Then we had to secure the straps to the crib for hoisting. We had to hoist them up to the hovering helicopter suspended over us, 50 feet in the air. This was a plus that Joint Base McGuire Dix Lakehurst had to offer. I'm not sure if they offered the same opportunity at Fort Sam Houston in Texas as they did here at Lakehurst Navy Station.

We waited while each one of us took turns hoisting up to the helicopter one at a time. The Medic up in the Black Hawk bore the task of strapping themselves inside of the helicopter while guiding the wounded into the hovering aircraft, securing them inside to prevent them falling out, and reevaluating their vitals and wounds.

This training was priceless. You could see the pride swelling up in all of our Training Instructors at the Program. As a Class, we had each other's backs. We were down for each other. We were down for the mission. On the learning curb, we were getting the Medic training down, all this Black Hawk training we had down!

Through the woods we hiked when they dropped off some MREs (meals ready to eat). The old school MREs came in olive green aluminum packets. They had delicious flavors such as spaghetti, chicken pot pie, peanut butter, and a meatloaf nobody believed was meat. These meals were not necessarily gourmet but they were satisfying to a hungry grunt. Military tradition included MREs since World War I. However, some corporate genius decided to change the traditional government contract with newfangled heater meals. Their claim to fame was that you could introduce a salt-water pack to a chemical pouch, insert the meal tray, and enclose all into a plastic pouch. The chemical reaction had the pouch smoking and heating the meal like it came fresh out of the oven. The only problem was it wasn't fresh. Flavor wasn't included in the government contract. The corporate geniuses were so concerned about heating the meal that taste and flavor became afterthoughts. After hiking through the woods, we marched into a mock city of empty buildings. The woods were the high ground and the city sat lower. We marched through in columns 2-by-2 like on road patrol. They had cardboard cutouts of people. Whether they were intended target practice or not, they were the recipients of several rounds of blanks my fellow Classmates and I fired off. We stormed into the rooms of the city using our newly taught 'Room Clearing' technique, looking for wounded and performing the field Medic training we received. After training, we gathered in a conference room with a giant television screen. It seemed there were cameras mounted throughout the city recording us as we treated the wounded. It was a training moment that pointed out the pros and cons of each Medic. Afterwards, we regrouped as we were hiking through the woods. We came across a box of the heater meals. The fat cats proved no turning back with the heater meals. We found that many of us were unable to digest the tasteless meals. We all threw up the meals as violently as they went down. Today, I tried eating half the meal and all the snacks for some sustenance.

After lunch, we hiked through the woods for another assault on the mock city. We spread out, kneeling and waiting for the final signal. While kneeling, I looked to the left of me to see my Sister-Soldier on her knees puking her brains out.

"Those heater meals make me nauseous," the Private First Class said excusing her behavior.

"They made me puke, too," I backed her up. "I only eat half of it now and the snacks." We all started trading war stories about the heater meals. They were too young to remember the MREs. "Don't worry little Sister. Nobody's going to hurt you on my watch," I said in jest.

"Shut up!" The Private First Class snapped back laughing.

"Let's go down here and rock this town," I chimed in. It wasn't my turn to be the NCOIC but I felt like being inspirational, even though the town was empty of people, not withstanding all the cardboard cutouts.

We marched into town, confident with our combat medic training. We were ready to search these buildings for any injured soldiers. We entered the building and got real tight for room clearings. Later, after video-reviewing our later performance in the conference room, we hiked back to the FOB (forward operating base). As a reward, they served us 'sea rations' from the Chow Hall. Real food came in metal pots and aluminum pans to keep them hot.

Training Day

Finally, the Army Combat Medical Specialist Course had come to an end. We were all certified to work out in the field as Combat Medics. Master Sergeant Cosmo congratulated our Class and inspired us in the future to provide the best medical care possible to our troops. He explained that at the end the course a Company Coin is rewarded the Soldier who showed tremendous heart, earning the respect of the Training Instructors and fellow Soldiers.

"This Soldier persevered, not accepting failure as an option. There is certainly 'no shame in his game.' The 65th Medical Support awards the Company Coin to Sergeant Bryan Porter," Master Sergeant announced to everyone. An unexpected thunder of applauds followed as I walked up to receive the coin. Next, Sergeant First Class Kurby came up, representing the Instructors from Fort Indiantown Gap.

"Fort Indiantown Gap would like to award the Company Coin to," he paused, "Sergeant Bryan Porter." To my astonishment, I received both Company Coins. Having the confidence and respect of my fellow Soldiers was one of the highlights of my career in the Army. Briefly, I spoke while accepting the coins as everyone there clapped for me.

"Thank you for your faith in me. I am so overwhelmed. I know that I am not the best Combat Medic but I will work hard to improve on my knowledge and ability to provide quality healthcare to our American Soldiers."

After finishing all three Phases, I was now a qualified Combat Medic ready to deploy. How I was removed from my line unit of the Jersey City's 113th Regiment and sent to Medical Command at Sea Girt was beyond me. Three months of Active-Duty pay had a brother's pocket's full. Iraq, here I come. It was about to be a Merry Christmas for all. I had to get Double K two Christmas gifts since he was both my nephew and my godson. He was presently surprised and there wasn't a lot of shopping during still what was a slow economic and a long Economic Recession.

While traveling to work at Macy's, I was feeling great so I decided to sing on the Light Rail Train. The train would be full people and I sang some songs a cappella. It felt totally free and I was at a creative peak in my life. I noticed Butch's neighbor on the train but he made no effort to acknowledge me as I drew all attention to myself with my marvelous singing voice.

A letter came from the National Guard Headquarter of New Jersey. The Air National Guard and the Army National Guard both fell under National Headquarters. Finally, news about my '20 Year Letter.' There was a printout of all my years of service in the Air Force. It included both Active-Duty and the Air National Guard. Under the rule reading accuracy of government employees and military preciseness, it was pointed out that I didn't qualify for 20 years of service in the Air Force. I only served 19 years and 2 months. Eight months shy of my 20 year milestone but the military wouldn't be forgiving that I fell short.

Christmas at Macy's was magical with all the decorations. People came from all around the world just to see it. Loss Prevention held special briefings about the security we would provide during the holidays. The onslaught of people came pouring through the doors like a river of water. It was like nothing I ever experienced before. I pulled out my cell phone to take a photograph of this unbelievable phenomenon. A store Executive in Loss Prevention saw me and it was immediate grounds for termination while on duty. She reprimanded me and I snapped back to my senses. It was training day all over again. This year, I was finally able to get my sisters some better Christmas presents. I purchased one a Coach purse and the other a DKNY. New Year's came and my birthday.

The Flower Show at Macy's marked the beginning of spring. On that Sunday, I wore my white minister's robe at Macy's on my lunch break. The visual change from my black suit to white was eye catching. The white suit gave a purity religious appearance. For lunch, I would fast and take Communion. Events were held at Herald Square where I received a vision of conducting a non-denominational Communion for the masses. I always desired to do great things for the Lord. No good deed goes unpunished. After work, I used to go get together with some co-workers, they weren't used to me being more open about my religious beliefs. Forgetting how everything was under video surveillance, I'm sure Control was giving the rumor mill and Management an earful. Since everything was under surveillance, they used to complain that I changed my tie on breaks. Changing into a white robe was sure to receive persecution.

Lil Big Sis invited me over to her house for Easter Sunday after church. This was rare and unusual but very nice. Frequently, I visited her home but Butch always invited me. Even at Macy's, work was going well. Things with the National Guard were good as well. My National Guard Unit assigned me to be the Non-Commissioned Officer in Charge (NCOIC) of Immunizations. They routinely developed leaders and conducted critical skills training. We were still vaccinating against the H1N1 virus, the swine flu epidemic. We also vaccinated against the annual flu shot, Hepatitis A, Hepatitis B, tetanus, diphtheria, pertussis (or Tdap), meningococcal, measles, mumps, and rubella (MMR). Hepatitis took a series of shots, both A and B.

My Army National Unit selected me for Warrior Training Camp (WTC). The requirements for selecting a junior Non-Commissioned Officer, NCO, was that they must be approved by the Unit Commander, show sound character, be promotable, and have to be recommended by the senior NCOs of their Unit. This was such a prestigious honor that my Commander, Top, senior NCOs, my Platoon Sergeant, and Squad Leader honored my hard work. Never had I missed a drill. I worked hard for this and showed them true commitment. This was the next step in my promotion to E-6, Staff Sergeant. My Unit surprised me by announcing that they scheduled to train me as the NCOIC of a mission. In it, I would be treated as the Top Ranking NCO. Our Medical Command Unit's mission was to process soldiers for deployment as well as manage the flow of soldiers processing. Everyone had to listen to me and I had some good ideas for improvement. Finally, it was my time to show them my experience in managing and how I could have a positive impact.

Houston . . .We Have a Problem

Our Neighbor Craig wasn't much older than me. Still, he felt the need to spy on me for my mother. He told her I was outside selling drinks to the other neighbors. He was so suspicious. How did he know what I was saying to the neighbors? How was it any of his business what I was doing anyway? I'm a grown man with 'no shame in my game.' Later, my mother confronted me.

"Craig told me you were taking my glasses out of this house and selling drinks," she said in the most condescending tone. She didn't purposely mean to demean me but she just couldn't see me as accomplished. She only saw failure.

"Why didn't you tell him that your son is a grown man who has all his owns glasses, dishes, and appliances," I fired back. Seems like I was always reacted instead of responding.

"Not in my house and you going . . ."

"Your house? I pay rent here," I replied like I had no rights. She treated me like I was a stranger, not family. "I do what I want. I go where I want." I didn't feel the need to embellish, confirm, or deny whether I was selling alcoholic drinks to the neighbors. Oh, the absurdity of it all! My clergy status didn't matter. My community standing didn't matter. My military resume didn't matter. They were trying to wreck my reputation, bearing false witness and making false accusations. 'A good name is more precious than gold' (Proverbs

22:1). I often reminded her, "I would remind them that whoever God blesses, no man can curse.

One day back at Macy's, while monitoring an entrance door, I started feeling strange. Suddenly my heart was racing and I couldn't breathe. Quickly, I moved to the telephone and called the Security's Command Center. I told them that I needed an emergency relief. They told me hold on that they were sending somebody right away. They asked me what was wrong but I didn't know what to tell them. I never felt like this before. Unknown to me, my unseen anxiety was making matters worse. When I called Command, I'm sure they had a camera on me.

All of a sudden, my eyes widened and my mouth gaped open with a look of horror across my face. My recent education in anatomy gave me enough knowledge to make my dilemma more excruciating. Wham! It felt like a bolt of lightning was shooting all through my injured brain. Wham! Sharp pain raced through the parietal lobe of my brain. Then wham! It shot through the frontal lobe. Next, I felt it shoot through the temporal lobe and then the occipital lobe. I could hear Control calling me in my earpiece. They had to be watching me on the surveillance camera.

"Porter, what's the matter? Are you okay?" Command asked. My heart kept racing, as I felt the electricity shot up and down my thoracic spine cord. I didn't know what was happening so I couldn't form the words to comment back.

"I don't know," I said as I walked off through a side door that led down to the stairwell for the holding cell, escaping the view of the public. To the floor I dropped, bewildered, and soon all the undercover security ran to my aid. I learned anatomy but I had no clue what was happening to my body.

"Are you all right?" They asked.

"Yes," I said. "I don't know." I was panting heavily sitting unconventionally on the floor. The expression on my face and my heavy breathing were symptoms of elevated respirations. Something was definitely wrong. My body was failing me. The Supervisor came by to check on me. He told me to punch out and go home. Standing in front of my locker, I took off my suit. What is going on now? It felt like my body was betraying me, just in a time I needed it the most. Every time I would make some strides, another obstacle would come. I was a man of faith, I know my God is able, but it seems like it's just one thing after another. The spirit was willing but my flesh was weak. Joy may come in the morning but there I was. For now, I was weeping all through the night.

CHAPTER 6
Betrayal

On my day off, I experienced another episode at the Radio Shack when I was looking to buy a new cell phone. My heart started racing and I was having some severe pain swirling around my head. Then the shocking pain started radiating, moving up and down my spinal column. After fifteen minutes, it stayed in my lower back, crippling me. Calmly, I sat down and asked the store clerk if I could call Butch.

Butch came to drove me off at the VA Hospital in East Orange. I could always count on him. He was the big brother I never had. On the ride out we talked about the family and life. Butch was always getting himself checked out, so he was all for me conducting some test. He felt that I could have sleep apnea when I told him about my insomnia and headaches. He was smart but he wasn't a doctor and then the car stereo started playing Lionel Richie's 'Truly.' This was one of the songs Butch knew how to play on the piano. Every time he was at my keyboard, he played and sang this song. His playing was much better than his singing. Butch was singing at the top of his lungs. I was feeling better and a little playful. We were stopped at a traffic light where I used to go to Medical Assisting School, in East Orange. This was familiar territory, so I opened the car door and took off running to escape Butch's off-key singing. I thought it was comedic brilliance. I was also training for my Leadership School, so I ran at a quick pace and high step through the parking lot across from the parking lot on Central Ave. As I was laughing, I saw Butch drive the car in the opposite direction that I ran. He drove into the parking lot of the Dunkin Donuts. I kept eye contact with him and waited for him to drive the car over because this was the way toward the VA Hospital and the direction I ran in. Butch drove off, still in the opposite direction of where the VA Hospital was. Was he punishing me for my joke? I had no cell phone to call him. After waiting, I started walking toward the VA Hospital. After a while, I thought that Butch would catch up soon, so I just kept walking. About 15 minutes later, I almost reached the VA Hospital. Butch finally found me pulling up slowly. He had this puzzled look on his face. We stared at each other in bewilderment. Immediately, I asked him where he went and he asked me what happened. I explained to him that I was joking when I leaped out the car. Butch stared at me, convinced there was something wrong with me.

They admitted me into the Emergency Room. After I explained my symptoms and history of Traumatic Brain Injury, I was immediately rushed to get a CT Scan. After my results came back, They diagnosed me with having migraine headaches. My limited medical knowledge led me to question this.

"Headache?" I inquired. "Well, I was a Medic in the Army. So why is it radiating," I asked. 'Radiating' was a medical term describing pain that travels from one part of the body to another. "First in my occipital lobe, then in my frontal lobe, then up and down my spine," I asked dropping some medical knowledge to justify my concerns.

"They are called cluster headaches," he further explained. People get them when they are exposed a lot to the sun or high-stressed, lack of sleep, or the weather. He went to his computer and searched for something as I sat on the hospital bed waiting to be discharged. Soon he arose with my discharge papers and some print outs. "This is some information about migraines/cluster headaches," the ER Doctor handed to me. He also prescribed me Percocet for the pain.

"Thank you," I don't care what anyone else says. The VA really took care of their veterans. This is something I need to hide from Macy's. The less they knew about it, the better. As a Visual Security Officer, working inside kept me from excessive exposure to the sun. Did not want the National Guard to find out. Did not want them to cut my orders to Fort Benning. Definitely did not want to take the Percocets.

In the news, U.S. Navy SEALs raided Osama bin Laden's compound in Pakistan on May 2, 2011. All this time, we'd been searching for bin Laden in Afghanistan and our pretend-to-be ally Pakistan had been hiding him all along. The News stations were reporting they had reason to believe the President was going to announce the death of Osama bin Laden soon. It took nearly an hour before President Obama officially announced that Osama bin Laden had been assassinated and his ashes had been buried at sea in accordance with Islamic tradition. There were crowds of people in the streets waiting to hear the news. People started wildly celebrating this momentous occasion. I was proud to post the news on Facebook and shocked to read the backlash from the anti-Obama enthusiasts. People were skeptic of anything positive and wrote that they wouldn't believe it until they saw the body with their own eyes. Four days later, al-Qaeda posts confirmed Osama bin Laden's death because they threatened to retaliate against the U.S. and Pakistan. Even al-Qaeda believed Osama bin Laden was dead but many Americans remained skeptical and wouldn't give President Obama any benefit of the doubt.

The Warrior Training Course (WTC) was coming up at Fort Benning, the NCOIC weekend Detail, moving out, and looking for EMT jobs. Maybe I could get Orders to Airborne School as well. Spiritually, I was looking to expand my ministry into full-time. Strategically, I was making new connections in New York. Meeting New York musicians, ministers, and churches was opening fresh new opportunities for me. When I was scheduled to work Sundays, I was starting to fast and take Communion on first Sundays during my lunch break. There was a vision I had seeing with all the people on 34th Street and Broadway sitting there. Many Christians made signs and stood out there all day ministering and telling people about Jesus. A couple of believers told me how they had to register their ministries and get a license to witness there. What if I registered and held Communion for the masses, free of judgment or denominational bias? Just simply minister the love of Jesus Christ.

Before my shift, I jogged down the long New York City streets of Manhattan preparing for WTC. My assignment at Macy's that day was to secure the Employee Entrance on 7th Avenue. One reason for their items remaining secured was that only the assigned Security for that day had access. Even all the other Security personnel were not granted access and subject to the same employee inspections of their bags. One of the Visual Security Guards had an Auntie or Uncle up in the Loss Prevention hierarchy. Let's call him Kiss Up.

The next step up in Loss Prevention was to become a Store Detective. You would wear plain clothes, not uniform, and act as if you were a shopper. You would follow suspected shoplifters around, aided by your earpiece and video surveillance. My role was a Visual Security Guard. Wearing a black suit and an ear-piece, we would call out suspicious shoppers and they would be followed by Control and the Store Detectives. When Kiss Up called out a suspicious character, Control would praise him so blatantly over the radio. It became common knowledge that Kiss Up was going to bypass everyone ahead of him and get the promotion to Store Detective.

This made Kiss Up act even more arrogantly. One day, he tried to just enter the 'secured area' where employees stored their personal items. Even Security had to wait outside if not assigned to work there to maintain confidentiality. Kiss Up was in his civilian attire. He must have been promoted to Store Detective. He tried to come in and get his own items on a day I was assigned to monitor it. I told him that I would get his items for him and to hand me his chip. He tried to walk in the room and I stood in the entrance, blocking him. He argued with me, even though he knew the policy. He tried to go around me and I moved to continually block his way. Control had every inch of Macy's under video surveillance. I called on the telephone to have Control take a visual look and tell Kiss Up to stand down. The arrogance of this guy, I remember the day they hired him. He had only been working there for a few months. Little Kiss Up started to cry and walk away. He had the maturity of a teenager despite his cocky attitude.

The next week HR called me to their office. James, the Executive in Charge of Loss Prevention, accompanied me. I thought it strange for him to be there but maybe he was going to stick up for me. After I explained what happened with the other Associate, I expressed how I never touched him or threatened him and did the job I was instructed to do, which is to not permit anyone into the secured area, which included Security personnel not assigned for that day. James just sat there in complete silence. Shockingly, Human Resources put me on a seven day suspension without pay. This shows that he wasn't there to help me.

Macy's had been so promising that I was thinking about getting out of the Military and pursuing an Executive position. This complete 360 showed me how easily everything could actually change. Opportunities were opening up for me in the National Guard, so I thanked God this happened and I was going to concentrate on the ARNG. After Warrior Training, I planned to move out and get my own apartment once I came back from Louisiana. Contemplating the move, I planned to start parting with some things, so I decided that I would sell my Wisteria Ancient Greece porcelain China set to start. Anticipating all the things coming up, the WTC in Louisiana, the NCOIC weekend Detail, moving out, and looking for an EMT job, I started waking up at five o'clock in the morning again, just like when I was in the hospital. My mother's take on it was that my mind was troubled, and that I couldn't sleep. Troubled? My life was golden. Promotion to E-6 coming up, military orders to Fort Benning, and selection for NCOIC (in charge) training. I would make around $3,000 to $5,000 in one month. Everyone should have my troubles.

It was early in the morning around five o'clock as I rose and gave God praise. Down the stairs I quietly went, bringing my China dish set. Despite me being laid-off, I had total peace about the situation. Downstairs, Mom had a beautiful dining room next to an equally stunning sitting room. She entertained in the dining room with a maple dining room table set with six matching chairs, an elegant tablecloth, and occasionally linen napkins. Also in the room was a beautiful glass cabinet where many family treasured pictures were on display from over the years. This would be the perfect place for me to take pictures of my Ancient Greece porcelain China set. There were eight setting in all of dinner plates, serving bowls, serving pitchers, to include a salt and pepper shaker. I was quite pleased and planned to entertain with dinners of my own. For now, I wanted to take some pictures in the dining room and sell the set on the internet.

Dressed in my silk bath robe, I took several photos on my Blackberry phone. The digital photo quality looked highly professional. This was going to be an easy sale. Then I heard someone coming down the stairs. It was still very early. The sun hadn't come up yet. I put the light in the hallway to help guide their way.

"Who is that?" My Mother cried out as she was coming down the steps. "Oh, it's Bryan," she replied with a sigh of relief. Shakur had been sneaking girls in the house, which my Christian mother was strongly against. She was trying to catch him in the act. After she used the bathroom, she stepped into the well-lit dining room. "What's this?" She asked puzzled seeing my porcelain China collection in full display on in her dining room. I was quite fond of this blessing from God that I purchased.

"Who said you can do that?" She shouted at me. I was shocked, since my mother wasn't much of a yeller. "What is all this?" She said in total disgust, seeing her beautiful dining room table handsomely set with my fine China. This was an expensive Wisteria China Collection.

"I was having a photo shoot," I was trying to explain. "A photoshoot?" She screamed in disgust. Her tone was extremely upset. I never heard my mother talk to people in this tone except when it came to me and I was growing quite tired of it.

"Yes, a photo shoot. I am going to sell this," I tried to calmly explain.

"You don't come in somebody's house and do things without asking permission," she fussed at me. Ask permission? Was I not a fully grown man? I was going to take my pictures and have everything back in my room before she woke up. What does she mean ask permission? And I know what she means by "someone's house," like I'm a stranger who walked off the streets. I paid hundreds of dollars in rent a month.

"I'm a grown man. Why do I have to ask permission to take a couple of pictures?" I foolishly tried to reason but I was unaware that all rationality was out the window.

"Because it's my house," she screamed.

"If it's your house, why am I paying rent every month?" I snapped back equal in tone and sarcasm.

"I don't care what you pay, it's my house," she repeated in that hurtful, disgusting tone. "You need to ask for my permission," she said, like I was a little child.

"I'm forty-four years old. I don't have to ask for permission to take some pictures," I said, declaring my independence and sounding like a little child arguing with his Mommy.

"You do if you're in my house," she kept yelling.

"Why do I have to ask permission to take pictures for something I was going to put back anyway? I don't ever leave anything downstairs. I keep everything I own in my room." You would think that after I explained that she would have understood. I wasn't trying to take over her precious dining room but my words fell on deaf ears. We were like two children going back and forth.

"You do have to ask permission as long as you're in my house," she kept driving at me.

"Well, I won't be in your house much longer. As soon as I come back from Fort Benning, I'm moving out of your house," I fired back. I had a bad habit of directing any attitude back while growing up in a house full of women. I was quick to mirror back any tone with attitude. She never talked to anyone else in such a negative tone. It was very hurtful. I started talking back in a disrespectful tone I never used with my mother before. "I'm a grown man and I'm sick of that nasty tone you always use with me."

"Well, you're a child to me," she felt in her logic.

"Provoke not your child to anger," I reminded her of a scripture but it would have no bearing in this conversation. "I'm sick and tired of the way you talk to me," I said as I removed my China collection from the dining room area. Most women would have loved to see such a lovely China pattern grace their dining room table. As I removed all my belongings from the room, back up the stairs I marched, continuing to rambling on. The walls were thin of our attached house, so I'm sure all the neighbors heard me. With all the constant attacks, once I got started, I could never stop. I kept saying things to my mother and she kept on, too. I was more like her than her daughters but she couldn't see it because of gender. She said more hurtful things and I went back with my angry words. After a while, I came downstairs and Shakur was there. She had called him from wherever he was sleeping that night and he came as she made him feel her life was in danger. He ran to the house like she was in jeopardy and I was upstairs far away from her. Shakur came in the house as she instructed him. He grabbed a bat as I came down the stairs unaware.

"Yo! You gonna have to get out of here!" He yelled at me, standing next to Mom, holding a bat, and shaking it at me. The nerve of him to threaten me yet again. I had enough of his disrespect. My mother stood right next to him in total silence, in total compliance, the instigator of this chaos.

"That bat don't scare me. I'm going to take that bat and shove it right up your @$!," I never spoke like that in front of my mother before. "I used to change your diapers and now you disrespect me and tell me to get out of a house I help build. You don't pay any rent or bills here," I started charging toward him.

"No, no, you don't. Stop it. Stop it," my mother intervened, after she instigated everything up to this point, standing next to him in silence while he was telling me to get out the house. She called Shakur on the phone. She stood by his side and didn't utter a word while he held a bat and threatened me. "Don't you fight in this house, you take it outside," she said.

"Fine, let me get some clothes," I yelled. I'm sure the whole neighborhood heard me now. Ever since my coma, I was known for my loud outbursts in the neighborhood. My voice became thunderous when I was upset. I went upstairs to change out my silk robe and put on my combat boots and Army battle dress uniform. I called the police, which was my natural inclination with family. They were supposed to be a neutral third party, which would moderate everyone's legal rights. This was always my naïve thoughts but all they saw was a Black man when they pulled up. This time, when I called, I told them that I would be wearing my Army uniform, that I was a sergeant in the National Guard, and I demanded them to give me the respect that I deserved. The 911 operator asked me to clarify again which one I would be. In my rage, I sarcastically yelled out, "I'll be the one with blood on his uniform," I hung up the phone. I just told her that I was the one wearing the Army uniform. Wasn't that enough indication which one I was? I was fuming with rage.

Army Battle Dress Uniform (BDU) - 2010

When I came downstairs, I went in the kitchen to let him know I was ready. "Come on you little punk. I'll be outside." By his eyes, I knew he wasn't scared of me but he didn't want to fight. Mom was gesturing to him and told him to stay in the house. I went outside and kept yelling but he never came out. If the neighbors didn't hear me, they heard me now. Part of me was glad, wanting revenge for all the previous fights we had, and all the times I had to go and get CT scans. All the times he made me go to the hospital, this was the last time. The police pulled up. I was easy to spot in my uniform, pacing back and forth furiously. The Officers were very respectful. They asked what happened and I told them that nothing physical happened, just that my brother threatened me with a bat and I wasn't going to take any crap from him. I should have been turning the other cheek. I should have been giving the soft answer like my Pastor counseled me. They escorted me back into the house to get a change of clothes and check on everyone inside. I told them of all the fights me and my brother had since I came out the coma, all the many times he slammed my head on the concrete or punched me in the face, all the times I had to run up to the VA Hospital, and I was tired of it. I'm not taking anymore CT scans for head shots again. I told them about my orders in July and how I was moving out when I came back. One of the Officers escorted me upstairs while the other went to the kitchen and talked with my mother. I'm sure she told them what she usually tells everybody, that I had a brain injury, that I was never the same since I came out of the coma. I'm sure she didn't tell them about Shakur coming at me with a bat, like she never told the police about Lil Sis and the butcher's knife. The fault was always mine even though I never hurt any of them.

"Wow! You have a lot of stuff," the Officer said. My room was jammed pack. There were multiple dishware sets, glasses, coffee mug collection, clothes, bookshelves, theological books, comic books, suits, shoes, silk ties, a telescopes, water coolers, ceramic clay flowerpots, vases, mic-stands, amplifiers, musical instruments, etc.

After getting some clothes, my cell phone, cosmetics, and my nap sack, I went back to work at Macy's. My locker would store my uniform for now with my suits for work. One thing was for certain, I planned to never sleep in that house again. Where I would stay I hadn't figured out but I knew where I wasn't.

After work, the only place I could think of was sleeping on a park bench in Lincoln Park. I didn't get much sleep that night. Not quite the warrior I wished to be. I was a product of the Air Force, not the Army. We slept in hotels, not outdoors. PTSD would not let me be vulnerable sleeping on a park bench for anyone to assault me in my slept. Dozing off, my eyes opened momentarily wondering where I was. With the brain injury, my short-term memory always took a moment. It was dark but there was still plenty of light in the public park. I decided to go before people started coming out. My mind raced on the events of yesterday, the constant betrayal of supposed loved ones. I can't just blame the Devil for when they played such a pertinent part. As daylight increased, I noticed that I didn't have my nap sack. Back to the park I raced but my nap sack was no longer on the park bench. So all my belongings, including my cell phone were gone.

Later, I managed to call Errold. I told him how I slept in Lincoln Park on the park bench and lost my nap sack with my cell phone in it. So, I forwarded all my calls to Butch since he was my Emergency Contact with the VA. Until then, I would purchase a calling card in the meantime. At least I would be able to make telephone calls on pay-phones on the street.

Butch invited me to go home with him and sleep in his basement. It would be refreshing not sleeping on the PATH train and changing trains all night. He wanted me to take the Percocet the VA prescribed. Curiously, I asked him why. Why was he so insistent about me taking Percocet? He shared none of my fear of drug addiction that ran in my family. I forgot what a hypochondriac he was. Upstairs I went to the kitchen to talk with her. Butch came into the kitchen and said that someone from the VA called about the CT scan they took. He started playing the message for me and then he hit some button by mistake. Unfortunately, the message accidently deleted.

"Oh man! I must have erased it," he frowned and looked down at his cell phone. "They want you to come in tomorrow to talk about the test they took in the ER." Then he told me to go downstairs. Downstairs he explained, "I don't want to get your sister upset so try and stay downstairs in the man cave," he said. Sadly, it was Butch that invited me because I was homeless, not my own sister. Butch treated me well and made sure I had everything that I needed. After dinner, he made sure that he witnessed me take the Percocet and dimmed the lights to the basement. The futon was turned down and my bed linen was laid out. Butch practically tucked me in as he sat in the dimly lit room. He kept asking how I was doing and saying suggestively, "Go to sleep." My senses were so keen. It was clear he was suggesting sleep like a hypnotist. "Go to sleep," he kept saying.

The next day was National Donut Day, June the 3rd. After a good night's rest I wanted to go by Macy's and get something out of my locker. There were some banking concerns I wanted to handle before my big weekend as the Non-Commissioned Officer in Charge. It took me two years of hard work in this Unit to finally receive recognition for this opportunity. Butch kept insisting to drive me over to the VA Hospital. I just looked at him. I had a full agenda for today.

"The VA Hospital is one of the last things on my mind," I told him. "I have to get something out of my locker at Macy's. My Guard Drill this weekend."

"Yeah, but I got to do some running around, so I got to take you now," Butch told me.

"I don't need you to get out to the VA. Let's get a donut cause it's National Donut Day and then drop me off at Newark Penn Station," I asked him.

"Man, come on. Let's go to the hospital first," he insisted. Why was this guy so insistent on going to the hospital?

"Okay, but I want to stop by Dunkin Donuts first." We left and stopped at the Dunkin Donuts off Route 22. We reported to the Emergency Room of the VA and announced that I was returning because a Doctor left a message about the CAT scans. The Admitting Clerk in the ER told me to have a seat as if she was expecting me. She led me to a bed and went back to Butch. I asked myself why she is discussing my personal medical information with Butch. This was a flagrant HIPAA violation. Sensing something was wrong, I left my bed and approached the Admitting Clerk.

"Excuse me, why are you discussing my personal information with him?" I asked. My paralegal background and my new EMT certification had me qualified to defend my legal rights. She had a nervous energy about her. She smiled to accommodate me but still continued talking directly to Butch.

"I just need you to sign this one thing," she asked him. Why would he need to sign anything about me?

"I'm not signing nothing," Butch told her but I was discerning something was truly wrong here.

"Just leave, Butch. Something is wrong here," I told him to leave. He had no legal authority in my medical affairs. Butch was my trusted Emergency Contact but that was in the case of me being unconscious.

This did not to give him legal authority to make medical decisions for me, especially while I was still conscious.

"Please, just have a seat over there," she told me. "And if I could get you to just sign one thing," she still was asking Butch.

"Butch, go ahead and leave," I warned him. This was upsetting. She never asked me to sign or see the documents she was handing Butch. I discerned something was terribly wrong.

Working in Security had heightened my sense of awareness. I noticed that there were five VA Police surrounding my bed. Never before had I noticed that police in hospitals possessed firing arms before. The top ranking Captain walked over to me and told me to take off my clothes. My mind quickly flashed to the medical rights they taught us in our EMT Course. "You haven't established mental incompetence or have legal consent. I refuse all medical attention," I told them declaring my legal rights.

"We heard that you threatened your mother."

"You heard what? Are you going by hearsay?" I responded. My sense of awareness was heightened. Anyone else that had to use the legal system would know that guilt must be proven beyond a shadow of a doubt. For a Black person, they just needed hearsay. Quickly, I assessed there was no physical way I was going to overpower these five armed VA police and fight my way through this. I asserted my legal rights and as usual they weren't being acknowledged. The VA had the Emergency room under video surveillance, so by complying I knew this was all being video-taped. There were no other options available, so I raised my hands showing compliance. Taking off my clothes, I began to undress and put on my hospital gown. The anger hit me so hard. The Doctor was there, supervising the entire event. We made eye contact as the nurses swabbed me and injected me with three shots. The tears streamed down my cheeks. It would only be minutes before I would be medically unconscious, so I lashed out the only way I could. I wish I could say that I prayed and showed my faith but I was too overwhelmed by my emotions. This was like the assault, being arrested, being attacked by my son and wife, fighting with my brother, fighting with my sister, being kicked out the house, and being jumped at Minister Roddey's house. Again, I was shackled, dehumanized, and stripped of my rights and dignity. Again, I felt violated and totally taken by surprise. I looked my newest attacker straight in the face while he stood at a distance in his dress shirt and rim glasses hanging off his eyes. As I felt the medications pushing through the needles as they were stabbing me in my shoulders, I called him a Nazi, lashing out in the only way I saw possible. My stare was chilling and he seemed to cringe. Then I blacked out under heavy sedation.

Next thing I remember when I regained consciousness was being in a hospital room, feeling extremely disorientated. A Nurse's aide was sitting lazily in the room with me. When I tried to stand, she suggested that I stay lying down. When I tried to stand up, it was hard to maintain my balance. My head was spinning, the room was spinning. So, I awkwardly twirled around the room, unable to maintain my balance. All I wanted was to stand still but I was too doped up. It made me wonder what kind of drugs they pumped me up with.

When I was finally about to walk around, I found that they Committed me to a locked Mental Ward on the 16th Floor of the VA in East Orange. They dressed me in pajamas and my shoes were removed and replaced with socks. We stayed in our rooms until they feed us in a room. There was a break room we had snacks and shared a television. The Nurse's Aide took over the television to watch their soap operas. The nerve of these women from Newark, blessed to have a job, many of them were in their sixties that should have been living on retirement. They had a hospital telephone on the wall to receive incoming calls. My memory was good enough to remember the telephone calling card that I had purchased. The telephone was able to make local calls and toll free. I called Steve Bryant, my friend and Pastor. I told him how Butch insisted and drove me to the East Orange VA Hospital. How they committed me to a Mental Ward based on only hearsay. I was committed without establishing any mental incompetence or having legal consent. Steve had been a life-long friend, so he knows the history with my family and had suffered many battles in life as well. As a Pastor and a mature man of the world, he handled this with great calm. He was not surprised or pleased when I shared how ballistic I became when my brother yelled at me to get out of the house with a baseball bat sanctioned by my mother, and how she went ballistic on me for taking pictures downstairs without her permission. I'm glad Steve had great respect for my mother. He referred to her as his mother as we were raised together. He would have the upmost respect when he would talk to her but he would not let her spin anything around on me, either. Steve was also at the hospital when I came out the coma. He came all the way from New Jersey to visit me. We stayed in constant contact when I still lived in Maryland, even when living out of my car. He made me a Steward in the AME Church. He became my Pastor for these past three years and had not noticed that I suffered any symptoms of traumatic brain injury. He didn't noticed that I was never the same after being beaten into a coma. These were delusions about me that my mother entertained. I held many responsible positions in the Community, the National Guard, the Minister's Alliance, and work. Sunday came and Steve was granted access into the locked Ward. He was dressed in a black suit and wearing a Clergy collar. He smiled and didn't say much. He only administered Communion. He was granted access only for that specific religious observance.

There I overheard a discussion about transporting me to Lyons VA Hospital. There I would face a Magistrate. A Magistrate was like a judge when on Federal property. My release could only happen after presenting my case in a Court Hearing. Curiously, there were no legal proceedings when they Committed me. The papers they gave me said that my sister and brother-in-law are the ones who said that I threatened my mother. I had two sisters, not sure which one but Butch did insist on dropping me off there. Once transported to Lyons VA, they placed me in another locked Ward. They took my shoes and insisted that I wear these anti-slip socks. The Nursing Aides refused to allow me to keep my shoes. These socks had no arch support. However, the Medical Community endorsed them. There was a long corridor, maybe a quarter mile long. There I could continue to train for my two mile run; running in my anti-skid socks along those cold hard floors. There was also a telephone on the wall, Praise God, and I memorized my calling card number and toll-free numbers. Now I had a lifeline to the outside world. There was plenty of time to kill in this hallway, maintaining readiness for Warrior Training and Airborne School.

My mind kept dwelling on startling revelations about time. The truth of time is quintessential. Time is of the essence, say the wise. Time is one of the most valuable commodities we have. It's more precious than money or gold. Some are born rich, some are born poor. "The rich and the poor have this in common; the Lord is the maker of them all" (Proverbs 22:2). Earlier, I referred to 'killing time' but time is too precious. It should never be 'killed.' We should never refer to time as being 'free.' Time is too valuable to be free. Time is always personal. The rich and the poor have things in common through time. They are both subject to 24 hours to a day, seven days to a week, and 12 months out of the year. One truth that one had to accomplish the most with the time that was given. My focus determined my reality, so I focused daily on push-ups and running in my socks preparing for the two mile runs.

If I could have kept this situation from my National Guard Unit, I would have. My attempt of getting released was not going to happen quickly but there was no reasonable explanation that I could give for missing the most important weekend Drill of my enlisted career. On the weekend, they were taking me into their confidence to train me as the Non-Commissioned Officer in Charge (NCOIC) of the Detail (mission). There was no getting around it. No way of escaping what happened. Still I was confident that they would vouch for my character, the character that made them select me for this honor, the character that I displayed showing that made them select me for Warrior Training Camp (WTC). The requirements specified that a junior Non-Commissioned Officer, NCO, 'MUST show sound character, be promotable, and recommended by the senior NCO's of their unit.' The junior NCO must be 'approved by the Unit Commander and promotable.' God was protecting me. So, I made the call to explain my absence. My Military Unit would get me out of here, I thought to myself.

Next, I called my Church members at Good News Bible Mission. Before I was committed, Pastor Lanier's health started declining. Errold even took me to see him at a Nursing Home before he came to stay with him. The Church had many members and we had a body of believers praying with me. I explained to Errold where I was and what happened to me. He wasn't pleased but he wasn't shocked to see the decline in relationships with my family. He certainly didn't see this trend of mental illness in me.

So I prayed to Heaven, "Father God, my enemies have mounted up against me. I am surrounded on every side. But thou, oh Lord are a shield about me. You are my glory; and the Lifter of my head. My family has forsaken me. Imprisoned me in this mental asylum. Break my chains and free me, oh Lord. In the name above all other names, Jesus the Christ! Amen."

At night, I was sure someone was entering my room while I slept. Was I being paranoid? So, I placed the waist paper basket behind the door as a makeshift alarm to alert to wake me up. It turns out that I wasn't being paranoid. A nightshift Nurse came into all the rooms and did an hourly observation of the patients. Later the next morning, a young Marine had a room next to mine. He was adamant, saying that I was purposely making noise at night to wake him up. He was an Iraqi Freedom Veteran who had Veteran who had serious Post Traumatic Distress Syndrome.

Yesterday, we were all watching UFC Mixed Martial Arts. Everybody was sitting in the break room. The young Marine was bored and started arguing. Then he directed his anger at me, saying that I had been making noises purposely at night. He got up and threatened me. The Nurse's Aides stood between us and tried to calm him down. He resisted them and someone called for the VA Police to come immediately. I stood next to the other Nurse's Aide. They tried to hold him back for twenty minutes and still there were no police around. One Nurse's Aide started backing me down the long hallway. With his six foot frame, he marched down the hall doing spin kicks. Ignoring her verbal commands for him to stop, he kept advancing. Where were the VA Police? When confronting him became inevitable, I told the Nurse's Aide to step back, so she wouldn't get hurt. There we eyed each other ready for combat, the Army verses Marine. He spun around with an impressive back kick. It was apparent that yesterday's UFC had an unwanted effect on him.

He spun again and I timed it perfectly, I stepped in and cracked him in the ribs with a right hand jab. It knocked him back and threw off his spinning back kick. It knocked the wind out of him. He laughed, momentarily stunned, and said, "Okay." He was impressed and not too serious about fighting. He was more bored for being locked up than interested in hurting me. He was in his twenties and in top shape, so he could have easily harmed me, but he didn't really wish to. He just kept smiling and walked back down the hall, meeting the VA Police that finally arrived. They escorted him back to his room.

The Nursing Staff told me that their procedures mandated that I be shot up with drugs again. I refused. I cooperated with them, and I didn't try to fight that Marine. I tried to walk away. I only engaged him so the Nurse's Aide didn't get hurt. The Nurse told me that if I didn't take the shot, I would have to be restrained. Although I hated to be restrained with my arthritis, I requested to be restrained. After they strapped me down, they shot me up with the drugs anyway. She lied to me. I wasn't a danger to anyone while I was strapped down to the bed. Laying there, my knees were in agony from me not being able to crack them every five minutes. The pain was excruciating, the whole experience was humiliating. Laying there with my knees aching was like torture. Before I knew it, I was knocked out from the drugs. Later, I called my Squad Leader Staff Sergeant Cruz and told him how the Marine tried to fight me inside. He told me that I had a visitor while I was drugged. Master Sergeant Saunders came to see me. On her own time, she made an effort to come see me. She is a true leader, and I enjoyed serving under her.

Later, when I went to the Magistrate, I had the Nurse's Aide accompany me to the Hearing to illustrate how dangerous I was. The Psychiatrist Iqbal testified that I was violent and refused to take my medication, that I threatened to kill my mother, and that I was so violent that I was in a fight the other day in my Mental Ward. It was all in her need to justify her position, science, and profession and continue to medicate me and keep me under Psychiatric Care.

When my Case was called, the Judge allowed me to express myself. There was no family there to help me. Mom, Lil Big Sis, or Butch never came to help me. I was sorry Steve went out of town.

The VA Doctors had their notes and documentation diagnosing me as Psychosis NOS (not otherwise specified). So, I clarified that I had a Traumatic Brain Injury and I was under a Psychologist care for over ten years. I told him that I was a Security Guard working at Macy's, a Licensed Ordained Minister, and a Combat Medic in the National Guard, selected to be trained as a NCOIC. As a Combat Medic, I was certified as an Emergency Medical Technician and they had no legal right to commit me. They didn't have legal authority to hold me in here. I was not a threat to myself, others, or property.

The Magistrate told me that I expressed myself well, giving a compelling case. He understood that I had no diagnosis for mental illness and National Guard training was this weekend. However, the Doctors' statements were contrary to mine and I didn't have one family member there to vouch for me. He would have to rule on the side of the VA Doctors. At the next Court Hearing, if I could produce a family member, he would release me. I was crushed. We went back to the locked mental ward. Instantly, when we were back in the Ward, the Nurse's Aide assigned to me was reassigned. The charade of me being so dangerous and needing a constant Monitor was quickly abandoned when I was sentenced back to the Ward. The Monitor was only for the manipulation of Dr. Iqbal to sway the Magistrate to keep me confined.

So, I reached out to my Pastor Stevie B to be a witness for me at the next Court Hearing. Steve called and talked with my mother and sister. Some things were said that I had some peculiar behavior. Steve knew my family from birth. He pointed out all the delinquency and turmoil my brother caused in the house and he was never committed or called out for his behavior. My mother and Lil Big Sis agreed they would come for my Court appearance. Butch told me he would come to testify as well.

When the Court date came around, Steve called and said he would be out of town on an AME Church trip. However, he talked with my mother and Lil Big Sis who said that they would be there. Then I talked to my mother closer to the date. Instead of being there, she and Lil Big Sis would write some letters that Butch would bring. Then, when the Court date came, no one appeared and no letters were sent. The Magistrate ruled that if I take the medication and comply with the Doctors orders, I would be released in thirty days. Later, when I spoke with Butch on the phone about it, he said the Cable Guy was coming by so he had to stay home. He left me in a Mental Ward over cable? My father's name was never mentioned. I asked him to help and he said he couldn't. I could never really rely on him my whole life.

An appeals lawyer came to visit to help me with my defense. She came to ensure that I would have a fair court hearing. She was making sure I had the opportunity to have someone testify on my behalf at the hearing. Anyone from my family, anyone from all my years of Church, or anyone from the Military could stand with me, just like the Children of Israel who stood up for righteousness, so many of them losing their lives. I told her that my brother-in-law couldn't make it that day. He told me that he decided to stay home for the Cable Guy to come instead. She looked at me strangely, acknowledging it was a pathetic excuse. We called Butch and explained that she was my appeals attorney and we were calling to ensure that I would have a proper defense. She again offered the opportunity for a family member to be present to vouch for my sanity, another opportunity to testify that I never threatened to kill my mother. Despite making my desires known to Butch, he said 'yeah' and then told me to put her on the telephone. She asked him again to come testify.

"Whatever the Doctor wants," he said. My jaw dropped open. I was shocked. He just lied to me. "Whatever the Doctor wants," he repeated himself several times to make himself clear. Butch's voice was strong and loud. His recent betrayal hurt. It confirmed that he was definitely involved with me being committed. My heart was so broken, the tears automatic started pouring down my cheeks. My appeals lawyer saw my expression immediately. All the telephone calls were terminated following the Magistrate's ruling that I would continue to be confined until the Doctor released me.

The lawyer tried to comfort me. It was apparent that I was totally broken in spirit. She reiterated that all I had to do was follow the Doctors instructions and take the medication, then the VA would have to release me. To pass the time, I continued to train for my two miles, running barefoot in my socks up and down the halls of the Mental Ward daily. Working out, I did my push-ups and sit-ups to keep in shape. When Warrior Training Camp came around or possibly Airborne School, I would be ready. Hooray!

My time was coming to an end at the Mental Ward. Mothers are so revered in the Black community. The Nurse's Aide was talking about my release. She asked where I was going to stay. I told her that I wasn't sure. She said, "Why don't you stay with your mother?" My mother? She was the person behind this scandal. Even if it was Butch, they were willful participants and did absolutely nothing to help me get out and maintain my jobs. She naively suggested I go stay with my mother. Black mothers could do no wrong in the Black Community. Tears started rolling down my cheeks. To be released, I would have to comply with the Doctors orders and take more drugs. In the days to come, I just continued training for my two mile run in the corridor and taking the medication.

Upon release, the realization set in that I had no place to go. I used the telephone in the hall to call Steve and Errold. Errold was glad to share in the victory that I would be released. Sadly, he informed me that Pastor Lanier, Sr., had finished his journey and gone on to be with the Lord. The news and occasion turned bittersweet. After I called Butch, he said that he would come to pick me up. I didn't have many people to rely on, so I had to move past the obvious question. Is he one of the people who had me committed into a Mental Institution? Well, I say keep your friends close and your enemies closer. I needed a ride and no one else was offering.

On the drive home, I confronted Butch but he denied any involvement with having me committed. He tried to switch it and told me that I was acting so irate with the VA Cops, they had to restrain me. I reminded him that the Emergency Room was videotaped and under surveillance like my security job at Macy's. With the cameras rolling, I knew to display total compliance with the VA Cops. The entire moment was videotaped and proved I wasn't irate. The decision to commit me was already predetermined before I even entered the Emergency Room. He thought he was so smart. He drove me home, but he took on a strange route, and he stopped in front of my cousin

Sonya's house. He was on his cell phone and my father came running out of the house. Butch was yelling 'yeah' like he had nothing to do with me being there. My father ran up and hugged me in triumph. All this crap, and when I needed them the most, they weren't anywhere to be found. My father didn't visit, call, help, or care. When I needed him the most, he wasn't there. I didn't want to hug them or forgive them, but I was forced to do what Jesus would do in the situation. So, I tried to move past my personal feelings and chose to forgive. But how can I forget?

Everything was happening all at once. I was just released from a Mental Ward. We were about to bury my mentor, my Pastor, my spiritual father, and my friend. I was staying once again in a house where I was unwanted. Emotionally, I was too numb from the mourning to concentrate on the rejection from the family. I didn't want to stay at all but I had no place else to go. My clothes were there, and there was just too much going on. My mother's church had service on Tuesday night. With nowhere to go, I was even more encouraged to make service. The service was nice. I had attended there since my youth. When my eyes and mother's eyes met, she was stressed. She didn't want anyone to know what they did to me. My stare back at her was painful from the betrayal. I kept biting my tongue so as not to tell the saints and everyone what they did to me, including the locked wards, the Marine attack, strapping me down like a dog, and all the psychotropic drugs they pumped me up with. Forgiveness and healing would take a while. For now, all I felt was the war within myself. The flesh and spirit were like those yellow and blue auras, one pitted against the other.

Reverend Lanier was so beloved that our church was not large enough to accommodate all the people that wished to attend his funeral. We had to rent my mother's church despite two days of viewing at Good News Bible Mission. The funeral arrangements were done with the highest of dignity and respect. Junior, Pastor Lanier's oldest son, was a professional singer. He had some of his professional musicians and singers accompany him. Errold and Junior had a special selection in which Errold played the keyboard skillfully as Junior blessed us with his talent. Surprisingly, Joel didn't play the organ. Deacon Butler and his wife sang a beautiful duet.

They were the best singers from our church. Remarks were made from several of our clergy. Evangelist Ida Harris eulogized Pastor Lanier. She was a prayer warrior and prayed with me through a lot of situations. With all the singing and remarks, the funeral service went on for hours. I had a mandatory Doctor's appointment following my release. I couldn't afford to not comply with any of the conditions of my release.

Staying as late as I could, I made my exit and went back to my mother's house to change. My niece was downstairs with her son, Jared. He was about two years old and ran into the kitchen to play with me. I called my Doctor to confirm my appointment. Jared was running around the kitchen and I was ready to leave. I couldn't get him back in the room with his mother. He started poking at the screen door like children do. I let my niece know, so could come get him to stop.

I was enthusiastic about seeing the Doctor to verify that I have no history of psychiatric episodes, no history of mental illness, and no history of violence or irrational behavior. I need them to help me salvage my reputation and good name. This would help in my lawsuit against the V.A. for wrecking my life, destroying my character and career.

Jared was poking at the screen hard. He was barely two years old. He had no understanding of how fragile the screens were. "Tia, come and get him. I'm leaving out the kitchen," the kitchen was a dangerous place to leave a child unattended with stoves and knives. She stormed in reluctantly and frustrated. She must have called my nephew because he came into the house yelling at me to get out of the house, just like Shakur with all this disrespect.

"Who do you think you're talking to?" I was in no mood for further disrespect from a nephew on the day I was burying my Pastor.

"You need to get out this house," he told me without even asking anything.

"Never tell me to get out of this house. This is not your house and you don't ever talk like that to me," I demanded respect from him. Then Shakur came in the door. He could tell from our stance facing each other and our expressions that there was trouble.

"What's going on?" He asked.

"Uncle Bee in here acting crazy again," my nephew said.

"Yo, you got to get out, Bro," he said, pointing at the door. I was leaving to go to a Doctor's appointment anyway, but with my brain injury, I couldn't switch gears quickly. If I felt that I was being attacked, I just reacted. The Enemy was the author of all confusion. My anger made me none the wiser. I didn't see the Enemy. All I just saw was my disrespectful brother, a disrespectful nephew, and a disrespectful niece. All of them had their diapers changed by me and I helped raise them. I paid rent in this house. I help rebuild it from the plumbing to the sheetrock on the walls. These are the mouths I fed, clothed, and protected, and this is how they treated me for stopping Jared from poking holes in my mother's screen door and insisting that my niece watch her own child in a kitchen unattended.

"No, you will never tell me what to do in this house or to get out," I said furiously pointing at them.

"Then we'll put you out," Shakur said. My nephew shouted 'yeah' in agreement with the challenge.

"I'd like to see you try," I reacted again. I was mourning, insulted, disrespected, and angry. There was no praying about this or wanting to be the bigger person. My nephew lunged at me or stepped forward. Whatever you call it, it was disrespect enough. God blessed me because I was too angry. My brother immediately grabbed by nephew to prevent us from fighting. I grabbed my nephew by the collar to pull him in. We all lost our balance and fell to the floor. We all got back up and Shakur was actually playing the peacemaker right now. When I saw my nephew, his lip was bleeding. Seeing that made me quell some of my anger back but it was too late. This was like my child and I saw blood by my hand. I didn't even punch him. How crazy was my family becoming? How crazy was my life? How far was my role in this? All I did was stop the baby from poking a hole in the screen door. I was just trying to protect my mother's property and now all this was blown out of proportion.

We all were staring at each other. Shakur, my nephew, and Me all locked in eye contact. It was like a Texas stand-off. The absurdity of the situation made us all take a step back. I didn't leave immediately, making it clear no one was putting me out. They could have tried to jump me but they came to their senses, not in fear of me, but as it should have been. I was his older brother. I was his uncle.

I left the house and headed for my Doctor's appointment. Now, my heart was heavy with more than just mourning my Pastor. My mind replayed all that happened. But this is the culture my family had adopted. Black men weren't respected, age wasn't respected, and I was certainly not respected. But I demanded respect. Later, when I saw my mother and sister, I told them how I was physically attacked again in this house. I reiterated that no one besides my mother had the right to throw me out of that house for which I had labored for decades. It all started from my niece leaving a toddler running around in a kitchen unsupervised and then getting angry because I stopped him from poking out my mother's screen door. You would think that my mother would show some appreciation for me trying to protect her home. But no, I was the problem. For her, I've never been the same after the brain injury. Their silence meant that they were compliant with all their actions. Houston, this meant we had a serious problem. I wasn't the type of person that waited for anyone's authorization for being respected. I was totally in charge of that. If the dog bites me the first time, then it's the dog's fault. If the dog bites me the second time, then it's my fault.

After I went to the mandatory appointments, I asked my Primary Doctor Park and Psychologist Weinstein why, with over a decade of treatment, did they not speak up for me and say that I had a TBI and that I wasn't suffering from mental illness. They seemed submissive to the diagnosis of a Psychiatrist who never met me, never properly evaluated me, and never talked with me for more than ten minutes. Doctor Park was my primary doctor for over ten years. He would always send my pamphlets about drug use because I had a fatty liver. It seemed highly judgmental and racist to me. Since the National Guard randomly drug tested I strenuously defended myself him that. The random drug test actually requested me every drill weekend. I felt their betrayal. I was under their care for ten years or fifteen years and they never noted any bipolar behavior. They didn't stand up to the Psychiatrist diagnosis. After a week of eye rolling and the hypocrisy displayed that 'I could come home,' I left voluntarily. I'd rather sleep in the streets than live unwelcomed in anyone's home.

So, I made a special visit to the Veteran's Affairs Office downtown at City Hall. They were trying to get me into a VA shelter. They said it might take a while because of a waiting list of homeless Veterans. The next day, I returned to work at Macy's. The PATH train system honored veterans, so all I had to do was flash my Military ID and they allowed me free access. Many nights, I slept on the PATH trains riding back and forth to Newark, Jersey City, Hoboken, and New York City all night long. I refused to sleep in that house again. Immediately, I went and rented a Storage Unit off Mallory Avenue by Westside Avenue. God gave me favor with the Manager at the storage. He authorized me 24 hour access and mentioned that, if necessary, I could sleep in my Storage Unit. They had a restroom in the Office where I could take a bird bath and shave in the mornings. Macy's soon terminated me because of unexplained absences from my holiday trip to VA East Orange.

Now without a home or a job, I had to come up with a quick means to gain some spending cash. Thanks to Mayor David Dinkins, New York City reenacted the five cent recyclable deposition bottles and cans. During my homeless days, I wanted for no good thing. Some nights, I slept in my Storage Unit. Other nights, I slept on the trains. Remembering that God was with me every step of the way. No matter how things seemed, I remembered the scripture, "I've never seen the righteous forsaken nor his seed begging for bread." My cousins would take me in right away. Some drank, some smoked, but my religious family wanted to see me grovel at their feet. They want to break me. But one thing is for sure, they didn't want to help and they didn't offer any. What doesn't kill you makes you stronger. Now I had strength beyond belief and they resented it.

The stores wouldn't take the recyclables unless they were in a recyclable bag. The maximum they would accept was 400, which totaled to $20. One day, I came across an unclaimed shopping cart to help me. Now I was able to haul hundreds of recyclables at times. I took a break and walked from midtown to downtown and back all day, and then from downtown back to midtown, to Herald Square, and Times Square. Everyday all of the time I felt the awesome presence of God as I was collecting recyclables in my shopping cart while singing songs of praise. I walked to Grand Central Station, then to Penn Station, and into the Port Authority building on 42nd Street. Occasionally, I would stop there and use the UFO for cold donated drinks, snacks, and the internet. Then it was back to walking and collecting cans and bottles to Washington Square. Then it was back to Herald Square, Times Square, and Madison Square Garden. It was hot. I was tired but I kept humping it out. "I have never seen the righteous forsaken; nor His seed for begging bread." My faith kept me going. My God kept me strong. Daily I would walk for miles and miles. Daily I would walk for hours and hours. The sun was dehydrating and I didn't sleep comfortably on the trains at night. Riding the crowded trains in the daytime forced me to stand. My body collapsed as it fell forward so hard, which used to wake me up. I never felt sorry for my predicament. Homelessness can be powerful. Homelessness could be liberating. Jesus spoke, "Foxes have holes, and birds of the air have nest; but the Son of man has nowhere to lay his head" (Luke 9:58). There is no one more powerful than Jesus. Jesus said there was no greater prophet than John the Baptist. John lived in the wilderness. John ate wild locust and honey. Jesus commissioned the 72 to go into all the world, preaching the Gospel.

According to Luke in the 10th chapter, Jesus commissioned the 72 because the harvest was plentiful. He sent them out like 'lambs among wolves.' Jesus told them not to take any extra clothing or greet anyone while they travelled. He further instructed them to bless any house they entered. They were to remain in that house to eat and drink whatever was given to them. They remained with believers and ate with them because they were homeless and were without steady means of financial support. They had no financial support other than ministering but they were the most powerful evangelistic ministry to ever grace the Earth. Jesus commissioned them to heal the sick and tell people the Kingdom of God has come. Whoever listened to them, listens to Jesus. Whoever rejects you also rejects me. Whoever rejects me also rejects he that sent me. The 72 came back, declaring demons submitted to Jesus name. People were healed in Jesus' name.

Jesus declared that all things have been committed to Him by the Father.

Jehovah Jireh, God provided for us. Stores threw out their outdated sealed quality food in clear plastic bags separately from the trash. Bakeries would set out fresh baked pastries in boxes. The homeless community was very generous with food. Everyone would share the fresh food with each other. We ate well every day and night. "Look at the birds of the air, for they neither sow nor reap nor gather into barns. Yet your heavenly Father feeds them. Are you not of more value than they?" (Matthew 6:26)

This time, I had to call the cops to get some of my belongings. My education in domestic disputes came by the previous Restraining Order fiasco, introducing domestic escorts. Since Mom wouldn't let me in house, this time, I wouldn't be denied. It's a shame the only sons she respected are those without a job or work history. When the cops came, they told me they would have to talk with my mother. I just needed to get some of my own clothes.

The Police Officer came back out and told me it was all right and they would accompany me. How embarrassing it was to me and to the whole family. When the Officer saw the many instruments, clothes, National Guard uniforms, dishware, sets of glasses, televisions, furniture, etc., here marked like the other Officer, "You sure do own a lot of stuff, Mr. Porter."

Of course, there was stuff. I was a man of accomplishment, a man respected in the community. Well, at least I was respected everywhere else. I was respected in the church, at the job, in the community, in the Air Force, in the Public School system, in New York, and in New Jersey. Clothes and uniforms were stuffed into duffle bags. Luggage bags and gym bags were filled with toiletries and shoes. I grabbed as many bags as I could as quickly as I could. Domestic escorts were on a time limit and could turn ugly. The Light Rail stop was down the corner. It's the story of my life. I played a game of leap frog with the bags, grunting it up. I boarded the Light Rail to get off at West Side Avenue. Again, I leap frog down one block to the Mallory Storage Unit.

Finances were running low. I was anticipating my income tax return. Then a notice came from the IRS that $1,230 was intercepted for Child Support. Well, at least it was going to my child, so I called Charity to let her know. I asked if she needed anything and told her of the amount of money that was just sent. She seemed confused, as always, when I talked about such matters. I told her to ask her mother about it and make sure she got whatever she needed. I wasn't sure what arrangements were made for rent and food but that money was for her needs.

A pattern started to develop. Whether I slept on the train or in the Storage Unit, I traveled to my Storage as early as six o'clock in the morning. When the Office opened around eight o'clock, I slipped in to use the restroom. My plan was to collect recyclables in Jersey City where the five cent recyclable was not in progress. The opportunity arose to go to the Big Apple with 400 recycles in my trusty deluxe shopping cart. I started right with $20 and got the ball rolling. I sat there waiting for the PATH Train at a familiar spot. Being homeless, you longed to appreciate some familiar surroundings. The sun shined beautiful in the sky. Praise the Lord! It was a nice day. It was not too hot, not too cold. Walking up and down the streets of Manhattan can be exhausting. Taking a moment to rest was just what the Doctor ordered. Suddenly, my Momma walked up to me. It was unusual for her to be there, not to mention that there is no parking at Journal Square.

"Bryan," she paused. Her voice was soft. I haven't heard her speak to me like that in a long time. "Bryan, this is not you," she said sympathetically. Since when had she become sympathetic? I've been sleeping on the streets for over a month now. Unwittingly, my sister worked up the Square and she must have seen me with my shopping cart. My mother had no knowledge or cares about my whereabouts. There was no other explanation for how she knew where to find me. She handed me an 'Obama phone.' This was the innovative government free cell phone program under President Barak Obama. A cell phone is exactly what I needed. Without it, I was cut off from the world.

Occasionally, I met some Veterans who claimed they knew how to get me a bed at the VA right away. All I had to do was make a false claim that 'I wished to do myself harm.' If I did this, I would betray everything about myself. This would justify their life shattering mistreatment of imprisoning me, confining me to Mental Wards, doping me up, and strapping me down like an dog. My trust in God led me to wait it out in faith. The VA finally called me with news that a bed was available for me at the PERC shelter on 36th Street in Union City. My own City was overcrowded with homeless people such that its own shelters had no room for me. I attempted to go time and time again. Finally, I didn't have to recycle bottles and cans for food all day anymore. Finally, I didn't have to sleep on trains or in storage units anymore after betrayal, after committal, after heartbreak, after watching my military career sabotaged, after unemployment and homelessness, after watching my dreams of a commission die, and after watching every other hope and dream die with it. Finally, after a long hard day and night, this week, after a long hard summer, I had a bed to sleep in. Thank God. It was not a bed of a friend, a relative, a cousin, or a sibling. It was a bed provided by the PERC shelter in Union City/Weehawken on 37th Street.

At the PERC Shelter, they fed me, gave me linen, and a bed at night. Finally, I could lay down my head on a mattress. Believe me, it felt so good. That night, I lay in my bed relaxed and was ready for a good night's sleep. Finally, after a long hard day, a long hard month, a hot summer now to sleep in. It was now my bed, not a storage storage unit, or a park bench, or a train. I was so very grateful. Hallelujah!

The PERC wasn't used to having serving members in the Armed Forces. There were no guarantees to save your spot for a bed. You miss a night, you might be removed from the program. My monthly obligation for the Army National Guard was coming up. The Director told me that I had to return with a letter justifying my whereabouts. When I returned to PERC, still in my uniform, my assigned bed was given away. For the night, I had to sleep on the foldout table. This is the respect they gave to a man in uniform. I saw young men in their twenties come and go. The Shelter's Director took a fancy to them. My threats to call the Veteran's Affairs Office to straighten things out paid off. Suddenly, a bed was available again. Some days,

I had to walk from Jersey City to Union City straight down Kennedy Boulevard. Most days, I took the Light Rail to the Bergenline stop.

My National Guard Drill came up at Sea Girt and I would have a safe place to sleep with my Battle Buddies for the weekend. The barracks were much more comfortable than the shelter. New Jersey Transit permitted free travel on its trains and buses while in military uniform. I traveled down to Sea Girt Friday night before anyone and slept like a baby. Saturday in the morning, when Colonel Burn saw me, she was furious and marched me into her Office. Without hesitation, she started yelling as soon as I entered the room. When I tried to respond, she stood me at attention. This meant I stood there with my hands pinned at my sides, not the slightest movement of my head. I wasn't permitted to speak. You couldn't even flinch. She told me I wasn't allowed to Drill with Medical Command anymore. Now I was ordered to report at Lawrenceville National Guard Post near Trenton.

Lawrenceville was spoken of often referred as a tomb for broken soldiers. From my observations, it was for Soldiers placed on profile, not fit for duty with their home Units. Jokingly, I referred to it as the island of misfit toys. Colonel Burn ordered me to take off my uniform and go home, as if me wearing the uniform was disgraceful. Take off my uniform? How was I going to afford to travel back home? She treated me with no dignity or respect. Our conversation consisted of her yelling at me and me marching out daring to say nothing. My Senior NCOs met me later.

As I went back to the barracks to grab my travel bag, Top, the Platoon Sergeants, and my Squad Leader were all there. They adopted a different tone than the Commander. They wanted to hear my side. They wanted to mentor me, not throw me away like the Commander did. They were more sympathetic to my situation but they could not override the Unit Commander's orders. Master Sergeant Saunders told me she was sorry for what was going on. She understood I needed to wear my uniform to get back home. Master Sergeant authorized me to wear my uniform to get back home after I explained that I didn't have much money on me. She echoed the Commander that my future Guard drills would be conducted at Lawrenceville.

The VA finally called and placed me in one of their Homeless Programs. Since the VA had me Committed, my documents were now red flagged. It was explained to me that, before I would be able to live in the Domiciliary, I must first voluntarily enter the CORE Program. All the Patients there suffered from mental illness and were kept in a locked Ward, just like when they committed me in East Orange. We would be given one hour a day to leave the ward for shopping privileges. My sacrifice for room and board was to swallow my pride or continue to be homeless. I willingly had to let them evaluate me, as if I was mentally ill, for ninety days until I completed the Program.

Personally, I mean no disrespect or insensitivity to people suffering from mental or behavioral disorders, *but* I suffered from Traumatic Brain Injury (TBI). My symptoms weren't the same as a person suffering from Bi-polar Disorder or Schizophrenia. The ignorance on Traumatic Brain Injury is widespread. My fellow soldiers, construction workers, and victims of car accidents, bicycle accidents, or motorcycle accidents, with TBI injuries, get committed to mental institutions by their family members because they can't tell the difference.

Traumatic Brain Injury can affect your thinking ability, emotional stability, sense of sight, sense of sound, loss of motor skills (walk or speak), PTSD, depression, and/or confusion. A person can suffer from one or more of these symptoms, so it is not the same for everyone. However, rarely does someone fall off a bike and become bi-polar, or suffers a physical assault and starts hearing voices. Normally, families are sympathetic and supportive. Individuals whose motives come from fear, anger, or sibling rivalry are not supportive. If their motives are impure, their actions will be impure. Families should be all love, but sometimes families are all drama.

As patients in the CORE Program, we were locked in the Ward. We were allowed one hour of free time to walk around the Lyons VA campus and to visit the Post Office, Cafeteria, or shop for personal items. All other times, we were in mandatory Psychiatric Wellness Classes, Stress Managing, or one-on-one Psychological Counseling. The Psychiatrist upstairs was a short Korean lady named Doctor Lee. She could be nice at times. But when Doctor Lee didn't get her way, she went nuts. She demanded that I take mood stabilizers. She ever observed me but she wanted me to take Depakote to help me manage my mood and behavior. I told them that I had God and I didn't need their medications. Doctor Lee insisted I take 1,500 milligrams of Depakote and something to help me sleep. Doctor Lee had no faith in me or God. She didn't like the four hours a night I was getting. She didn't like when I refused her sleeping pills. From my Medic experience, I told her that I would be willing to take 500 milligrams of Depakote daily, only because it was mandatory to take prescribed medication in the locked Psychiatric Ward. I agreed to take them for 90 days until I could get into the Domiciliary. Doctor Lee slammed her open hand on the desk.

"No! No!" She stood up but she still seemed only waist high, yelling and slamming the desk. Who was the one who needed the mood stabilizers? "You need more than 1,000 milligrams to make the medication effective." At this time, the VA operated in a Patient Orientated mode. The Patient's rights and opinions were enforced in the diagnosis. Doctors were not ready to share their power.

The holidays were very nice at the VA. Several patriotic agencies came to give us holiday treats. Every week, we had pizza parties. One week, the Disabled Veterans of America (DVA) came with their families. They told us that they had ordered lots of pizza and cookies they would bring to us. My Battle Buddies and I sat there shoving our faces with delicious pizza. After a while, I reached over to my friend in astonishment. Never have I seen such generosity before. I started feeling guilty about all the pizza I was eating.

"I can't believe how much pizza I ate," I grinned with a full belly. "I must have had six slices," I boasted to a friend.

"I had seven," he grinned, leaning over at me. It was a great night to be a Vet.

"Why don't you get one more and you'll have a whole pie," I said in astonishment.

"Nah," he fired back, "I'm saving room for cookies." We just both laughed and laughed.

Soon. my 90 days of good behavior and compliance with taking the Depakote were up. After graduation, I was sent to the Domiciliary. The Orientation period was 21 days. At the Domiciliary, my roommate was a huge muscular brother who was recently released from prison for murder. He used to sneak alcohol into the room of our drug-free, alcohol-free hospital Domiciliary.

Part of the agreement to stay in the Dom was to attend morning and evening Alcoholics Anonymous (AA) meetings, followed by morning and evening Drug Addicts Anonymous (DAA) meetings five days a week. In between, we had breakfast, lunch, and dinner. Another part of the agreement was to take the prescribed medication. In the Domiciliary, I stopped taking the mood stabilizer. Weeks later, a blood test revealed that I stopped taking the medication. They warned me if I wanted to stay on the VA campus, it was mandatory that I comply. Like my grandfather, my middle name is Joseph. I am a Dreamer. After they committed me I lost my jobs, my promotion, my military orders, my hopes, and my dreams. Then one day in the domiciliary, I saw a face from a dream from my youth. The face of a man God gave me in a nightmare in a dark place, with dark thoughts, and dark feelings. The face of this man was full of wisdom and peace. I drew strength from his smile.

It took some time to be processed into the Lawrenceville National Guard. It gave me ample time, so making my monthly drills wasn't a priority. By the time I received letters telling me when and where to report, I finished the mandatory AA meetings and moved over to the Compensated Worker Therapy (CWT). In CWT, we were given work on the VA Hospital campus. We were paid $8 an hour tax-free because it was funded as therapy. It wasn't considered a job. They placed me in Housekeeping. Housekeeping was assigned to cleaning the hallways, restrooms, medical offices, cafeterias, polishing floors, and emptying trash.

News traveled that my Battle Buddy, Specialist Steven Lauther, overdosed. The post-traumatic stress of Iraq haunted him until the day he died. Without Jesus to lift those heavy burdens, 'He who keeps the city labors in vain.' To get to Lawrenceville, you had to get on five o'clock NJ Transit train to Trenton. There, at six o'clock, there were vans to drive us to Lawrenceville. At Sea Girt, I used to walk every drill from the Manasquan Station. The Secretary at Lawrenceville, Ms. Cox, kept insisting that there must be some hidden diagnosis why I'm living there and not because I was simply homeless, as I had stated, since my address was at the Lyons VA. She thought that she was so clever. The VA didn't force me to live there. It was my choice to live there. They weren't keeping me there because I was a danger to society.

The Compensated Work Therapy (CWT) initially was to employ Veterans for six months while they found jobs in the economy. This was great for homeless or unemployed Vets to come to the VA and receive immediate financial assistance. President Lincoln was quoted about employing and caring for our Veterans. Many Veterans applied to become Federal employees while we were working CWT. Unfortunately, the economy wasn't opening up for Veterans like many companies had advertised. Vets worked in the six month program for five to seven years without finding gainful employment. The job proved stressful on my body at this age. To ease the back pain, I tried to get cortisone shots to help me make it through the workday.

My efforts allowed me to graduate the Domiciliary and move into building 53. Some agency had a grant to house Veterans on the VA Campus for a uniquely affordable rent while we worked our CWT jobs, waiting for permanent jobs and HUD VASH. HUD VASH was a special funded program to house homeless veterans. The Department of Housing and Urban Development (HUD) Veterans Affairs Supportive Housing (VASH) provided Section 8 funding to assist or pay rent for Veterans. While staying in building 53, Veterans received the opportunity to find gainful employment, build savings, and establish credit.

Praise be to God my Section 8 for HUD VASH came through and I moved to New Brunswick. I stopped taking the Depakote medicine they forced me to take as a mood stabilizer. This meant I didn't have to see the Psychiatrist anymore. Rutgers University had a Theological Seminary there and I felt compelled to attend. Getting a job there should be relatively easy. There were hospitals, restaurants, and hotels. It should be easy to replace this minimum wage job. Working in fast food would easily replace it. The state's minimum wage was $7.87 and I was only making $8. Until then, I would take the seven hour daily commute to Lyons. Any minimum wage job would be better to erase the daily commute. The CWT program would be my primary source of income until I could do better.

So, I kept working and making my monthly drill weekends. One time at drill, they prepared a document for me to sign. The document stated that I was suffering from a closed head injury with residual effects and was unable to perform the daily functions of my job. What a fabrication! I were deemed unable to perform, I could not qualify for WTC, get the recommendation of my senior NCOs and Unit Commander, and have them sign on my promotion. This would show that Colonel Burn is contradicting herself. I refused to sign.

The Swine Flu epidemic was causing great alarm. By 2010, there were 60 million cases and over 12,000 deaths. My Lawrenceville National Guard Unit asked me to implement an immunization program. I would have to vaccinate everyone with the Flu Shot and H1N1. They asked me to sign a document stating I was unable to perform the daily functions of my job, and then they asked me to perform my job for them. Pondering the situation, I thought of the irony of it all. My response to them was that I would implement an immunization program only if it would be documented on my evaluation. A promise was made to me. I was already performing my daily functions at Lawrenceville. The Appeals Board should see right through the charade of it all.

CHAPTER 7
The Magic of St. Peter's

Month after month, I kept getting computer generated job search emails that I was not being considered for the positions I applied for. How could I not be considered? How many other paralegals had specific automated litigation support experience, Paralegal Certificate from the University of Maryland, and the Secret Security Clearance? I left the company on good terms. Then this world-wide company makes millions, if not, billions on government sensitive contracts, so they have to ensure all their employees pass Secret Security Clearance standards. The company aggressively recruited Veterans because they are in possession of a Security Clearance or could easily be cleared. Security Clearances cost thousands of dollars for each employee. Even more money is lost when an investigation is conducted and a person does not qualify.

The legal firm that I worked for in Washington D.C. had paralegal job openings in Newark, New Jersey, and New York. I became very enthusiastic. My faith told me that this is the reason why I didn't get so many other jobs that I was overqualified for in the past. This is why I was fired while still on military orders. This is why I went through the Great Recession and couldn't find a job for two years. This is why that NJ Transit Urinalysis Monitor position fell through. This is why the County Prison Health Tech job fell through. This is why I still had a seven hour daily commute for a minimum wage job. This was God's plan for me to gain back the job I lost, the job I trained for in college. The job I lost when they lied to keep me from my children. It was the paralegal job of my dreams. After all these years, my God was still faithful to his promises that I could still be restored back. The fact that I had automated litigation experience working for this company was promising but having a Secret Security Clearance from the National Guard just placed me ahead of the class. My faith was never more realized and I was voicing it to everyone I could.

Believing that this was my blessing, which I had to claim and fight for, I tweaked my application and reached out to the Litigation Project Manager that I worked for. The firm's Veteran Recruiters allowed me to email them directly to alert companies that I possessed previous internal work experience. Although my faith was that God would bless me and give me back the job I lost through a bitter divorce, I still applied to other jobs while I waited. As the months went on, nothing materialized. Even the minimum wage job I had on the VA Hospital campus was being terminated. My dreams of going to Seminary would have to be placed on hold.

Meanwhile, Ms. Cox continued her personal witch hunt to dig dirt on why I lived on the VA Campus. My claim of being homeless wasn't sufficient enough. She felt there must be some mental health reason behind it. Her job as Secretary was just to process forms with office support. I could overhear her demanding things from the Commander instead of just following his orders. They all worked under Colonel Burn, which was a constant red flag to me. On my monthly Drills, I was requested to sign paperwork that I couldn't perform my Medic duties. Instead, I filed an appeal for their outlandish request. The Appeal's Board was approaching, and an Army attorney was assigned to me. He suggested that I ask my mother to write a letter. When I asked her, she didn't want to get involved in clearing my name from false accusations, which was unsurprising. So, I coerced Mom into writing me a letter to present at my appeal. She wrote a letter stating that the accusations of me threatening her were untrue and that she didn't try to commit me.

After a full day of work on Friday at the Lyons VA, I traveled back home to New Brunswick. One night, I got off the train and started walking home. Weary and worn, I walked back down George Street from my three and a half hour commute from work. Dragging my feet, I was dreading getting up at four o'clock in the morning for my National Guard Drill. There was a metal grate in the concrete that led into a basement. As I walked passed it, I avoided stepping on this grate. A young man in his twenties was standing there. He was very skinny and started to mumble, "You don't have to be afraid of no grate." So, as I continued to walk. I noticed him following me. He was still mumbling out loud, "You don't have to be afraid of no grate." He came and stood in front of me. Looking at him, I marveled how young and skinny he was. Quickly, I assessed he posed no threat to me. As I looked him up and down, I turned the other cheek and walked away. As we walked, we passed a group of college students. He started taunting the college students sitting along the wall of the park in front of the Heldrick Hotel. He walked across the wall like on a trapeze while the college students jobbed off, avoiding his bizarre behavior. He stepped in front of me for the third time. This time, I tried to punch him in the face but I just didn't have the fight in me anymore. He started reaching in his pockets while still mumbling about walking on the metal grate. He could have a weapon. I couldn't take that chance. I wasn't going to the hospital anymore. Relentlessly, I started punching him in the face. I snatched his monkey behind up and body slammed him to the ground. I was pounding him over and over again none stop. Never in my life, from fighting in my youth, have I repeatedly hit someone like that in the head. The fact that I was too old for street fighting quickly sank in. Fatigue started to set in but I continued my onslaught, beating him in the head until I felt something strike me in the shoulder plex.

Instantly, I was rendered powerless. My hands were paralyzed and all the fight was taken out of me. When I looked up, I saw a giant of a police officer standing over me with his baton raised up. This seven foot cop was menacing in stature alone but the baton was skillfully placed and took all the fight out of me. The young instigator immediately popped out like I hadn't been wailing on him for the last five minutes. He darted off like he felt no pain. He had to be high as a kite but he would feel it in the morning.

"I am a Veteran and I want to press charges on him," I declared to the police officer. I wanted him to apprehend the instigator before he got away.

"Ah, it's all right," he said, getting out of his responsibilities.

"I want to press charges," I said as he was escaping down the street. Anxiety was kicking in because of my Traumatic Brain Injury and short-term memory loss. If he retaliated with his drug dealing friends, I wouldn't remember his face. My attacker would have the jump on me just like my attackers from the coma. This made me more vulnerable and more anxious. "What if he and his friends come back and attack me?"

"Believe me," he paused. "He is not going to attack you again," he replied to my allegations.

"I want to press charges," I insisted, asserting my rights.

"Believe me," the Officer insisted. "He is not going to bother you again." After witnessing the beating I gave him, the Officer was convinced the instigator would not be back again. I, on the other hand, was not reassured with a memory I couldn't rely on to alert me if my attacker was standing right next to me. It was just like when I got out from the coma.

Once home, I stared in the mirror and attended to my fresh bloody wounds. My elbow and knee were busted. Maybe it was the long day but I felt that I was too old for these physical battles. I set the alarm for 4 a.m. to catch the train to Trenton for my Army National Guard Drill in the morning. I got up and made the trip to Trenton in my battle dress uniform, so I could travel for free. Since I just was doing battle last night, my wounds were too large for traditional band aids. But I didn't have gauze or medical tape to improvise. I felt the bloody knee and elbow rubbing against the inside of my uniform. My fear was that it would soak through and reveal my blood stains. They kept me under a veil of suspicion anyway. Thankfully, nothing was seen and I went back home Sunday only to repeat my sixteen hour day Monday at Lyons. It became harder to replace my minimum wage job than I thought. My one-way three and a half hour commute gave me sufficient time on my cell phone to apply for paralegal and medical assistant jobs on my way to work.

A recent influx of homeless Vets was draining Federal funds. So, after two years, I was released from the CWT program. After a long summer and a daily regime of job hunting, I started looking for other areas of employment. No more seven hour commute and nine hour workday. As my memory was deteriorating, my love for music began to subside tremendously. I was struggling to recall words, chord progressions, and playing notes were becoming increasingly more and more difficult. Whatever I would play the day before would become absent from my memory when I sat at the keyboard. I realized I was primarily a bass player. I got off the keyboard and picked up my bass guitar. It was hard to make this old bass talk again. It was in need of new strings. The action was way too high that it affected the timing of the fingering. The action is how hard or high it is to push the string to the fret board. On home equipment, it was impossible to sound like the professional bass players on the radio. Inside my house, I felt totally dead. I was wrestling with the internal voices in my head.

My struggle was more than just the struggles in my head but the struggles of life. My efforts to gain sufficient employment were fruitless no matter how much I prayed. Financing the Bible Seminary seemed impossible even with faith. Until God show me another way, I must stick with working. My college degrees, paralegal certificate, EMT certificate, phlebotomy certificate, EKG certificate, Medical Assisting certificate were all meaningless in gaining employment. In the interim, I was still applying for jobs at hotels, restaurants, warehouses, and transportation, but the doors were being constantly slammed in my face. Multiple resumes were continuously being tweaked but to no avail. Past companies had me on their computer generated employment status, so I reapplied as frequently as I could for new employment opportunities. As I went to medical appointments or law offices, wondering why I couldn't get a job as less qualified people could.

The blessing of being on the Veteran's Section 8 took the fear away from being homeless again. God didn't open the doors of employment as I wanted but all of my needs were met according to His riches in glory. My housing needs were met. I received a miracle thousand dollar credit on my utilities bill and I received monthly food stamps. Satan's last attack on my finances had me once again hand washing my laundry in the bathtub. It is both grueling as well as tiresome. Using heat and electricity sparingly helped spread that heating credit throughout the year. When I was working, I was always near cancellation but now I was safe in His arms.

My Paralegal background wasn't the only career area I was seeking. My certifications in EMT, Phlebotomy, and EKG had me actively pursuing positions in the local hospital, Robert Wood Johnson. This hospital had notoriety in the State as one of the top trauma and cancer treatment centers. One day, I was out walking and putting in applications with the local colleges. The Human Resources Office of St. Peter's Hospital was across the street and I put in applications for the open positions of Medical Assistants, Phlebotomist, and EKG Technicians. There were openings for Patient Transportation. I never did hear back about any of the medical positions that I was certified in. I never did hear back from my old law firm in Washington D.C. (CACI). Working in Newark or New York would not become a reality for me. As I prayed for guidance, the job openings I asked for weren't happening. After all avenues were exhausted, I decided to put in an application at both local hospitals for the same Housekeeping job I held at the Lyons VA Hospital.

This 4th of July, I was watching the news with my mother. They talked about the NYPD Officer, Miosotis Familia, who was fatally shot in the head and killed by Alexander Bonds. Bond's girlfriend called the police saying he was acting depressed and manic. Reports later came that Bond's girlfriend told that he complained that he felt like killing someone. The hospital sedated him and released him. Butch kept calling me. How ironic that the hospital released this man to kill a cop while I was committed even though I threatened no one. As we continued to watch the news, I too asked what was said by the weatherman. Sarcastically, I was so snipped that I couldn't concentrate. I talked about how the VA committed me, a Veteran, over nothing. Yet they let this man free to threaten and kill people.

At August Guard Drill, they gave us our Annual Evaluation. In order to keep a paper trail on us Misfit Soldiers, they gave us average or below average evaluations. My Evaluation was a 3 out of 5. It was the kiss of death in an enlisted career. They lied to me and didn't include implementing an immunization program of both H1N1 and the Flu shot. The only reason I did this work for them was that it would be included on my evaluation. But they had no honor and honor was all I had.

I never received my appeal against my discharge from the Army. I never did hear from any Paralegal jobs in New York. I never did hear from the Medical Assistant jobs in Princeton or New York City. The Hilton and Hyatt positions weren't answering back. The jobs at Newark Airport weren't answering back. It seemed like I would return to the seven hour daily commute of Housekeeping at Lyons VA Hospital. Then suddenly in November, I received a miracle call for an interview with St. Peter's Hospital for an opening in Housekeeping. Staying in New Brunswick would reduce the seven hours a day commute and making the $8 minimum wage wasn't hard to replace.

President Obama was leaving office but the Nation was definitely stronger than when he took office. I was unemployed before his eight year tenure began, as were many in my Medic Class from all over the country. There were many notable accomplishments, such as him winning the Nobel Peace Prize. Despite public recognition to the alarming number of homeless veterans, there was a 47 percent decline since the implementation of the Open Doors Program. The Dow Jones was 7,949 points and now in 2016 it had tripled. The 80 billion dollars bailout was paid back with interest and the auto industry was saved. The federal deficit was reduced from 9.8 percent in 2009 to 3.2 percent in 2016. Osama bin Laden was located and executed in the war on terror. Under his leadership, we cut in half our dependence on foreign oil.

The Republican obstructionists refused to support any policy by President Obama. Senator Mitch McConnell stated, "The single most important thing we want to achieve is for Barak Obama to be a one-term President." Speaker of the House, John Boehner, was quoted, "We're going to do everything – and I mean everything we can do – to kill it, stop it, slow it down, whatever we can do." President Obama said in a speech in Rhode Island, "So I hope that my friends on the other side of the aisle are going to change their minds going forward, because putting the American people back to work, boosting our small businesses, rebuilding the economic security of the middle class, these are big national challenges. And we've all got a stake in solving them. And it's not going to be enough just to play politics." His words fell short and the Congress lived up to their threats. The government shut down in October 2013. We were authorized not to report for Drill and I could have used that paycheck. In the mail, I received a letter informing me of my official retirement from the Army National Guard.

My prayers were finally being answered. It was not the job I wanted, but I finally had a job. The money was barely over minimum wage. But after being homeless and working for minimum wage, this too was a blessing and a step up. In addition, I wouldn't have the seven hours of daily commute and the $300 a month I would save in transportation cost. The Employee Health Department gave me a thorough examination. The Doctor was curious about the scar on my trachea. Now I had to explain about my closed head injury and being comatose for a month. This allowed me to make it to two services on Sunday at Church and the blessings started pouring out. The blessings started overflowing. There was a magic at St. Peter's, a blessing that this Catholic hospital had in sustaining life and in living life. It seemed like small little things, like lunches and food, but they all impacted life. While I worked, my thoughts often reflected on Jacob and how God blessed him tending Laban's flocks.

When Laban told him that, for his payment, he could keep the speckled and spotted cattle and goats, God multiplied them. The wages weren't the best, especially in comparison to Robert Wood Johnson Hospital but there was a blessing that was on St. Peter's Hospital. Even in my orientation, a person high in Administration was returning from Robert Wood Johnson Hospital and the higher pay wasn't worth the aggravation it came with. After orientation, I had a full medical examination at Employee Health Office. My Doctor who signed off my closed head trauma, coma, and tracheotomy was an Indian. She was a believer in Christ and shared her testimony when I shared mine. Glory be to God!

They hired me at a higher rate than my CWT minimum wage salary. They told me that they hired me at a beginner's rate. They were glad I had previously waxed floors. I reminded them that I had over 15 years of experience. My response was quickly downplayed, as if I hadn't even mentioned it. Well, thank God for His timing. My first paycheck was right around Thanksgiving and I had something to contribute. Jehovah does provide. Thank you, Father. Thank you for your Son, Jesus Christ. Especially around this time of Thanksgiving, when families gather and share, we should acknowledge the blessings in our lives. My children were missed and I knew they had to miss me, too. We had too many memories together built on Godliness. We had too many memories surrounding the joy of this season. We had too many memories giving thanks this holiday.

Quickly, I caught on to all the routines for Housekeeping. One day, I worked in the Neonatal Intensive Care Unit. There, I prayed for all the premature babies. The medical staff was award winning and rated one of the highest in the State. There were two cafeterias I had to clean every night. There were also Doctors' offices, a Dialysis Unit, the Maternity Wards, the Operating Rooms, and the Emergency Rooms.

Everything was going well. On my way to work, I noticed how warm it was in February. I experienced a few days of crippling arthritis pain. My Supervisor was a sweet Filipina woman who was so kind. She wore a white jacket over her clothes to signify that she was a manager. There were other nice women supervisors wearing their white lab coats. The only male supervisor was an Italian man, Michael, who only wore dress shoes and a silk shirt. It was quite pretentious for a Housekeeping Supervisor. The white lab coat was the distinguishing factor to tell everybody in the room who was the supervisor. Soon, the various departments were pleased with my work and requested me to work extra days in their units.

Time came for my first Employee Evaluation at St. Peter's Hospital. My Supervisor gave me 4 out 5 for the simple reason that it was my first evaluation at the hospital. She brought up that I was a new hire at the hospital but I reminded her that I wasn't new to the work. I had been high polishing the finished floors since I joined the military in 1986. The Management at St. Peter's liked my experience and quick adaptation in polishing the floors. Michael approached me weekly and offered me overtime to polish the floors in certain areas.

The weekly overtime made up for the low salary they offered me. Since I was still certified in Phlebotomy and EKG, it was easier to get hired internally once you were employed by St. Peter's. I asked Perry, the Director of Housekeeping, if he would sign a transfer after six months. He thought about it and remarked that I never had any complaints in my five months of employment. It was a long hard road but I was finally getting a medical job.

One night at St. Peter's, Michael made me sign the Routine that he previously read the day before taking even more time from my work time. He wasn't motivating me and it was highly insulting. He was taking other people's word against mine without even asking for my side of the story. He was exhibiting racist behavior but I couldn't prove it. He became so flustered when I came to work dressed in a dress shirt and tie. He questioned me and wanted me to explain why I was wearing a dress shirt, as if a Black man had to give justification for why he wasn't wearing a sweat suit or a tee-shirt.

Mike would leave at nine o'clock p.m. but I would get off sometimes after twelve. All the employees saw how hard I worked. They would tell me that I didn't have to work as hard as I did. I felt a sense of pride in how shiny I would buff the floors of the Cafeteria. Mike wasn't my Supervisor. My VA Section 8 Counselor came to the apartment for my monthly visit. She looked at me and was highly concerned since I lost over twenty pounds in two weeks. The stress of the job gave me insomnia and my arthritis was becoming crippling. It became as when I was first diagnosed with the cluster migraine headaches again. The pain swirled around my head for ten minutes, then traveled up and down my spinal cord (thorax) to finally rest in my lumbar region of my back for twenty minutes. It became increasingly difficult to finish my housekeeping routine. Several days of work were missed and I injured myself and went to St. Peter's Emergency Room. My Counselor made an appointment with my Primary Doctor. She had been my Doctor for over a year now. She dealt with the cardiac arrest, muscle spasms, hypertension, high blood pressure, diabetes, and arthritis. Explaining my recent symptoms, I requested a medical leave. The Doctor asked me how long I needed leave, so I requested two weeks. She wrote me a letter authorizing a medical leave and I would return to work on April 16th. The HR Benefits

Coordinator at St. Peter's for my Section 8 Counselor drafted me a letter for my short-term disability. I signed a lot of papers to start my short-term disability. It was necessary to disclosure of my traumatic brain injury to explain my need for a medical leave.

My body was healing but my pockets were draining. My request for the Family Medical Leave was denied because I only worked four months when twelve months were required. So, I drafted a letter requesting the ADA to document the high stress at work, loss of a cousin in a car accident, loss of a co-worker, and the aggressive arthritis. This free time just gives me the opportunity to focus on the piano. I would be in beast mode by the time a concert came. Feel me! While on my time off, I rekindled my love for the keyboards and bass guitar. While praising the Lord through song, I felt the Lord leading me to give a concert. A beautiful melody of praise and worship songs cascaded through my mind. Maybe I could finally ask Charity to dance at my concert. I called Pastor Errold on a short notice. It was rare that scheduling this late would be granted but it was.

The April and May disability checks still hadn't come. I didn't want to go back to work but I needed the income. Charity contacted me back that she would come but she needed to cover her transportation cost. This meant Daddy had to get back to work. As I tried to return to work, the Employee Health Department wouldn't clear me back for duty. It seems that my disclosure of my traumatic brain injury had backfired on me. The letter from my Primary Doctor alone was not sufficient for them. Now they were making me go get an examination from a Neurologist.

When I saw the Neurologist, I made it very plain, "I have to get back to work for my daughter, Doc." I was very eager. After talking with a Resident, I waited awhile until the Resident walked back in supervised by the Attending Physician.

"Hello, Mr. Porter. I'm Doctor Nygard. Doctor Foal tells me," he pauses with a puzzled look on his face, "that you are requesting to go back to work." He repeated my request to make sure it was accurate.

"Yeah, Doc. I have to go back to work because my daughter needs the money," I was proud to say.

"It is rare that I find someone who wants to go back to work," said Dr. Nygard. "How are your headaches?" He asked.

"They're all right. I can make it through the day," I was lying. God forgive me but I had to get back to work to finance the concert. My face was insincere as I spoke.

"Have you ever taken Depakote?" Doctor Nygard asked, still evaluating me.

"Yeah, but I don't need that," I diagnosed myself. "They tried to make me take that as a mood stabilizer," I replied with resentment.

"Well, a study for people suffering with traumatic brain injury found that taking 1,000 milligrams a day helps greatly in reducing headaches," he informed me.

"I'll take it," I responded without hesitation, so quickly I don't believe he thought I understood.

"So, you are agreeing to a 1,000 milligram daily regiment?" he reiterated to verify my comprehension.

"Yeah, Doc. Give me the candy!" I said. Everybody in the room burst out laughing. This is how we talked in the military. "I have to go back to work for baby girl." I wanted my daughter at my concert. I haven't been to church with her since she was eight years old.

My Neurologist, Doctor Nygard, wrote me a letter to go back to work. So, he wrote a letter that I could return to work under light duty. This time, Employee Health couldn't deny me. It couldn't have come at a better time. My Landlord called to inform me that my March rent check bounced and I was two months behind now. Section 8 paid their portion and I had no other recourses to pay rent. I had to go request Dr. Jewels to sign a medical form to help process my short-term disability benefits.

I returned to work to catch up on my past due rent and the concert. The medication was helping my headaches but work was still demanding. Perry and Mike pointed out there was no light duty. It challenged me. Should I ask for accommodations for my disability? I decided to refrain from more disclosure but had difficulty getting all the routines finished. Mike kept bumping heads. He tried to dictate every procedure and the instructions he gave would only take more time in a time sensitive routine. One day, he started getting smart. He tried to tell me I was new. I pointed out that I worked at another hospital and I was buffing floors since the 1980s in the military. He told me I wasn't in the military anymore. Then we continued to get loud. I didn't use the soft answer like Rev used to teach me. I told Mike that he didn't have the experience, intelligence, and the education to instruct me on work procedures. Michael had no management degrees, certificates, or training. He only felt privileged and wore dress shirts. We had to go to HR after I filed a complaint. In front of my HR Representative, Mike started yelling, pointing, and repeatedly calling me a liar when I recapped what he said. His lack of professionalism and immaturity were blatant at the work dispute in front of Perry. At work, I had another accident. I went to the ER and was later discharged. My headaches returned and it was clear I went back to work too soon. Still, I was glad to be back at work but I bumped my head in the therapeutic athletic center. After that, I was sent home. It was difficult finishing most of my work assignments.

By June, Perry and Mike called me into the office and told me to sit down. They fired me for unacceptable work performance and behavior. So why did Mike authorize so much overtime if this was true? They documented that I demonstrated an inability to follow directions and carry out work outlined. They said that I was insubordinate, behaved in an unacceptable manner toward employees, was difficult to work with, and made coworkers feel uncomfortable. I was fired for only the second time in my life. Now I would have nothing interfering with my practicing for the concert.

CHAPTER 8
The Shadow of Death

The songs I selected for the concert ran through my mind night and day. Fred Hammond's 'You Are My Daily Bread' was a great song to start a worship service. The introduction was a masterful musical piece of percussion. It had drums, congas, and bongos beating in a rhythmic processional. My bass guitar would be my weapon of choice for this song. Everyone could sing along and hopefully Alan Cherry would be there for the keyboards. Chris Tomlin had two songs I was going to play on my acoustic guitar 'How Great Is My God' and 'Holy Is The Lord.' I reached out to the Praise & Worship Team at Calvary Chapel Riverside to help me play these songs.

Weeks went by and one Sunday morning, I traveled to Good News for worship. There I personally thanked Pastor Errold, Dr. Carla Collins, and Reverend Dr. Jeffrey Roddey for their support allowing me to have the concert there. I asked them for continued prayer concerning my 30th year worship celebration. I hinted that my daughter could be a surprise guest with her dance ministry. I was hoping that everyone who I had blessed these past 30 years in music would come worship with me. This was what I desired, the beginning of many more concerts. The Porter Family reunion would be that very same weekend and it would be nice if everybody would come out and support me.

I made an appointment for the State's Division of Civil Rights in Newark to file an appeal concerning my termination at St. Peter's

Hospital. They worked me an average of ten hours overtime weekly. My 50 hour work week was proof that my work was more than satisfactory and I had a record of the pay stubs to prove it. Ever since I disclosed my disability, they started discriminating against me. They were prepared to fire me once I experienced some medical complications. When I stopped by the office, I found out the Supervisor for my ADA appeal was on vacation.

One day by the strip mall near my Mother's house, I ran across Double K's friend Jermaine. All the boys in the neighborhood called me 'Uncle Bee." All the boys were men. He wanted me to meet his pride and joy. Little Maine, his son.

"Uncle Bee," Jermaine called out walking up giving me a fist bump and hug. He smiled with his dred-locks looking down lovingly at his son. "I want you to met my son, Little Maine." This handsome little guy was all smiles, with dimples, and dred-locks like his Dad.

"Hey little man," I knelt down and shook his hand and a fist bump. "How are you doing?"

"Fine," Little Maine worked the courage to say. Still too shy to make eye contact and playing with his finger in his mouth.

"Well it's a pleasure meeting you little Maine. I know you Dad loves you and is doing a great job of rising you I hear," Jermaine was proud to hear that we were being the fathers we wished we had. The fathers the strong women of our single parent homes raised us to be.

Concert time came at Good News Bible Mission. I was so excited about launching a musical career. However, everything seemed to be going wrong. But this celebration was not about me. It was about worshiping my God. For the moment, my feelings were insignificant. So, I must concentrate on magnifying the Lord. This was a celebration of 30 years in music ministry: ministering in music, singing in the choir, playing drums, Directing a choir, playing the bass guitar, playing in local Jersey City churches, playing bass for McGuire AFB Gospel Choir, the Glassboro State Choir, Lajes Field Portugal Gospel Choir overseas, playing the bass for Pentecostal churches overseas, playing for the Men's Choir overseas, playing outdoor events for the people of Terceira Island Portugal, playing for Gospel Workshops, playing bass for Travis Air Force Gospel Choir in California, and singing and playing bass for the Praise Team at Calvary Chapel. Yet, none of the churches, musicians, choirs, or praise and worship teams came out to support me. All the time spent blessing their Choir anniversaries, Pastor's anniversaries, and Sunday worship services for 30 years of faithful service and no support for me when it was my time. All the music would sound flat and one-dimensional. Fred Hammond's 'You Are My Daily Bread' was out. There weren't enough instruments to support this and no practices with the drummer. Anyway, I thanked all who came out and gave my testimony of how God spared my life. I grabbed my acoustic guitar and played 'How Great Is My God' by Chris Tomlin. Chris' love for God was unmatched. My daughter was in college now and independent. She made it her decision and danced at my concert. The few people that showed up were amazed by her dance talent. My Aunt Clara happened to be there from Pittsburgh. I asked her to have words at the end of the service. An old high school friend named Roland came all the way from New York. I hadn't seen Roland in over twenty years. My cousins Josephine and Louise came. They also sang background for me on 'Jesus Is Love' by Lionel Ritchie. I played the keyboards and my friend, Dee's son, was on the drums. Although hundreds of people lived next door at the housing project, less than ten came over to my celebration. Surprisingly, this was still the most financially successful concert I ever had. Obedience to God is better than sacrifice. Dee had a car and she drove me home. We ate some takeout and I nodded off in the car. Her son was excited and a big help. It gave the music more punch with percussion.

At home, I stayed up preparing some food for the family reunion tomorrow. With the abundance of food from the pantry, I never knew a hungry day. The next day, I brought some dishes for the family reunion. After everything was cooked, I loaded up my boxes and called a taxi to the New Brunswick Train Station. I took the NJ Transit Northeast Corridor train to Newark Penn Station to switch for Jersey City. When the train pulled into Newark Penn Station, the platform is on the same level as the PATH Train to Jersey City, Hoboken, and NYC.

All the PATH trains were shut down for some technical reason. All passengers were stuck at Penn Station Newark in larger than usual crowds. My niece was there with her boyfriend, Bootsy. He had just got out of prison but I wanted to speak encouragingly to him. I complemented him about building up his physic in prison. He said they had nothing else to do. Meanwhile, I was playing with Jared who was older now and was leaping into uncle's arm. They were about to go out and celebrate Jared's birthday. Bootsy must have become jealous and started giving me side-eye. I was baffled, wondering why this little midget was popping yang. I turned the other cheek and continued to speak to him.

"I am the uncle," I said, setting some boundaries of respect for this little street thug.

"I don't give a fl@ck who you are." This little jail bird wants to do a little something?

"Who are you talking to like that?" I asked shocked at his disrespect. Still, I was using words but my body language prepared for battle. Ever since I came out the coma, I always had to be prepared for war. I just never knew where it was coming next. My niece stood by silently. Then, all of a sudden, Bootsy lit up my jaw like a Christmas Tree. I never saw the punch coming.

"No! No!" You could hear my niece yelling. But it was too little, too late. She ran to get in between us, trying to restrain us. I'm not sure why. Maybe out of respect, maybe out of fear of what I was capable of doing to him. I put up my dukes in my best Mike Tyson, Floyd Mayweather pose. Next thing I knew, all I saw was the second punch coming back. I never saw the punch but my jaw was throbbing now. My niece continued to get in between us and the crowd started to draw. There was no train, so might as well have some entertainment. Since I had kids older than him, he had the advantage of speed. My Rocky days were over. I put up my dukes like the old 1920s boxers. Jesus said turn the other cheek but I ran out of them.

"Move out of the way," I told my niece. I didn't want her to get hurt for what was about to come. The cocky little inmate thought he was a contender now but he was only a pretender in disguise. I raised my fist above my shoulders. Mighty Mouse swung another haymaker at my head. This time, I grabbed his fist and pulled him in. Now it was his four foot strength against mine. I snatched him up like a baby and body slammed him to the pavement. Carefully, I pinned one arm down with my knee like the UFC Mixed Martial Arts fighters. Then, I pinned the other arm down while I straddled on top of him. He laid there defenseless and it was payback time. I raised my fist and started coming down. This was for his disrespect. This was for the coma. This was for the mental wards. This was for the false arrest and not seeing my children. I was going to beat this boy to a bloody pulp. I felt the adrenaline pumping through my veins. The only outcome to satisfy my desires was to see him on his way to the hospital. My fist came crashing down when all of a sudden someone came and knocked me off him. My opportunity for sweet revenge was ruined.

My reflex response was a spin kick to knock my new assailant off me like a fly. Momentum spun me around and I was about to finish him with my fist, which was still locked and loaded. However, to my surprise, it was the police and I never felt more sorry to see them. Immediately, I showed no aggression. They instantly started manhandling me.

"Officer. I'm a Veteran and he assaulted me first." This wasn't my first rodeo. I knew the drill.

"That little guy? Why, he's just sitting there cooperating. You're the one on top of him," they said as they handcuffed me while Bootsy sat handcuffed sitting on the curb.

"I'm a Veteran. He assaulted me first and I want him arrested." It was just like in New Brunswick, getting equal protection under the law. They took no heed to what I said and started steam rolling me into the concrete wall outside Newark Penn Station.

We were speeding face first into the wall like a freight train. They propelled me toward the wall, an Officer on each arm. Bootsy just struck me in the head twice. The Doctor said I wasn't supposed to get hit in the head anymore. Just as my face was about to slam into the wall, I raised my foot up. The three of us all jolted backward. They were surprised and angered by my actions. The nerve of me, not letting them slam my face into the wall.

"Congratulations, now we're going to arrest you for resisting arrest," he wisecracked. Resisting arrest for not letting them slam me face first into a brick wall? Having traumatic brain injury, I'm not supposed to get hit in the head. The cops pushed me down to the entrance door like a perp walk for the crowd to see. Their agitated state could be seen in the way they pushed me faster than my feet could step, so as to empower themselves and dehumanize me. Looking at the situation, I guess they were upset that I kicked one of the cops off my back, but not nearly as upset as I was. They started reading me the riot act and told me they were sending me to Secaucus Correctional Facility. Again, I acknowledged that I was a Veteran. I had the right to defend myself, and Bootsy struck me first. Based on my experience in Security, I verified that they could look on the video cameras for proof. When they emptied my pockets, they came across my Military ID card. Now my Veteran status was starting to be taken seriously. My head was throbbing from the stress, the punches, and the cops. I asked for something for my headache.

They put me in a holding cell but Bootsy went free and I was so stressed that I paced back and forth none stop. I was given some medicine for my headache and released shortly after. Thank God for setting me free. The PATH trains were working again. You could kiss the dishes I made for the family reunion goodbye in all the confusion. Lil Big Sis came over to pick up my niece and the kids. Of course, Bootsy was unreliable and couldn't provide a ride. When I saw my sister, I was still in the same angry mind frame. She didn't like my tone and she was angry after I was going through my ordeal. I told her what I was going to do to Bootsy the next time I see him and to tell Mommy because that could happen in her house. She just took offense like she was the one who was sucker punched twice and left me in Newark. My jaw felt like it was broken. She gave Bootsy a ride home but I just got an attitude.

I made a process of cleaning, organizing my apartment, and/or inventory. Inventory produced documents and dates to help in my upcoming Court battles to get back to work. Now I would have to wait until July for the paperwork to be processed before checks would be cut. Victory! The Division of Civil Rights called yesterday for me to come sign the legal papers. When I arrived, while waiting in their lobby, I read their mission statement, which was hanging on the wall. Their goal was to eradicate illegal discrimination based on race, religion, color, national origin, handicap, age, and sexual orientation. The Division maintains that if illegal discrimination negatively affects any one individual in New Jersey, it negatively affects every individual in New Jersey. Thank you, God! This made me confident that I would receive retribution.

When around my mother's house, I was always leery. So many physical confrontations I was never supposed to bring up in conversation. So many times I was told to be quiet like a child. So many times I was told to get out like a dog. The loving moments far outweighed the bad, but the bad times linger in the echoes of one's mind. In the Lord's Prayer, forgiveness had to be applied as Jesus said. The latest assault came from my niece's boyfriend. He almost broke my jaw. I couldn't chew on the right side for a month. It bothered me to see him walking around my mother's house. It bothered me but it didn't bother my own mother what he did to me. She said that he never did anything to her. It bothered me to see that little smirk on his face and the only thing that stopped me from stomping him into the ground was my faith in Jesus. My pride was mortally wounded by being cursed out, the lack of family concern, the arrest, the assault by the police, and by the relenting Court hearings.

I received sad news from my mother's side of the family. Uncle Howard passed away and we all had to go down to Maryland for his funeral to honor this Patriarch. It's as if we had a big family reunion in Maryland. Everyone was there except my children. Charity and Gabriel were in their home state but their relationship with me and the family was still in need of repair. These are the scars that eleven years of Supervised Visitation will bring you. Mostly all I had was spent in travel. By June, my health was declining as poorly as my finances. The Department of Community Affairs kept paying my full rent in addition to making payments for the utilities.

On Saturday, August 8th, my High School classmates were having our 30th Year Reunion on the River Lady dinner cruise. I had no money for this but my bestie, Michele Costello, and Alex made provisions for me. There I ran into Master Sergeant James Hogan from my Air National Guard Unit. He hadn't seen me since I moved over to the Army. It was great seeing all my old classmates again like Kerri. Eric Ragno, Lisa, and Kevin were friends since Elementary

School. We stayed in frequent contact on Facebook. God provided but life on a fixed income felt little excitement.

This year on my birthday on January 13th, a letter was sent following an inspection of the unit. Community Affairs continued to pay my monthly rent payments according to the Section 8 program. SSI was not a possibility. Seminary at Rutgers was still an improbability but my body was healed enough to look for employment. My feet hurt the most and I had to look for work with no prolonged standing. I gave up on the Department of Civil Rights hearing. There would be no retribution for St. Peter's firing me. My mother told me over the phone how Bootsy was coming to the house all the time when she was gone. Little did she know, he kept parking in her complex's private parking lot. He got in a dispute with a neighbor who reminded him that he wasn't supposed to park there. He threatened the neighbor and when my mother heard of it, she was quick to defend her neighbor. She was awed how Bootsy felt he could come to her home and disrespect her neighbors. She let him know he wasn't allowed back if he continued. She didn't see any irony in saying this to me. It's as if they were blinded. Anything said or done to me was alright, my fault. I couldn't chew on that side of my jaw for a month. Well, I had to forgive but it wasn't alright with me. And I wasn't going to be silent about it anymore.

Pastor Lanier had a brother I called Uncle Ernest. He would come for a vacation every year and stay with his brother. I made sure to visit regularly when he came. He was funny and lived a full life. He passed away and his son Ricky was making sure he was laid to rest properly. At his funeral I saw Evangelist Ida Harris there. She was our prayer warrior, unofficial Assistant Pastor, President of the Women's Day fund raising, Building Fund, CO-Op Food Sharing Program. She was pillar, she was everything. She called out my name in prayer daily. She sat in the back at Uncle Ernest funeral. I sat near her briefly to confess my undying love for this church Mother.

"How is my prayer Warrior!" Evangelist Ida led noon day pray around our alter 7 days a week.

"Fine," she smiled in her Southern belle glory. We didn't have to say much to communicate beyond mere words. "I told myself he doesn't know. He never said anything," Mother Ida said with her Southern style smile.

"Doesn't know what Mother?' I asked.

"Inez," she paused. Inez was her daughter. Mother Ida knew I had a huge crush on Inez but either she was in a relationship or I was in a relationship. "Inez passed away," she still sat there like a prayer warrior. Sat in strength even with a broken heart. Even in the valley of the shadow of death!

My reactions gave it all away. If she didn't know how I felt about Inez everything was revealed as I sat there with my mouth open slumped over with tears rolling down my cheeks. She saw me pain. "I said he didn't know. He would have said something to me." I couldn't look her in the eyes.

"I'm sorry for your loss," I was too choked up to say it properly.

"Her and my son Larry died at the same time. We had to have their funerals together. Their caskets side by side," she sat in dignity my little personal guardian prayer warrior. I would be dead without her prayers over my life and 2 of her children were gone. I moved away and sat mourning throughout the funeral.

My Pastor Erwin Lanier, Sr. and my father were brilliant men. These Bible scholars taught me that the speed of light is 386,000 miles per second. The speed light travels, the power of it, and its mighty presence are unfathomable. Yet, no matter how fast light travels, darkness is always there first. Still, God's universal law is that light will always conquer the darkness. People hesitate and at times doubt the existence of God but there is very little doubt that evil exists in our present world. At the time being in Newark, New Jersey, I see so many things interwoven in the fabric of the Newark Court System. Many people are arrested or have family in the Court System on a daily and weekly basis. There are so many citizens of the Urban Community in the Criminal Court system that for them it has become a way of life. Their thoughts and lifestyles will make them perpetually institutionalized. God help us all. For God so loved the world that He gave his only begotten Son. That whoever believes in Him should not perish but have everlasting life. For God did not send His Son into the world to condemn the world, but the world through

Him might be saved. He that believes in Him is not condemned, but he that does not believe is condemned already, because he has not believed in the name of the only begotten Son of God. Jesus is the true light and the light of Jesus is the life of men. And this is the condemnation that light is coming into the world, and men simply love darkness rather than light, because their deeds are evil. These are the thoughts expressed in the Gospel of John, the first and third chapters. The first chapter expressed that in the beginning of all time was the Word, or in the Greek the Logos (or the written Word). The same was in the beginning with God or in the Hebrew (Aramaic) Elohim, a plural word. In Genesis, when God spoke, He always spoke, "Let us create man." Judaism is a monotheistic religion. It does not suggest that there are three distinct Gods but one God existing in three distinct individuals: God the Father, God the Son and God the Holy Spirit.

When I lived on the VA Campus and they forced me to see the Psychiatrist, they didn't approve of my belief in God. They frowned upon the fact that I could hear God's voice guiding me. They felt hearing the voice of God was a type of schizophrenia. I stood on my faith no matter the consequences. Yes, I was a Christian having to defend my belief in God and standing alone with no support from the church. I was fighting the good fight of faith all alone against these Psychologists who did not believe in the God whom I served. After being denied four times for my VA Service-Connection, I followed the suggestion of one of the HUD VASH Crisis Team Counselors and filed for Social Security Insurance (SSI). Against their advice, I hired a lawyer to increase my chances for success. For about two years, I was physically unable to work and on General Assistance. Doctor Weinstein, my VA Psychologist, gave his expert medical opinion that I should never work again. Months had passed until the decision came and I received a letter. The Judge disregarded the Doctor's medical opinion.

My perspective was looking for light at the end of the tunnel as my health was starting to spring forth, not at the speed of light but quite quickly. It was evident that God's will was not for me to collect Social Security Insurance. The road ahead of me would be the traditional 40 hour work week.

I noticed these mini-vans traveling around the city. They displayed an M&T Medical Transportation login on the side. When I contacted M&T, they told me there were driving positions available. At M&T, we transported Medicaid patients to their Medical, Dental, and Counseling appointments. Driving allowed me to stay off my feet and put in long hours at work. God knew just what I needed.

The Jewish synagogue, Poile Zedek, was erected here in New Brunswick during 1928. The historic century-old synagogue caught fire on October 24th, 2015. The Rabbi ran into the synagogue to save one of the sacred scrolls. Tragically, nine Torahs and hundreds of religious and prayer books were burned in the fire. In accordance with Jewish tradition, the sacred scriptures will be buried in the synagogue's cemetery. Double K called one day crying and said that Little Maine got run over by a car like Tré did. He died instantly. I was on my cellphone walking down the street crying like a baby. It seems like I just met him. I told him to be strong. To tell Jermaine he can still see his son in the Kingdom of Heaven, sitting by Christ Jesus.

Meanwhile, driving alone at work, my Seminary training began. When driving, I was in God's seminary listening to audio recordings on the Book of Job, Creation, Albert Einstein, and Isaac Newton. Einstein didn't start from greatness. Like King David, he started from very humble beginnings. He had a simple job in the Patent Office. Einstein's job provided him the opportunity to published four revolutionary papers. They built a strong foundation for modern day physics. He proposed innovative concepts of space, time, mass, and energy. His theories helped in the acceptance of the existence of atoms. He proposed the theory of relativity. He won a Nobel Prize.

I studied Isaac Newton's theory of light and laws of motion. Newton found that white light is composed of all seven colors of the rainbow. When God said "Let there be light," it meant shedding light on many other things we couldn't comprehend. Not only did light come forth but the colors of the rainbow appeared with it. Time, space, and matter were all created. It would take centuries for man to comprehend. Knowledge would be revealed precept upon precept over time. Yet enough information was given since the dawn of time for men's understanding to comprehend. "In the beginning, God created the Heavens and the Earth."

The Bible goes on to say that "The Earth was without form or void. And the Spirit of God moved upon the face of the waters." Although it says the universe was not formed, one of the sharpest minds ever still believed that God created the universe (the Heavens and the Earth). Isaac Newton explored the universe with a primitive telescope and his intellect. With his gift of intellect, he created calculus and the laws of motion. His calculations were used by NASA to further space exploration. Newton wrote more about religion than any other subject. "The most beautiful system of Sun, Planets, and Comets could only proceed from the counsel and dominion of an intelligent and powerful being" (Sir Isaac Newton).

One morning, I received a hysterical phone call. Lil Big Sis said that Stacey called her and said that she had to bring Trė to the hospital. Trė made frequent trips to the hospital with complications from him being a quadriplegic. This was not a routine hospital visit. Stacey was told by the doctors that Trė didn't seem like he was going to make it. Once again, the burden fell on me to contact Shakur.

Was I his father or mother? Was I his only sibling? Why did the burden always fall on me? When I called my brother, he seemed like he was in a good mood and glad to hear my voice. Now, I was going to break his heart and ruin his good mood. I let him know that Stacey called and she had to rush Trė to the hospital. The Doctors are suggesting that he come right away. His intelligence let him derive a familiar fact that his son was dying.

Things got real emotional. He asked if he had to go through this again. From his pain, it was just like the experience when Trė was struck by the car. We never expected him to live that day and the pain rushed right back. No parent should have to live through this but this was the second time for Shakur and there was nothing I could do to stop it. It was all in God's hands.

I encouraged him to go see his son while he still can. "Go and I will be by your side," I told him. I didn't know it but I was actually ready for Trė's suffering to end. Maybe that could shed some light in this dark moment.

"Okay, where's he at?" He responded like a soldier, like a loving father. I told him Trè was at University Hospital in Newark. I took off work to be by his side. At the hospital, Mom, Lil Big Sis, and Butch were there with Stacey. Shakur couldn't take watching him helplessly like that, so he left.

Trè laid there in his hospital bed. He had been lying in a bed for the last ten years after the horrific car accident. His eyes were tightly closed expressing pain riddled on his face. His panting for breath showed he was in the fight of his young life. Later, we were told there were complications from Trè's feeding tube into his stomach all these years. Being untreated, the undigested milk rotted in his stomach and had to be removed. I had seen this kid live through unformed limbs, leg braces, tracheotomy tubes, and feeding tubes. This seemed too much but Mom and Lil Big Sis were praying that God would heal Trè. How was he supposed to live without a stomach?

Life resumed and we all went back to work. After a couple of days, Trè continued to fight on for dear life. The Doctor's decision gave him days. On October 10th, after a long shift, Lil Big Sis called and asked me if I was still working. I asked her to just tell me. She said Trè had passed away and Mom wasn't taking it well. Trè had finally earned his wings. Life was a fight for him and he was a fighter all the way through. The rest of the day was dreary. Hours later, my sister called me again. I wasn't as sad as I was earlier. I was looking for light.

"Hey, Bryan," she spoke.

"Hey, Sis. Who died now?" I joked sarcastically. My family and I share a pretty morbid sense of humor with each other. The silence on the phone was deafening. It seemed like it went on forever, but it gave me my answer rhetorically. "No," I pleaded. "No!" How could this be? They say death comes in threes.

"Lynn went to see Keith and they found him dead in his apartment tonight," she said. I was awestruck.

"Keith and Trè in the same day?" I was in denial, baffled, and broken.

Trė was sixteen years old and we had a small funeral service for him. Finally, after fighting since birth, his struggles were all over. 'Suffer the children unto me, for of such are the kingdom of Heaven.' Trė survived ten years after the accident. What a fighter! After we buried him, I buried myself in my work the following weeks with thirteen hour workdays, and six days a week.

The Dispatcher, Jason, called me the day before and explained the pickups that he scheduled for the next day. Not trusting them to my memory, I wrote them down, so I wouldn't make a mistake. The next morning, I tried to pick up my first passenger on time deep in South Jersey. I called the client as I went down there but no one answered, so I left a message. Finally, I reached her home. Despite the several phone calls and messages I left, she answered the phone complaining that I was too early and she wasn't coming out until twenty minutes later. Now this was going to mess up the whole schedule. Later, she complained that the Dispatcher called her at 5:15 while she was in the shower. I waited until six o'clock for her to come out. When she entered the van, she was raging and turning beet red.

"You guys keep calling me," she blurted out. "Calling me at 5:15."

"I didn't call you until 5:30, Miss," I quickly defended myself.

"Well, someone called me at 5:15 and told me you'd be coming early and I told him 'no' and that is when I jumped into the shower." Now things were starting to make sense. "I told him I wouldn't be ready until six o'clock and you pulled up at 5:45 and told me you're outside."

"That's the time they told me your pickup was," I said for clarification.

"I'm supposed to be going to get a Stress Test and you guys are stressing me out." Immediately, my Combat Medic skills started kicking in. I needed to alleviate her stress.

"I'm sorry, Miss. Don't upset yourself. Let's keep you calm, so your blood pressure doesn't rise anymore," I said attempting to calm her down. A soft answer turns away the wrath of scorn.

"I know to keep calm. I was a First Responder," she mentioned. I took that as an opportunity to converse on a common interest.

"I was a Combat Medic in the Army," I said proudly. "I was trained as an EMT," saying for clarification. "You were a First Responder?"

"Yeah, an EMT," she said as she were calming down. She started a grim tale with me hanging on every word, "One day, I was driving home and this guy crashed right in front of me. Crashing straight through his front windshield. He laid there with a severed carotid artery on the hood of the car."

"Did he bleed out?" I asked curiously. The carotid was a major artery.

"I had to pinch his carotid artery off," she said. I was in awe of her heroics. "I had to release it every four minutes."

"Why?" I asked her but I faintly knew the answer.

"So his brain would breath," she responded. Blood flow to the brain was necessary to deliver oxygen. They taught us that in training but rarely did we have an opportunity to apply it.

"How did you remember to do that?" I asked in amazement. I was remembering our training for these scenarios for blood supply to the brain. He would have gone brain dead without continuous blood flow.

"I don't know," she paused unemotionally. "I just did it."

"I believe God was with you," I shared.

"They said he would have never made it if I hadn't packed his head with snow." Her keen skill continued to bloom.

"You did what?" said I.

"The Doctors were amazed how I did it."

"Well, did he make it?" I was totally engaged in her story.

"Yes. We kept in touch. He called me every year. And 70 years later when I needed a liver, he called me to offer me one of his." Don't tell me God doesn't perform miracles. The fact that they are a match, preserved for 70 years.

Great news, Charity finished school and earned her master's degree. She wanted to move back to New Jersey. She had missed growing up around me and her family. She had many female cousins around her age. Even better news was that she was expecting to have a baby. Tia moved out with her kids and Charity moved into Mom's house with the baby.

Before you know it, nine months passed by. The night before Charity was scheduled for her C-Section, I called and asked how she was feeling. She seemed a bit nervous. So, I offered to be there with her. At the Hospital, they asked if I wanted to be in the Delivery Room with her. I witnessed Charity's delivery, which was such a blessing. Charity was so brave and the miracle of birth was such a beautiful moment. The Doctors even let me cut the umbilical cord. The miracle of birth is not without its challenges. Charity had to undergo two blood transfusions. Praise be to God! Sugar drove up and we were all so happy for our new addition to the family. It had been decades since Sugar was up here. She saw Mom at the hospital and asked about Dad. Dad was in the hospital in Bayonne. Sugar wanted to visit him, so we took a trip over there. She walked into his hospital room. Dad was all smiles looking at his daughter-in-law. He gave a grand smile. He was a grand dad.

Through the experience of life, I pondered why some people are abundantly wealthy while others suffer extreme poverty. Why are some skilled with strength and athletics while others struggle with their health? The Scriptures say, 'the poor and the rich the Lord makes.' Many people I knew got on a fixed income and decided not to work harder or earn more income to lose that benefit. With my faith, I didn't mind rocking the boat. My desire was to seek first the kingdom of God and the riches would be added to me.

It became time to renew my Section 8. I would be forced to submit my W-2 forms showing the massive amounts of overtime. There was no way of hiding the fact that I made too much money to be on the HUD VASH Program. My only options were to have my hours cut back and live my life on a fixed income. My faith was stronger than that. I believed God for greater. I knew my value. So, I gave up Section 8 and moved out of my George Street apartment.

Sleeping in the Company take-home van and showering at the 24 hour Planet Fitness gym.

Lil Big Sis decided to have a 70th birthday celebration for my mother. We were going to book an extravagant hall and make it a gourmet catered affair. The problem was that we had limited seating and a large family. Having a close Church family didn't make things easier. In addition to my weekly overtime, no monthly rent, and security deposit, I planned to help Charity with her bills and help my sister pay for my mother's 70th birthday celebration. One benefit about being homeless meant I had no fear of giving up my apartment. I could sleep a couple of nights at my mother's house and the rest in the company's take-home van.

Every week, I was anticipating receiving my security deposit. Lil Big Sis needed it to make a deposit to hold the date. It was approaching thirty days and still no word. This year on Juneteenth 2019, I was upset and texted my cheap landlord to do what's right. She owed me my rent deposit. A month and a half rent was going to be a hefty check with seven years of interest. After thirty days, I called the Section 8 Crisis Team. At first, the Landlord's wife told my HUD VASH Counselor that she would put the check in the mail today, but today seemed to never come. This prompted me to call. The husband got on the phone and started telling me that basically they have 90 days and they were extending me a courtesy. Immediately, I cut him right off.

"No, Rizzo. I am a paralegal," I remarked stating my legal authority. "The lease we signed directly states 30 days after." Then he mentioned again how he is doing me a favor by returning my full deposit. Normally, he takes off a hundred dollars for cleaning. "The lease states that my deposit was supposed to go into an escrow account. It should have compounded seven years of interest." Rizzo knew he couldn't challenge the lease. When they finally released my rent deposit, I was loaded. Now I could give Lil Big Sis the money to rent the hall for Mom's 70th birthday celebration. Now I could finally buy the electric guitar that I've been dreaming about for years. I could use so many different songs and techniques that I couldn't use with my acoustic guitar. This was my reward. I owed this to myself.

Everyone thought I was nuts for sleeping in the company's van at night. When you worked 13 hours of the day, it mattered little. Some nights during the week, I drove up to Mom's and checked on Charity and my new grandchild. I made sure the house was always taken care of. I mowed lawns, did repairs, and kept the refrigerator full. Everything was going fine, but then tragedy struck. Charity's car was in an accident and her front end was totaled. It would take weeks to fix, so I had to loan her my car while she was waiting. After all, she was a mother now with a baby to take care of.

Then came the death of a matriarch. After over twenty years of battling cancer, Aunt Clara finally passed away. She was not only my mother's older sister but also her best friend. She was like a grandmother to us all. Shakur and Charity rode with me back to Pittsburgh for her funeral. Mom had great inspirational words to say. You could hear how confident and comforting she was speaking at the church. We had the opportunity to visit Uncle Joe while we were out there. He was battling cancer himself.

Before you knew it, Mom's birthday celebration came around. The Lee family from the Pittsburgh area came out to join us. Uncle Joe was too sick to travel. We had to select from our guest list. Not everyone was invited and not everyone was happy. I wanted to cater a cookout in the backyard for all the local family that was not invited to the hall. I was out voted and unsupported. Mom's friends from church came, some Jersey City relatives, all her children, and grandchildren. To my surprise, my father came after he was invited with her permission. A lot of those cousins from Pittsburgh hadn't seen him in a minute. Charity danced for Grandmother. I sang a song and played the piano but we needed a choir and people just wouldn't sing with us. Thank God for my cousin Josephine backing me up again with her vocals. We tried our best. It was Mom's favorite song. I played on her birthdays and on many occasions when I visited her. My friend Steve was there with his mother.

Months went by and I hadn't heard from my brother. He kept himself away from the family. Then I heard my Uncle Joe had lost his battle with cancer. We journeyed back to Pittsburgh and Aliquippa to bury Uncle Joe. My Mother always bragged her brother was named after 'Joe Louis,' the famed boxer. She was named after 'Marva,' his wife. The White people of that time wouldn't let them put these names on their birth certificates. My Mother had to wait until she was a grown woman to change her birth certificate from 'Margaret' to 'Marva.' One day, I got a call to come pick him up on the Turnpike. He was stranded. I questioned him how he got stranded on the NJ Turnpike. It seemed as if his friends kicked him out because he chocked somebody. If it's not one thing, it's another. I had better ways to spend my time and my gas. He was stranded. What was I going to do? What would Jesus do? My cousin Quincy was shot and killed on Claremont Avenue after leaving the Dog Pound on Orient. Charity moved back to Maryland to teach dance. I was going to miss her but I think she would do better down there. There would be less distractions for her. Charity happened to be there when I picked up my brother.

"What could you possible do now to get negroes to kick you out on the Turnpike?" I was waiting to ask him.

"Me and some girl was arguing and she said something about my son and I started to choke her." The silence was deafening. Charity and I had no words to say with the shadows of Tré's death still lingering.

"You can see your son again," I smiled encouraging him to get his life in order. "You can see him in the Kingdom of Heaven with Jesus Christ.

I wasn't going to sleep in the van tonight. Butch, Shakur, and myself all celebrated Dad's birthday together. Butch barbequed in his backyard. It was nice that all the men were together. Shakur didn't normally hang with us. It was a nice day with Dad. We should get together more often.

As I was driving Shakur home, he began to express anger at Dad. What brought this on? He chose to spend the whole day with Dad celebrating his birthday and now he was yelling in my car. His eyes were black and soulless but they still had an eerie glow.

"What happened to you? You've been celebrating with him all day," I was baffled.

"Don't make any excuses for him! He never did anything for his wife or his kids," Shakur grunted while pointing his finger. This had some truth in it. But why did he spend the whole day with Dad if he felt like this?

"Well, he wasn't that bad. He had done some good things," I chimed in being sentimental.

"He was never there for us," his rage continued to increase with the volume of his voice and the gestures of his hands. I glanced at him while I drove. He had to be on something given how quickly his demeanor changed.

"Look," let me try to calm this down. I didn't like him yelling at me in my car while I'm doing him a favor and driving him home. "Just be quiet and I'll take you home or else you're going to get out," I told him. This was my incentive to stop yelling at me, transferring all your anger at me in my car.

"If you don't take me home and put me out this car, I will slash all your tires," he threatened me. I couldn't pull over fast enough. I'm not going to do you favors and you disrespect me like that.

"Get out," I told him. He got out and a sped off to show a little more attitude.

In the morning, the Lord spoke to me that my brother needed counseling following all the deaths of his son and my cousins Keith, Quincy, and Biz. As I came out to leave for work, I found out that all four tires were slashed. Shakur had delivered on his promise. I wasn't going to get to work on time today.

I didn't go back to Jersey City much after that, with the War on Terror, Iraqi Freedom, Enduring Freedom, the war on crime, and all the spiritual warfare. The Enemy comes in like a roaring lion, seeking whom he can devour. The Enemy comes to steal, kill, and destroy. He desires to sift us as wheat or shake our faith. We are in a battle of spiritual warfare with evil but people are not woke. If the blind lead the blind, they both fall into the ditch. Unfortunately, we can't see the spiritual darkness. However, we can see the mass shooting at shopping malls, shootings at schools where children were, shootings and killings at churches in South Carolina, shootings at Jewish synagogues in Pittsburgh, police shootings, unarmed Black civilian shootings, people pushed on to train tracks, anti-Asian attacks, subway slashing, violence against women, hate crimes, anti-Semitism, discrimination against Arabs, over 930,000 abortions, one person sexual assaulted in the U.S. every 68 seconds, 1,152 women raped everyday in the Congo, etc. People may question the presence of God but evil is running rampant in our godless society. Just as fear and anxiety are unseen, a new pandemic hit the world called COVID-19. By April of 2020, the Church of God In Christ reported the deaths of thirty prominent Bishops and Pastors by COVID. No part of society was immune to this deadly disease. Churches ceased their in-person gatherings. Multi-millions of people died throughout the world. God still promised, "if my people who are called by my name, would humble themselves and pray. Then I would hear from Heaven and heal their land"(2 Chronicles 7:14).

My family and I were still healthy, even family that contracted the virus. We had no COVID related deaths. You beat COVID, death and prostrate cancer Dad! For Father's Day, Butch and I took Dad out to breakfast. Then we took him down to the Korean Memorial, downtown in Jersey City, so he could see the stone they dedicated to the Korean War Veterans. Shortly after, he had to go into a nursing home. He couldn't chew well and seemed to have lost his taste for life. My cousin Lynn traveled from Pittsburgh to visit him in the nursing home. Charity came up from Maryland to see her Grandfather. Later that day, Dad finally passed away. I was glad she got to see him. He too had battled cancer for twenty plus years but God gave him victory. He died of natural causes. May your neighbors respect you, trouble neglect you, the Angels protect you, and Heaven accept you. Be at rest, Dad.

Lynn and Joy traveled from Pittsburgh for his funeral. Gabriel and Sugar surprised us and traveled as well. They were missed over the years and were well received with much love from all the family. Jermaine hadn't seen Gabriel since they were little. The words of the Bailiff came true that day, time heals all wounds.

I took a leap of faith and quit work to start college at Rutgers University for the Fall semester 2022. It would be my first experience in music theory in my thirty plus years of musical instruction. It wasn't easy with the curriculum at Rutgers. Given my traumatic brain injury, my ability to quickly recall information was limited. I had to work jobs with a temporary agency around my schedule. It took away from my studies. The Agency sent me to clean up the Giants Football Stadium, the New Jersey Devils Prudential Center, Six Flags, Ryder University, and various other venues. It took me away from my studies. I was unable to take higher amounts of student loans to supplement my income.

My mother had a necessary hip replacement. She required more hands on care, so I chose to forsake my college studies that day to go attend to her. Lil Big Sis came by after work but I would be the one to give Mom full attention for that day. After class, I drove up, cleaned the house, and made sure that her meals were prepared for a couple of days. I didn't leave until I was sure there was no further reason for her to go back downstairs. As I went downstairs to leave, I noticed the mailbox was opened. You could see the stack of mail that was delivered. No one checked the mail to bring it to my mother with her bad hip, so she wouldn't fall on the stairs. I wanted to just drive home. There was a lot of studying and papers I had to catch up with.

When I reached for the mail, I wrestled with my feelings and chose to take my mother's mail up the stairs. I checked the names to see if I had anything. The VA often forwarded my mail there. One envelope had a certain appeal. It was a manila envelope, the kind you get the government with your income tax checks. The return address read U.S. Treasury. My eyes widened and my mouth opened in awe. The paper inside the envelope had my name printed on it. The paper it was printed on was definitely the type government checks were written on. With anticipation, I opened the check. To my delight, the amount was so high. It brought an instant smile to my face. So many answers came by reading the amount. Despite all the various agencies in the Government, it could only be the VA. It was an amount that answered many questions: why I didn't received the jobs that I applied for, why I didn't get the jobs that I was qualified for, why God allowed me to suffer, why I was homeless, unemployed, and had to rely on Section 8. The Heavenly Father answered the questions to the direction of my life. Why did God send this check after the semester ended? Why didn't God send this check when I was applying to Seminary? Why were all these fresh battle scars, years of pain, suffering, test of faith, and struggles I went through? It felt like the prophet Job. At the end of all his test, he was blessed far above all he had lost. This soldier was anointed for the battle. The believer must remember, when you are going through overwhelming circumstances, that God has already prepared you for the victory. A brother/sister has been born for the adversity you are facing. The prayers of the righteous avail much. No weapon formed against you shall prosper. No Enemy can defeat you. Greater is He that is within you, than he that is in the world. Hallelujah! Since Jesus Christ took the keys to death, Hell, and the grave, I will live on, even when my body is laid to rest. We will fear no evil. We are warriors for Christ! And we have been anointed for battle!

www.ingramcontent.com/pod-product-compliance
Lightning Source LLC
Chambersburg PA
CBHW071712120626
46550CB00001B/197